Filmmakers and Financing

Praise for *Filmmakers and Financing:*

"An excellent, insightful guide to attracting financing for indie films. Louise Levison takes a sane, balanced approach to research, comparables and projections, achieving honest outlooks in business plans that are accurate and convincing to equity investors. An important tool for filmmakers and producers seeking innovative financing models."

—Danny Glover, Actor/Director/Producer

"Thank you so much for all your help from the business plan to the emails and introductions. You have helped this film become what it is today."

—Rob Cowie, Producer, *The Blair Witch Project*

"How to raise funds for independent films was the best-kept secret in Hollywood until Levison's book was published."

—Rick Pamplin, Producer/Director, The Pamplin Film Company

"If you are an independent filmmaker trying to raise any private financing for your film, you absolutely must read, absorb, and understand the material and advice in Louise's book. . . . I tell all my clients to buy a copy, because they will continually use and refer back to it. . . . I do."

—Harris Tulchin, Entertainment Attorney/Producer and
Co-Author: *The Independent Film Producer's Survival Guide*

"*Filmmakers and Financing* is an indispensable navigational guide to successful financing, production and release of independent films. Louise Levison has synthesized her years of professional experience into an invaluable roadmap for the filmmaking community."

—William Nix, Chairman, Creative Projects Group,
Executive Producer, *The Prophet*

"Need money for a movie? Here's the road map every indie filmmaker needs to find it. It worked for me!"

—Paul Sirmons, Director/Producer, *The First of May* and
former Florida Film Commissioner

"If Louise Levison's *Filmmakers and Financing* were only about business plans it would be worth more than its cover price. In addition, Levison gives sage, savvy and clear introductions to every important aspect of film business—marketing, distribution, varieties of investors, financing options—it's all here, including a sample business plan. This book is a 'must have' for any filmmaker's bookshelf."

—Morrie Warshawski, Consultant and Author of *Shaking the Money Tree*

"A 'must have' educational and reference tool to help you conquer current industry practices regarding finance, production and distribution. Louise has consistently delivered a plethora of information that is easy for a beginning filmmaker to understand, while at the same time very useful to the entertainment veteran. NO filmmaker's library would be complete without it."

—J. David Williams, Distributor, *Shiloh* and *The Omega Code*

"Levison's book gives filmmakers an inspiring and coherent merger of plain English, film lingo, and traditional business-speak. It helped me create a straightforward and thorough business plan that ultimately raised $2 million for my new project."

—Stu Pollard, Producer/Director, *Keep Your Distance*

Filmmakers and Financing

Business Plans for Independents

Seventh Edition

Louise Levison

Focal Press
Taylor & Francis Group

NEW YORK AND LONDON

First published 2013
by Focal Press
70 Blanchard Rd Suite 402, Burlington, MA 01803

Simultaneously published in the UK
by Focal Press
2 Park Square, Milton Park, Abingdon, Oxon OX14 4RN

Focal Press is an imprint of the Taylor & Francis Group, an informa business

Notices
Knowledge and best practice in this field are constantly changing. As new research and experience broaden our understanding, changes in research methods, professional practices, or medical treatment may become necessary.

Practitioners and researchers must always rely on their own experience and knowledge in evaluating and using any information, methods, compounds, or experiments described herein. In using such information or methods they should be mindful of their own safety and the safety of others, including parties for whom they have a professional responsibility.

Product or corporate names may be trademarks or registered trademarks, and are used only for identification and explanation without intent to infringe.

Library of Congress Cataloging-in-Publication Data
Levison, Louise.
  Filmmakers and financing: business plans for independents/Louise Levison.—7th ed.
    p. cm.

ISBN 978-0-240-82099-6 (pbk.)—ISBN 978-0-240-82137-5
1. Motion pictures—Production and direction. 2. Motion picture industry—Finance. I. Title.
    PN1995.9.P7L433 2012
    791.4302'320681—dc23
                                    2012034550

ISBN: 978-0-240-82099-6
ISBN: 978-0-240-82137-5

Typeset in Palatino
Project Managed and Typeset by: diacriTech.

For Leonard the Wonder Cat,
who has left us but continues to inspire . . . .
For Buffy and Angel, who inspire me every day.

Contents

7

Distribution: Nontheatrical and the Wild West   143

8

Risk Factors: Truth in Advertising   151

9

The Financial Plan: How It Works   155

10

The Financials: Forecasting Without Fear   189

11

Sample Business Plan   205

12

Breaking the Rules: Documentary, Animation,
and Large Format   245

13

Other People's Money: Them That Has the Gold Makes
Some of the Rules   265

www.focalpress.com/cw/levison

Companion Site Contents

(Note: Check the site for updates)

Ch. 11

Foreword

Despite the near hero worship accorded successful independent film producers and studio executives, not one of them would be able to function without a strong backup team. The myth of the one-person band is just that—a myth. Without the talent and hard work of the lawyers, bankers, accountants, development personnel, and administrative staff—not to mention the literally hundreds of people involved in actually making the films—no independent producer could survive, much less succeed.

To marshal all the disparate talents involved in mounting a major film production, the most important element is a common vision of the ultimate end product. In the same way that directors need a storyboard to communicate their vision of what the film will look like, producers need their own version of a storyboard (that is, a business plan) to explain their objectives, hopes, aspirations, and, yes, even their dreams.

Gone are the days when a business plan was regarded as inappropriate for an artistic endeavor such as producing a film. These days, the risks are too large, the competition too intense, and the sophistication of investors too great to "leave the details until later." Completion guarantees, discounted cash flows, letters of credit, foreign sales contracts, domestic distribution deals, internal rates of return, gross deals, rolling breaks, third-party participants' security interest, bank discounting, residuals, and cross-collateralization—all these terms, to name just a few, have become part of the regular vocabulary of today's independent producers. Without a detailed business plan to coordinate all these elements, it would be virtually impossible to produce a major film. So, dear independent producer, read on …

Jake Eberts

Jake Eberts has helped develop and finance films that have earned 64 Oscar nominations and received 27 Academy Awards. He also is a partner in Allied Productions East. Among the films on which he has been Producer or Executive Producer are *Chariots of Fire, Gandhi, The Killing Fields, Driving Miss Daisy, Dances with Wolves, A River Runs Through It, The Legend of Bagger Vance, The Education of Little Tree, Chicken Run, James and the Giant Peach, Open Range, Journey to Mecca, The Illusionist*, and *The Last Empress*.

Acknowledgments

To all the clients and students who have taught me as much as I have taught them

To all the industry professionals who have generously given of their time in classes and seminars to share their knowledge

To Rick Panplin for his ongoing encouragement and many contributions to the book

To Jake Eberts for graciously contributing to this book

To Thierry Baujard for his contributions on European funding

To Michael Donaldson, Bill Whitacre, Michael Norman Salesman, Robert Seigel, Karen Corrigan, Dr. Linda Seger, and John Johnson, whose comments on and contributions to the text are greatly appreciated

To Patrick Horton for his advice and always reminding me that the story come first, whether in a script or a book

To Suzy Prudden and Terrel Miller for helping me keep my mind and body in balance after spending hours at the computer

To Tracy and the early morning crew at The Coffee Roaster for helping feed the mind as well as the body

To Bill, Helen, Jeffrey, and Carl for their support and understanding

To Faryl Saliman Reingold for her editorial contributions and comments and her tireless efforts to keep me on track

To everyone at Focal Press for their patience and understanding

And last, but not least, to the late Leonard the Wonder Cat, my inspiration for the cat tales

Introduction
Controlling Your Destiny

A business plan always evolves

—ROB FRIEDMAN

Co-Chair Motion Picture Group. Lionsgate Entertainment

WHY SHOULD YOU BUY THIS BOOK?

King Ferdinand of Spain appointed a group of consultants to advise him on Christopher Columbus's enterprise for sailing to the Indies. This scholarly group of astronomers, mariners, and pilots pored over charts and graphs. They determined not only that the world was flat but also that the ocean was too big to be conquered.

"Ergo," they said, "if you try to sail to the Indies, you will fail." But Columbus had done his homework and planned ahead. He replied, "I have researched my own charts and graphs, spoken to other sailors, and obtained years of technical experience that proves otherwise. I believe it can be done." Columbus was the prototypical entrepreneur. He examined his proposed business venture and made forecasts regarding pros and cons and plunder versus expenses; he decided to move ahead and control his own destiny.

Neither Columbus nor any of his friends or enemies knew that he would run into the Americas on his journey. Nevertheless, he seized his opportunity and took appropriate action. By keeping abreast of the situation on his ships and the changes in the outside environment, he was able to make an informed decision. When he landed in the wrong place, Columbus looked at the opportunity, measured it against his goals, and decided that he had discovered a better place than he had originally intended.

From the dawn of film—actually, from the dawn of time— there have been individuals who have wanted to do it their own way. People who are not content to live by the rules of others continually strike out on their own. Here we are in 2012. The world is in turmoil with terrorists and strange viruses, governments are changing, corporations are failing, and the number of independent filmmakers keeps growing.

ABOUT THIS BOOK

Whether you use this book as a step-by-step guide for writing a plan or as a test of your own ability to be in business, it will help you meld creative thought with business fundamentals. It has been written in language that is accessible to those who are not skillful with business jargon. Understanding business is not that hard.

Whether you want to take the time to learn about business, or even want to be bothered with the noncreative aspects of filmmaking, is another question, one that you will have to answer for yourself. What if, after reading this book, you decide you would be better off selling your script to a studio or directing for one? Have you wasted your money? No. You will have saved money by reading this book first. It is better to find out now, rather than several months or thousands of dollars down the road, that running a business is not for you.

Goals of This Book

My goal in writing this book is to give you, the independent filmmaker, an introduction to the world of business and to provide a format to help you present yourself and your projects in the best possible light. People want to know who *you* are and what you will do. Dreams are good; the nature of an entrepreneur is to be a dreamer. Your plan will bring the dream and the reality together.

There are many filmmakers with projects who are struggling to obtain equity (private) dollars. Being able to see your project from the investor's viewpoint and being able to present it to the financial community in a recognizable form will give you a useful edge on the competition.

Throughout the book, I emphasize that this is your plan. When I write a business plan, it is also the client's plan, and that person or group must understand it.

A Constantly Changing Medium

My friend Jerry Quigg suggested calling this book *sex, films, and investing*. Good title. It is clear, informative, and to the point. All the elements for a book or a business plan are there. Your finest hour will come when an investor says, "What a sexy idea! It will make me money. How much do you want?" This book is sexy, too, in its own business-like way. It will bridge the gap for you between the passion of filmmaking and the day-to-day realities of creating a successful company.

As you read this, the motion picture business is changing right before your eyes. For four editions of this book, the big news in the "industry" chapter was which company was buying Universal Pictures. That company has remained part of the NBC family since the third edition; however, the rest of the industry seems to be buying, selling, and making new alliances at a pace faster than ever before. Much of this is due to the continued growth and presence of the independent sector as well as the rapid application of new technologies to the film business. The "paradigm" (an in-vogue word meaning "pattern") shift that has been predicted for over 20 years is taking place and its overall business effects are debated constantly. What hasn't changed is the audience. No matter how many products divide the finite viewing audience, theatrical motion pictures keep chugging down the track. Product is needed to fuel that engine, and you can be the one to provide it.

People go into independent filmmaking for many reasons. They are driven primarily by the subject matter, theme, or style of the pictures they want to make. I have talked to thousands of people who have told me what types of films they want to make. No two people have had the same vision, but they all share the same goal—to own their project and control it. Whether a filmmaker decides to make one film or many, it is up to him or her to understand how the business world functions. Of course, your goal may not be feature films at all. Instead, you may focus on other types of films—direct-to-home video, Internet, or any of the myriad new electronic/wireless devices. All of these are important, and all the principles stated in this book apply equally to them; however, their business models differ from that of film.

With new opportunities appearing for the independent filmmaker, more and more people want their own companies. Books and articles have been written about the ins and outs of writing or finding the perfect script, how to do the budget, finding the best location, and what camera to use. None of that information is in this book. The question before us is not how to make a film, but how to get the money.

You might argue, "But I'm making a film. This is different from other businesses." The details of any business may differ from industry to industry and from segment to segment, but the principles are the same. Movies involve lots of people, all of whom expect to get paid. Raising money involves intermediaries such as agents, finders, and lawyers, who expect to receive a fee for what they do. And do not forget the investor, who hopes to see a return on his investment. All films need certain standard ingredients to get going and stay alive. To get the show on the road, you need to put together a business plan.

It is true that independent films have been made and found success without a business plan. Many more films without one, however, have not been funded and never see the light of day. No plan can guarantee the thrill of victory, but not having a plan could bring you closer to the agony of defeat. When you read about all those productions setting up shop with a large influx of capital, which of these scenarios do you believe?

> *Scenario 1:* Louise, you've had such extraordinary success at Megalomaniac Studios that we would like to give you $100 million. Have fun and send us our share.
>
> *Scenario 2:* Louise, you've had such extraordinary success at Megalomaniac Studios that we would like to explore the possibility of having you head your own company with $5 million in seed capital. Why don't you get together with Victor Visionary and create a business plan? If we agree with your product analysis and the numbers look good, we're in business.

Trust me (a famous Hollywood term): Scenario 2 is far more likely. Wealthy people do not throw around big bucks on a whim. An investor may say, "Louise, you have a great idea." However, before that impulse leads to cash in your bank account, many questions will be asked. Eventually, someone will ask you for—you guessed it—a business plan.

The purpose of this book is to show you how to make all that thinking and analyzing into a coherent story. It is more than just an outline, however. The standard business plan outline has not changed for over 100 years. Open any book on business planning and you will see the same types of headings: Executive Summary, Company, Product (Film), Industry, Markets, Distributions, and Finance.

What do you do next? This book will help you take the next step to expound and polish your business plan within those guidelines. It specifies not only what you need to include but also why and how. I will give you samples—both good and bad—for writing the individual sections of your business plan.

Movies as a Business

The biggest misconception about the movie business is that the *movie* is more important than the *business*. Many of us tend to think about filmmaking not as a business at all but as an art form; in that case, it would be called *show art* instead of *show business*.

A movie is a form of art, but a very expensive one. Often the most difficult concept for filmmakers is looking at the movie as a commercial enterprise. The word *commercial* can be viewed in two very different ways. When it comes to artistic endeavors, many people give the word a negative connotation. The strict definition is "prepared for sale," but in many people's minds, the words "without regard to quality" are added to the end of that definition. Looking at the term in the broader sense, however, the filmmaker trades a seat at the film for someone else's dollar ($4, $9, or $15, as the case may be). Whether this trade occurs at a multiplex mall theater or at a video store, the buyer expects to get value for the trade, and the value is definitely in the eye of the beholder.

The Blair Witch Project, which earned $300 million worldwide and of which the business plan (yes, the filmmakers had one) called for raising $350,000, was always considered a commercial project. Audience evidently liked it a lot; other filmmakers were more critical. But the filmmakers made the film they intended to make consistent with their vision and were successful in their effort. They were innovative not only in the filmmaking but also in their use of the Internet. The point is that they made a film that brought profit to themselves and their investors—the real meaning of the word *commercial*.

The definition of *independent film* depends on the speaker's agenda. Filmmakers often want to ascribe exclusionary creative definitions to the term. When you go into the market to raise money from private investors (both domestic and foreign), it doesn't matter if your film is a mini-budget production or a $200-million blockbuster. You are still finding your own financing. Sometimes filmmakers on panels declare that someone else's film is not independent by being "a genre" or "in a specific genre" (i.e., horror, comedy, and family). This drives me crazy. In the end, esoteric discussions don't really matter. We all have our own agendas. If you want to find financing for your film, however, I suggest embracing the broader definition of the term used in this book: An independent film is one made by those individuals or companies apart from the major studios that assume the majority of the financial risk for a production and control its exploitation in the majority of the world.

There are plenty of successful filmmakers who manage to find their own financing to do things their way—John Sayles, Woody Allen, George Romero, and the Coen brothers, to name a few. They make films on whatever subjects please them. While some of their films with relatively small budgets may have a limited distribution and other are taken wide, they try to keep their budgets at levels comparable to the likely box office receipts for that type of story.

It seems to be a simple concept. If you produce a gizmo designed to lose money, you go out of business. Why would it be any different with a film? Many films lose money (ask the studios), but many films have success also. Film investors have a right to expect to earn back their money at least. Unfortunately, many auteur filmmakers find the concepts of creativity and attracting an audience mutually exclusive. If you suffer from this malady, take two aspirin and rethink your position. Even relatives have their limits; they don't want to lose money either. You are using *other people's money*. Be respectful of it.

People Get the Money

A question frequently asked of me by students and clients is: "How much money have your business plans raised?" My answer is: "None. People raise money. Business plans are only a tool." Some of the best business plans I ever wrote are stored in drawers; they haven't raised any money. In addition, although you may have the most well-written and well-presented business plan ever done, to raise the money you have to:

1. Be ready to go ahead with the film.
2. Understand the contents of the plan.
3. Look until you find the money.

To be ready to get your project off the ground, you have to be focused on your goal. If you are arguing with your partners, are not ready to make decisions, or are unwilling to look for money, the quality of your business plan is immaterial. The biggest consulting firms down to the smallest ones have plans stored on shelves gathering dust, because the client was not ready to be serious about taking on partners or making changes. Business plans do not find money by themselves.

Once you track down your "prey" and deliver this terrific plan, you have to explain what it is all about—how it represents you. A plan is only a guideline with strategies and forecasts. You have to demonstrate to others that you can carry out the steps described within. Unless you understand every step of the plan—rather than just handing over a document written by someone else—you will not be able to do this.

Finally, are you adept at handling business in a professional and impressive manner? When all is said and done, the company is only a reflection of your demeanor and presentation. After all the numbers have been added up, investors are still betting on people. If they are unsure or wary about you, no checks will be written.

All consultants have clients whom they would like to keep hidden. Sometimes it would be ideal if the entrepreneur and the investor never met. Some clients like to argue with investors and generally have a take-it-or-leave-it attitude. I once had a client—a successful studio screenwriter—who actually said to an investor, "I'm doing you a favor by giving you this opportunity. Take it or leave it." The investor left it.

How Does the Economic Climate Affect Financing?

When I wrote the sixth edition, we were in the middle of a recession. Now in 2012, we are still there. While people always go to the movies (and will continue even with all the new media available), they usually go more often in difficult times. As of the end of June, the total box office was 6 percent more than the same period last year. The independent portion of that box office was 42 percent ahead. To put it in perspective, however, *The Hunger Games* accounted for 26 percent of the increase. Nevertheless, if we ignore that film as a reason, the indie box office was still 15 percent ahead of 2011.

The short explanation of the box office going up during difficult economic times is just that. If you are putting together a business plan in 2015, the economic picture could be different. Since this book tends to be published as we are going through a national election, making definitive statements about the general economic picture is impossible. You easily can do the research on the Web and find many quotes as to what is happening. In addition, I publish a newsletter and write blogs for Focal and Baseline that will tell you how the independent box office is faring. It always is important to give an analysis of the big picture for your investors. To update the quotes, go to the Motion Picture Association of America (http://www.mpaa.org/press). Currently, I use this paragraph in the Executive Summary of business plans:

> Widely recognized as a "recession-proof" business, the entertainment industry has historically prospered even during periods of decreased discretionary income. "In mature markets such as the United States, the business can be more cyclical in the short term, driven by product supply and distribution patterns," National Association of Theatre Owners President John Fithian stated. "In the long term, however, domestic revenues continue to grow ... 2012 looks to be another growth year." Senator Thomas Dodd, Chairman and CEO of the Motion Picture Association of America (MPAA), stated at the December 2011 Asia Pacific Screen Awards, "I am proud to report that the film industry remains a key driver of economic growth around the globe."

Can Anybody Do This?

Developing a business plan involves the proverbial "10 percent inspiration and 90 percent perspiration." In other words, anybody can do it. Unfortunately, I have found that most people lose interest when faced with the amount of research and work that is required. If you want to make your own films, however, this is part of the price of admission.

To find financing for your films, you do not have to be part of the business world, have an M.B.A., or be an accounting genius. This book will help you bridge the gap between right-brain creative thinking and left-brain math stuff. All you need is the desire to be in control—a powerful motivation.

Hollywood Is Only an Attitude

"Hollywood" is not a specific place. This book does not restrict the term *filmmaker* to those toiling in Burbank, Century City, or other areas of the southern California movie scene. Moviemaking is a worldwide event. The person in Cincinnati, Ohio, with a camcorder who aspires to make a documentary or a feature film is as much a filmmaker as her counterpart in Brisbane, Australia. Watch the film festival rosters and you will quickly see that there is a lot of moviemaking going on outside of Los Angeles in places like Omaha, Boston, Orlando, Mexico City, Taipei, and Galway. My client Rick Pamplin, who owns The Pamplin Film Company, lived and worked in Los Angeles for a number of years until reaching a different level of success in Florida.

An Entrepreneur Is an Entrepreneur...

For most entrepreneurs, the idea of boiling down a vision into a neatly contained business proposal is as foreign as the notion of taking a job. Nevertheless, the recipe for success in today's competitive business environment demands that we act as managers as well as artists. The most common blunder that entrepreneurs make is to assume that a business plan is a creative piece of fiction used to trick a rich person into giving them money. Even worse is the assumption that creating a business plan is an interesting hobby for someone who has nothing else to do. The biggest mistake made by independent filmmakers is to see themselves not as businesspeople but as only artistes—creatures whose contact with the murky world of business is tangential to their filmmaking and unimportant. Nothing could be farther from the truth.

When a person has an original idea and develops it into a product, an entrepreneur is born—a person who has personal drive, creates an intimate vision, and is willing to take risks. Entrepreneurs want to make the decisions and be in charge of the show; they want to do what they want to do when they want to do it! I have never met an entrepreneur who was not convinced that he was right, who did not believe that the world couldn't live without his film, and who did not want to control his own destiny. Independent film-makers are the best kinds of entrepreneurs, because they want to push the edge of the envelope and seek new horizons. They are major risk takers.

Film investors are the biggest risk takers of all, however. They bet their dollars on an idea and help it become a reality—a contri-bution not to be taken lightly. Too often filmmakers believe that investors should donate their money and then quietly go away. Of course, this attitude is not unique to filmmakers. Most entrepre-neurs feel that their ideas have more value than the capital needed to make them a reality. Think again, or you won't see any cash.

Rick's Story

Independent filmmaker Rick Pamplin has had his own film com-pany since 1994. After selling scripts and projects to studios and major independents in Hollywood, and after teaching screenwrit-ing, low-budget producing, and directing for nine years, Pamplin moved to Orlando. "It wasn't easy and most of my friends and fam-ily thought I was crazy. At the time I had a wife and small child and no income. But in my heart I knew I was an independent filmmaker and believed in my talent and myself." Unfortunately, such struggles can play havoc on a family, and eventually the Pamplins divorced.

"My first project was with a partner. Although we had a script, raised development money and attached talent, we could never get the film off the ground. We then raised money for a comedy concert film, *Michael Winslow Live*, by asking everyone we knew and every-one they knew for money." The film was sold to the STARZ pre-mium cable channels, Australian television, and received American and European DVD deals. Recent sales have included Netflix streaming, multiple Video-on-Demand deals, and iTunes.

Their second project, *Hoover*, starring the late Academy Award–winning actor Ernest Borgnine, had a small theatrical open-ing and is now available on DVD, Netflix, Video-on-Demand and iTunes. A third project, *Magic 4 Morons*, an award-winning instruc-tional video, debuted on the Home Shopping Network, got a distri-bution deal, reached several foreign markets, and is also available on DVD, Netflix, and Video-on-Demand.

Pamplin and Business Strategies then developed separate business plans for three feature films and set out to find production funding. "We had raised the money for our first three projects in a relatively short period. Raising money for independent films is a marathon, not a hundred-yard dash, so you'd better be prepared for it. Luckily our business plans were solid, investors liked our packages, we signed Borgnine to a three-picture deal, which gave us credibility, and we have been able to raise development funds to sustain us during the lean years." Each of the projects attracted talent, development money, and endless meetings. A New York company, a Tampa (FL), homebuilder, and a doctor all came to various stages of contracting for the financing, but the deals never closed. In June 2006, Pamplin and investor Harry Green signed deals for financing the three films. Unfortunately, a month later, Harry, who also had also become a good friend, passed away unexpectedly. Then a fund-raiser from Palm Beach was interested, a South African source got involved, and so on and so on.

"Over the years we have reduced the budgets, raised the budgets, changed casts and constantly updated the business plan," Pamplin said. Once again, as this book goes to press, the saga is unfinished. Pamplin has signed contracts for funding the three films in his safe, a verbal commitment from a Philadelphia group for $25 million in production funding, interest from an Executive Producer of a baseball film, and a Swedish investor he's known for seven years.

"People come and go, contracts are signed and not funded, actors, development investors, relatives and partners pass away, yet the projects live on and we keep finding qualified investors that are interested in funding them," Pamplin says. Orson Welles once said, "It's about two percent movie making and ninety-eight percent hustling. It's no way to spend a life." Pamplin agrees with the first part but seems strangely optimistic that his funding will come through before this book's manuscript is set for printing.

In the last edition, I asked Rick if we should keep his story, knowing that his intention from the beginning was to show filmmakers that, like any business, getting a film made is 20 percent inspiration and 80 percent perspiration. His response was, "We have made four movies, all of which are in worldwide distribution and have won awards. We are a successful indie company. I have survived doing script doctoring, consulting and living as a frugal filmmaker. I just finished my first documentary feature and it has been released on DVD." "I'm still in the game, making the movies I want, controlling my destiny, and living my dream. Was it a good decision? YES. Would I do it again? YES. Did I ever imagine it would be this hard? NO."

I asked Rick if he still felt that way.

"YES, the only way to finish the marathon is to not stop."

WHY BOTHER WITH A BUSINESS PLAN?

Art Versus Profit

Lately, this topic has been in heated discussions on social networking and entertainment industry sites. Such activity is often the result of any film festival or market. At the 2010 Los Angeles Film Festival, James Stern, CEO of Endgame, stated three rules when making a film:

1. Make smarter movies.
2. Respect the money!
3. Before rolling cameras ... think "market."

Which one is more important—one's artistic expression or money? My view has always been that both are. If you are using your own money, you can do anything you want. On the other hand, if you are using someone else's money, it doesn't mean that you automatically have to forgo your artist intentions; you just have to make clear to your financial source what the chances are that they will ever see a return on their money or profit. Then it can be their decision, which is more important.

The Role of the Plan

The business plan is the entrepreneur's single most valuable document and his or her best safeguard for success. The majority of businesses that fail usually have paid little attention to proper planning. In Jake Eberts's book, *My Indecision Is Final: The Rise and Fall of Goldcrest Films*, he mentions several times that the company, which he founded, had no business plan. Although its first film, *Chariots of Fire*, won the Academy Award for Best Picture, the company (different from the one in operation today) did not succeed in the long run. Would Goldcrest have fared differently had the company had a business plan? No one can say for sure, but it is obvious from reading Eberts's book that this group of very talented people had widely divergent professional and personal agendas. They also had very different business styles.

Whether you are making one film or several, you have to identify who you are, where you are going, and how you are going to get there. The business plan allows you to plot this path. It gives you the opportunity to develop a clear picture of the growth and bottom-line prospects for your film company. It also enables you to make more effective decisions and helps everyone follow the leader. When you have a clear course laid out, you have guideposts to follow that will show you where you are vis-à-vis your goals. While you may find this secondary to raising money, it really is a priority for fulfilling that goal.

The ideal length and depth of a business plan vary. You have something to accomplish and a specific path you must travel to accomplish it. The steps that you take along that path are defined in your plan. Before beginning any business, you want to know the nature of your goals and objectives, the desired size of the company, the products and/or services it will sell, its customers and market niche, the amount of revenue likely to flow, and its sources. When you think of a business plan, your first thought may be how to impress the investor. Before you worry about the bank or the distribution company or the wealthy investor, however, you have to make a personal business plan. For all of those people—and for yourself—you have to come up with an agreeable course of action, and you have to stick to it. This book will help you do that.

Is This Book for Someone Making One Film?

In a word, "Yes." After six editions, people still call or email and ask me this question. Any movie proposal—whether for a single film or a company—that seeks to raise money from private investors needs a business plan. If you are doing a single film, the outline is exactly the same, except you have fewer numbers to project and there is no separate overhead. While production for one film is estimated to be one year, distribution can take another year or two. Once the film is distributed, you will see 80 to 100 percent of your revenues being returned in two years. It is essential to remember that before going into business, you must find out for yourself whether business is your thing. One film is a business and the producer (or executive producer) is the manager. You have the same responsibility to investors as if you were making four or five films. Reading this book will help you determine if a business is what you really want.

The Facts and Nothing But ...

The structure of a business plan is standard, but the contents are not boilerplate. Each film has its own unique qualities. All plans must be substantive, promotional, and succinct, with a length generally about 20–25 pages for a one-film plan—that is, comprehensive but not too long. The business plan needs to contain enough information in a readable format that excites, or at least impresses, potential investors. Perhaps even more important, however, is that the plan clearly represents you and your ideas. Copying someone else's plan is like copying someone's test paper in school. You may give the right answers to the wrong questions.

Several years ago, an acquaintance of mine wrote a business plan that was very professional and cleverly laid out. He found that he had to keep it under lock and key, because other producers kept making copies of it. What they failed to recognize was the specialized nature of his company. It was structured to fund development money, not to produce films. The payback to the investors is quite different with development money. The "borrowers" of the product were so enamored of the text and graphics that they were blind to the obvious: The business plan promoted a type of company that they did not plan to run. How they ever managed to explain the relatively lower return to investors we will never know.

NEGOTIATION STANCES

The first strategy that I suggest in negotiating with an investor is to leave the negotiation deal points out of the business plan altogether. By doing so, you keep yourself open for the best deal. Notice that the financial examples in the sample business plan in Chapter 11 do not show a breakdown for the split with investors. They simply show the pretax dollars available for sharing. How the interested parties decide on equitable shares will depend on the number of parties involved, the types of entities involved, and proposals not foreseen by this plan. Even if you have a limited liability company (LLC) or limited partnership (L.P.) (or any other offering memorandum) that specifies shares, you may find an investor who wants to put in all the money. In this case, he will probably want to negotiate one on one with you and your attorney. Several of my clients have had this happen.

I advise my clients to hold their cards close to the vest and to let the other person go first. Even though you have determined your needs and expectations in advance, a situation may arise that you had not anticipated. For example, one group that I worked with assumed in advance that they were looking for an investor in the company as a whole. I convinced them to forego detailing this investment share in their business plan. In the beginning, equity investors for the whole amount were hard to find, but the filmmakers knew several people who would invest in individual films. This option was better for them in the end. They kept control of the company, as there were no new partners, and they found the resources for financing features on an individual basis.

The Investor Wants How Much?

It is always perplexing for creative people who have put their hearts and souls into a project to give away 50 percent or more to an investor. A common complaint is, "I'm doing all the work. Why should he get 50 percent?" Your decision has to be based on whether the amount of investment money is worth giving the investor that large a share of the profits. I cannot answer this question for you. Your priorities and goals are part of this decision. A standard business plan ploy that seldom gets funded is the 70/30 or 60/40 split in your favor. There may be someone out there willing to take it—never say never—but chances are that you will give your business plan to a variety of people, so reserve the bargaining for the individual. If potential investors seem unsophisticated, you can try it. If you are lucky, they will only laugh. If you are unlucky, they will laugh while leaving the room. At least, the thought is not written in stone in your Executive Summary.

Specialized Financial Instruments

If your company is a L.P., LLC, or other private placement, the amount of ownership is set ahead of time in the prospectus. Many entrepreneurs think that the business plan and the prospectus are one and the same.

The business plan is a marketing and sales tool. It has to be factual. There will be additional explanations about what to include and what to say (or not) in each chapter of this book. Of course, the financial projects are forecasting the future. However, they need to be based on the best data that can be obtained from the most credible sources available.

Your private placement (PPM), which is the most usual form of legal document used when raising money from equity investors for film, is a nonpublic (not sold on the stock exchange) document that is your legal agreement with investors. It is separate from the business plan. The PPM includes arrangements for selling, discounts and commissions to dealers, subscription agreements, how monies are to be distributed, and responsibilities and rights of company management and investors. You cannot write your own by pasting together wording from previous documents. I don't care what your financial circumstances are. An attorney familiar with the format and the film industry *must* write this document. Otherwise, you run the risk of unintentionally opening yourself to accusations of fraud and future lawsuits.

Even if you plan to use one of these business structures, I recommend keeping the business plan a freestanding document. The business plan is part of the total package and being able to circulate the plan separately could come in handy. You never know what opportunities may come your way.

BUSINESS PLAN OUTLINE

This book is best described as a movie within a movie. To find financing for your projects, you will have to describe how your production or company will function. Accordingly, this book describes how the business works as well as instructing you on how to put the business plan together.

The book is arranged so that the numbered chapters follow the steps of the business plan. They appear in the order that the sections of your plan should follow with chapters (6, 7, 9, 12, and 13) giving you additional information. As you will see in the sample business plan, I don't include the subtitles of the sections, either.

1. Executive Summary: A Short Version of Everything
2. The Company: Who, What, When, Where, and Why

3. The Films: The Investor Needs to Know the Whole Story
4. The Industry: The Facts and Nothing But
5. The Markets: The Spin
6. Distribution: Theatrical and Managing the Changing Landscape
7. Distribution: Nontheatrical and the Wild West
8. Risk Factors: Truth in Advertising
9. Financial Plan: How It Works
10. The Financials: Forecasting Without Fear
11. The Sample Business Plan
12. Breaking the Rules: Documentary, Animation, and IMAX
13. Other People's Money: Them That Has the Gold Makes Some of the Rules

Note that the subheadings in these chapters do not have to appear in the business plan. This outline has been the stuff of business plans from time immemorial. Finally, a sample business plan for a fictional company appears in Chapter 11.

There are two new chapters. I've added Chapter 12, which moves the information about documentaries, animation, and large format from the market, and distribution chapters of earlier editions. While the general format is the same for these films, there are additional genre and market approaches, as well as slightly different financial formats. Chapter 13 expands how to work with investors.

No matter how independent you are, when writing your business plan, do not fool with tradition. You should make it as easy as you can for potential investors to read your plan. They are used to seeing the information in a certain way, so humor them. It is in your best interest not to be an auteur with your business plan. As you devise your plan section by section, you will find yourself being repetitious; likewise, you will find the chapters of this book somewhat repetitious. Think of the plan as a series of building blocks.

ADDITIONAL INFORMATION ON COMPANION WEBSITE

Focal Press has a companion website for *Filmmakers and Financing*. It contains files with additional information that can be downloaded to your computer. Don't go to the files until you have gone through the book. The most comprehensive set of files is the Financial section, which contains explanations and worksheets of my method of forecasting. I have used *Len's Thrill*, one of the films in the Sample Business Plan in Chapter 11, for a step-by-step explanation of how I develop the forecast. The contents and how to access the website is on page ix.

1

The Executive Summary: A Short Version of Everything

"Begin at the beginning," the King said, gravely, "and go till you come to the end; then stop."

—LEWIS CARROLL
Alice's Adventures in Wonderland

READ THIS CHAPTER LAST!

This admonition is like saying, "Don't open this package until Christmas!" You are, right this minute, ignoring me and reading this chapter anyway. Fine, but when it comes to writing your business plan, write the Executive Summary last. Typically, investors will read the Executive Summary first; nevertheless, it is the section you want to write last. It is the hook that pulls readers into your net, and it must represent your future plans precisely.

The Executive Summary is the place where you tell readers what you're about to tell them. Am I confusing you? Remember that old advice about writing term papers: "Tell them what you're going to tell them; tell them; tell them what you told them." You do the same thing in the Executive Summary. It is a condensed version of the rest of your proposal. This is not a term paper; this is your life.

The beginning of your business plan is the section about your film (or films, if you are starting a multifilm company). You give a brief overview of the people, the products, and your goals. In the rest of the sections—Company, Film(s), Industry, Markets, Distribution, Risk, and Financing—you provide more detail about how the company is going to function. The last section you write is the Executive Summary, which is just a summary. It presents a review of the plan for the reader.

WHY TO WRITE THE EXECUTIVE SUMMARY LAST?

Developing a business plan is a process of discovery. Until you actually put your business plan together, you cannot be sure what it will contain. As you will see in the rest of this book, much research, thought, and skill go into a proposal of this type. The total plan is the result of everything you learn from the process, and the Executive Summary is the culmination of that full effort.

The Executive Summary is written last for the same reason that you prepare a full budget before you do the top pages. You may have a problem with this comparison if you do the top pages of the budget first or if you do only the top pages. At best, filling in numbers on the top pages is a "guesstimate." Only when you actually work out the real 20 to 30 pages of the budget, based on the script breakdown, you know the real costs.

Perhaps your guesstimate will end up being right on the mark. I don't think anyone has worked out the precise odds on that happening, but you might be more likely to win a lottery. A more probable scenario is that you will have backed yourself into a corner with original numbers that are too low. The real budget will turn out to be greater than your estimate by $500,000, $2 million, or even more. When that happens, your potential investors will be extremely unimpressed. If you are not sure how their money will be spent, ought they to trust you with it?

A business plan is the same situation magnified a thousand times. All the reasons outlined in the Introduction for writing a business plan come into play. You may be setting parameters for yourself that are unrealistic and that lock you into a plan you cannot carry out. In putting together the proposal, your investigation of the market may cause you to fine-tune your direction. Learning more about distribution—and we all can—may invite a reworking of your film's release strategies.

Even when inventing a fictional company, as I did in Chapter 11, the Executive Summary must be written last. I did not know what I was going to say in the summary until the rest of the plan was written. Although I invented the company and the statistics for the sake of an example, my Industry, Markets (except for the cats), Distribution, and Financing sections are all real. I did not know which facts about all those elements would apply to my particular situation. Likewise, until I worked out the numbers and cash flows, I could not summarize the need for cash. The most difficult task for many entrepreneurs is resisting the impulse to write five quick pages and run it up the flagpole to see if anyone salutes. A business plan is not a script, and you cannot get away with handing in only a treatment. Your business plan must be well thought out, and you must present a complete package. Think of this as a rule. Other guidelines are suggestions that you would be wise to follow, but this is definitely a rule. Go through the process first. By the time you have carefully crafted your document and gone through all the steps outlined in this book, you will be able to proceed with as few hitches as possible.

This process has to be a cautious one, not a haphazard one. You want to be sure that your proposal makes business sense; you want to be able to meet any goals or verify any facts that you set forth. Passion does count. The film business is too hard, and it takes too long to tackle projects if you do not have a passion for your story and filmmaking. However, business facts are the glue that holds everything together in a tidy package.

Investors are the second reason that you write the Executive Summary only after you have carefully devised your business plan. Before you approach any money source, you want to be sure that your project is reasonable and rational. Potential investors do not accumulate their money by chance, and they are not likely to give you money on impulse. If you appear rash and impulsive, your 15 minutes of fame will run out before you know it. Treat potential investors as intelligent people, even if you are approaching the stockbroker's favorite group—widows and orphans. They'll have a business advisor who will read the proposal.

Often an investor will ask to see the Executive Summary first whether you are making one film or forming a company. In order to present him with the summary, you have to write the entire plan first, or there is nothing to summarize. Since a crucial part of the two or three pages is going to be a financial summary, how will you do that without running out all the data first? You would be making it up, which is not a good idea. The investor will be making initial assumptions based on those numbers. You don't want to be in the position later of saying, "Gee, we were a little off. Our budget is $5 million rather than $2 million, and the net profit is $3 million rather than $15 million." You will have lost an investor.

Besides, 5 will get you 10 if the investor likes what he sees in the Executive Summary, and the next communication will be, "Let me see the rest of the plan." That person means today—now. As I pointed out earlier, he assumes that there is a body of work supporting your summary; therefore, the summary and the complete proposal have to match. You do not want to have to tell potential investors that you will have the complete plan in a month. When equity investors ask for a business plan, you must have all the market explanations, facts, and figures at hand and in order.

STYLE OF THE EXECUTIVE SUMMARY

The image experts say that you have 30 seconds to make an impression, whether it is at a job interview, in a negotiation, or at your local party place on a Friday night. Your business plan has a similar amount of time. First impressions count; they will make the reader either want to read further or toss the proposal aside.

Cicero said that brevity is the charm of eloquence; this thought is a good one to keep in mind. In a few paragraphs, you must summarize the entire business plan to show the goals driving the business, the films, the essential market and distribution factors, and the major elements for the success of the project. Each chapter in the outline has its own summary. I know that it is hard to understand this repetition; students and clients ask about it all the time. That is why I keep coming back to it.

Earlier I said that the Executive Summary is the hook; you can also think of it as the bait that attracts the fish. You want the reader to be intrigued enough to read on. You need not try to rival John Grisham or Stephen King as a writer of thrillers or horror stories. You should not expect to keep readers on the edge of their seats. Simply provide the salient points in the Executive Summary: Less is more. If the Executive Summary of your plan is as long as this chapter, it is entirely too long. You can be long-winded later. All you want to do in the summary is give your readers the facts with as little embellishment as possible. Remember that this is a business proposal, not a script.

LAYING OUT THE EXECUTIVE SUMMARY

Follow your outline when writing the Executive Summary. Give the basic information of each section. Do not deviate from the path that you have already chosen. Anything you say here has to appear in more detail somewhere else in the proposal. Refer to the Executive Summary of the sample business plan in Chapter 11 while reviewing how to lay out your own summary.

Strategic Opportunity

Typically, the first section of the Executive Summary is called "Strategic Opportunity."

The Company

This section describes the outstanding elements of your goals and plans. Here, the reader finds out what is the name of your production company, what type of film or films you are making, and who you are.

A short introduction to your *production team* is included to give investors an idea of your team's experience and expertise. If you happen to be starting a company, you may want to call this the *management team*, as it will include executives who aren't involved in production per se. Indicate any notable attachments—director, producer, and/or actors—but save their bios to follow in the longer Company section. If you have a company plan in which each film has its own director and producers, you may want to include their bios with each film rather than in the Company section.

As we will discuss later, be sure to include only people who have given consent to be involved in your project in some written form. Do not include people who you would like to work with but who have never heard of you. Typically, you can include consultants, such as the business plan advisor or attorney, in the longer Company section; however, if you feel it is important to put them up front to add immediate credibility for your team, do so.

The Film

In this section, give readers only the most important information about your proposed film or films. Normally, I include one or two lines that have some punch or are intriguing while still giving the investor the essence of the story. Look at some of the one-line plot summaries in www.imdb.com. For example, for *Juno*, they have written, "Faced with an unplanned pregnancy, an offbeat young woman makes an unusual decision regarding her unborn child." This sounds much more interesting than if they just said, "The film is a coming-of-age story about a pregnant teenager." Both are correct, but you want to pique your investors' interest. It is also likely that the fuller explanation will make your investors ask what the choice is. If they like it, fine. If they don't, it saves you time. They won't like it any more later, after they have read the complete synopsis.

The Industry

Before describing your specific segment of the marketplace, it is necessary to give an overview of the industry. Just a short paragraph to show the current shape and financial growth of the industry will do. Include such things as the U.S. box office, worldwide box office, total admissions, and size of the independent film market.

The Markets

In this section, you should give readers a feel for the markets for your films. Spell out target markets (genres, affinity groups, etc.), as well as typical age groups. In addition, include any self-marketing methods you intend to use, with explanations of their value.

Distribution

Simply saying "We will get distribution" is not enough. Don't laugh. I've seen this in plans.

If you have distribution attached, give names here. Don't be shy. However, do be circumspect, as with the body of the plan. Mention only real companies from which you have received actual written commitments. Phrases such as "We have interest from many companies to distribute our films" are public relations jargon.

If potential investors think that they will find such meaningless generalizations in the rest of the plan, they may not read on. If you are planning to self-distribute your film, mention it here. Hiding that fact until readers have worked their way through 20 pages or more of the business plan will not help you at all. State your reasons and describe in a few sentences your knowledge in the area of distribution.

Investment Opportunity and Financial Highlights

This section summarizes all the financial information in your plan. The first item to include is that all-important fact that hundreds of people leave out of their plans—how much money you want. Do not keep it a secret. The whole point of handing this plan to potential investors is to relieve them of a little of the green stuff. They know that; they just want to know how much.

Follow with a summary sentence indicating the worldwide box office and projected profit. Whether you are making one film or several over 5 to 10 years, the details will be in your Financing section. Many of your investors will have business experience, whether or not it is in film. They are likely to look directly from the Executive Summary to the tables to see the details of revenues and expenses.

Notice that I continually use the words *projection, forecast*, and *estimate* throughout the financial sections. Always qualify any expressions of future gain with one of these three words. I also include a phrase saying that there is no guarantee. For example, "Using a moderate revenue projection and an assumption of general industry distribution costs, we project (but do not guarantee) …"

WHAT DOESN'T BELONG HERE

If by chance you skipped the Introduction, go back and read the Negotiation Stances section. The business plan is a freestanding document. It should not include any investor negotiations or legal language relating to how money will be distributed. The business plan is a marketing document that is part of a total package; however, it is not the total package.

2

The Company: Who, What, When, Where, and Why

To open a business is easy; to keep it open is difficult.
—CHINESE PROVERB

STARTING IS EASY

To start a business, all you have to do is choose a name and have a phone; ergo, you are in business. To be successful, though, a business involves much more. A company, according to the *American College Dictionary*, is "a number of people united for a joint action … a band, party, or troop of people." The lone screenwriter is an island of self-absorption; the filmmaker is king—long live the king! When she becomes the producer of even one film, though, she is running a business.

Running a business embodies a totally different set of skills. It is a special kind of collaboration in which dictatorship does not work. For a business to run successfully, everyone must agree on its purpose, direction, and method of operation. This goal requires a lot of planning and communication.

I always like to recount my first seminar in which I started the day with a discourse on "Common Blunders in Business Planning." At the break, my assistant overheard someone say, "What is all this esoteric nonsense? We came here to find out where the investors are." To make my meaning clear, I started each full-day seminar by putting a list of companies on the board. I asked the seminar participants to tell me what these companies had in common. After attempts by several attendees, one observant person finally recognized that they all had declared Chapter 11 (bankruptcy with reorganization of the business) or Chapter 7 (bankruptcy with liquidation of the business) or shut the doors in some other way.

Now it is more appropriate to discuss specialty divisions that have become brands within a studio or the more complicated dissolutions of international conglomerates that caused their production or distribution divisions to become stand-alone companies with their own financing.

The first reaction from independent producers was that these companies were all big and that somehow their size contributed to their downfall. In reality, the reason companies—whether big or small—failed was the same in either case: lack of planning. Anyone can have bad luck. Part of planning, however, is looking at the future result of current decisions. In doing this, you can build in ways of dealing with bad luck and other problems. Granted, some crises are beyond your control. A bank failure or the bankruptcy of a distributor, for example, is such an outside event. But careful planning can help you anticipate even these external occurrences.

The business plan diagrams a path for you to follow. Along the way, there may be forks in the road and new paths to take; flexibility in adjusting to such changing conditions is the key. On the other hand, taking every highway and byway that you see might take you in circles. In that case, you will never get a project completed and in the theaters. A balance is needed, therefore, between flexibility and rigidity. Planning provides this balance.

KNOW YOURSELF FIRST

When asked what they want to do, many filmmakers (or entrepreneurs of any stripe) reply either "I want to make money" or "I want to make films." There is nothing intrinsically wrong with either answer, but there are more questions to be considered. For example, what is the nature of the films you will make? what are you willing to do for money? and, ultimately, who are you?

Before characterizing your company for yourself or anyone else, make sure that you really know yourself. For example, one filmmaker told me that she intended to live and work in Georgia; she would make her films there and seek all money there. For her, this goal was nonnegotiable. This position may seem rigid to some people, but you have to know the lines you are not willing to cross.

Goals 101

Having and keeping a clear vision is important; it is as easy or as hard as you want to make it. Ensuring that you understand what you are truly about is the first step. A full course in Goals 101 would be too long to include here, but we can quickly review the basic principles with a minimum of academic jargon.

Setting goals merely means clearly stating your main purpose. Objectives are often shorter-term accomplishments aimed at helping you meet your main goal. For example, writing this book was my ultimate goal; teaching university classes was a short-term objective to help me reach my goal. I felt that the best way to establish credibility for a book contract was by teaching at University of California at Los Angeles (UCLA). From the beginning, I knew that the pay would be low compared to consulting and other work; however, over the short term, the book was more important. Teaching at UCLA, then, became a greater priority than making lots of money.

The business and personal aspects of your life may mesh quite well, but any conflicts between the two need to be reconciled at the beginning. Otherwise, those conflicts may interfere with your success in one or both areas. Covert agendas are sometimes good to use with competitors, but fooling yourself is downright dangerous.

Formulating Your Goals

Formulating your goals may seem complicated, but it involves just two simple but essential steps:

1. Take a meeting with yourself at the start. (In Los Angeles and New York, everyone "does lunch.") Think about your plans, look at them, dream about them, and then set out to test them against reality.
2. Write your plans down. Entrepreneurs love to declare that they can keep everything in their heads and do not have to write anything down. Big mistake! If your ideas are so clear, it will take you only a few minutes to commit them to paper. Anything you cannot explain clearly and concisely to yourself will not be clear to someone else. Writing down your goals allows you to see the target you are trying to hit. Then you can establish intermediate objectives or a realistic plan to accomplish these goals.

A word about money is in order. John D. Rockefeller said, "Mere money-making was never my goal;" other successful executives have made similar statements. Many talk shows have brought together groups of entrepreneurs to find out what motivates them. They almost always identify making the product, negotiating the deal, or some other activity as their main motivation; the money followed when they did the things they liked. Do something that you enjoy, that you are passionate about, and that you are good at; then the money, according to many popular books, will follow.

Whether or not you become rich, I cannot stress too often that filmmaking is not an easy business. Be sure that it is the filmmaking that draws you—not just the tinsel, glitter, and high-revenue prospects.

Personal Goals Versus Business Goals

Finding fulfillment is an elusive goal. To start, you must list and prioritize your goals. Unless you know where you are heading, you will be severely hampered in making decisions as you walk down your path. People have both business and personal goals, so it is crucial to look at both categories.

First, take a look at your personal goals to make sure that you do not inadvertently overlook something you want. This question has been the hardest for students and clients to answer. Someone will say that it is to move to Los Angeles to pursue film or hire a good director. Your personal goals have nothing to do with work per se; they are your private desires, your plans about your lifestyle, your dreams that will bring a feeling of satisfaction outside of work. Can you identify your personal goals? What is important to you? Is it family? Church? Riding horses in Montana? Consider the pursuits and activities that you find meaningful. Decide which are important enough to have time for outside of pursuing your business.

If the idea of personal objectives still perplexes you, take some time to think about it. Being passionate about films is one thing; having nothing else in your life is something else. Once you can identify your personal goals, continue on.

List your personal goals on a piece of paper, not in your head; writing in the margins of this book is permitted. Describe as many or as few goals as you want, as long as you have at least one. Here are some examples to help you get started:

1. Improve my standard of living.
2. Live and spend quality time with my family in Council Bluffs.
3. Play in poker tournaments (my list).
4. Work out with a fitness trainer on a regular basis. (Should be on my list!)
5. Volunteer at a local food bank every two months.

Now identify your filmmaking (i.e., business) goals. Again, make a list using the following examples as a guide:

1. Make inspirational films.
2. Form a company that will make action/adventure films with budgets less than $10 million.
3. Win an Academy Award.
4. Create a distribution division in four years.
5. Make a feature documentary that will influence national health care.

On another piece of paper, list both the personal goals and the business goals side by side; then rank them in order, with "1" representing the most important to you. Only you can set these priorities; there is no right or wrong way to do it. Once you have made the two lists, compare them. What conflicts do you see? How can you reconcile them? Accomplish this task, and you will be ready to write the story of your business. You also will be ready to draw any lines in the sand about work that conflicts with your combined list.

GETTING IT ALL TOGETHER

Putting together the story (or script) of your company is like making an extended pitch only longer. (Chapter 13 has more on pitching.) You want to convince an unknown someone of the following:

1. You know exactly what you are going to do.
2. You are creating a marketable product.
3. You have the ability to carry it off.

Essentially, you are presenting the basic "plot" of your company. The difference is that a script provides conflicts and resolutions as plot points. By completing the previous writing exercise, you should have resolved any conflicts. "All we want are the facts," as Sergeant Joe Friday of *Dragnet* would say.

Remember what your teacher taught you in high school English: who, what, when, where, why, and how. These questions are your guidelines for formatting the Company section of your business plan. Before you go any farther, ponder these questions:

- Why are you making films?
- Who are you?
- What films or other projects will you make?
- When will you get this show on the road?
- Where are your markets?
- How are you going to accomplish everything?

Note that the standard order is changed a bit. The *why* needs to come at the beginning to set the scene for the rest of the story.

Why?

Now that you have listed your personal and business goals, you can identify the underlying aim of your company, known in corporate circles as the "mission statement." This statement describes your film's or company's (remember that even if you are only making one film, you are a company) reasons for existence to you, your partners and managers, your employees, and, most of all, your money sources. It allows those marching forward with you to know whether you are all marching to the same drummer.

A major reason for failure is lack of agreement on where the management/production team is headed. A film is always a group project; there is far too much to accomplish for one person to do everything. It is important to ensure that company personnel do not go off in three or four different directions. Many companies that fail do so because of lack of focus; your company does not have to be one of them.

Do you have a specific philosophy? What do you want to do? Make the greatest films ever made? Make children's films? Make educational videos? Clearly define your philosophy for yourself and others. As long as people can identify with where you are heading, they will not get lost along the way.

When your philosophy or major goal is down on paper, stand aside and take an objective look. Does this sound doable to you? Would it sound reasonable if someone else presented it to you? Most of all, would you take money out of your own pocket for it?

By the way, in writing up this description, you are not required to incorporate all your goals for the world to see. Your personal goals are yours alone—unless they affect the production significantly. Suppose, for example, that you are active in animal rights organizations. For that reason, you are adamant that no animals ever appear in your films. Everyone working with you has the right to know about this dictum. It may affect scripts that have even innocuous animal scenes. Investors need to know about any major restrictions on your projects. Whether or not you put this in your business plan for investors, I will let you decide.

I am often approached by producers who have strong feelings about the source of investment money (how it was earned) or about certain countries to which they refuse to distribute their films. These countries always end up being major markets, so this credo strongly affects the company's potential revenue. Distributors do not like to give up lucrative markets, and investors do not like to give up potential profits. You have a right to your principles; if they affect future profits, however, you must tell your investors what they are.

This brings us to a brief discussion about honesty. What if you intend to make, say, environmental films, but fear that you will lose potential investors by being explicit? Should you keep your true plans to yourself? Should you claim to be making some other type of film, such as action/adventure? This question has come up in seminars and classes repeatedly. In one class, the following conversation took place:

STUDENT: If I tell them that I'm going to make environmental films, they won't give me the money.
L.L.: What are you going to tell them?
STUDENT: I won't tell them what kinds of films I plan to make.
L.L.: You have to tell them something. No one is going to buy a pig in a poke.
STUDENT: I'll tell them that I'm going to make action films. Those always sell well.
L.L.: Then you would be lying to your own investors.

STUDENT: So? The idea is to get the money, isn't it?

L.L.: If lying doesn't bother you, how about fraud? The best-case scenario is that they will take their money back. At the very worst, you can be liable for criminal penalties.

STUDENT (with shrug of his shoulders): So?

You may think that I invented this conversation to make a point. I wish that I had. Unfortunately, it is a true story. Is it surprising that, at the same time, the university offered an ethics course and no one signed up for it? My job is not to lecture anyone, although it is tempting. Your moral values are your own. Suffice it to say that fraud is not a good offense to commit, and most investors do not respond well to it.

Who?

By this time, you ought to know who you are, both personally and professionally. Now you can use the mission statement to define your company. Start the Company section of your business plan with a short statement that introduces the company. Give its history, ownership structure, and details of origin. Include the following in the statement:

1. Type of company: limited liability company (LLC)s and limited partnerships (L.P.s) are the usual format (and name of state where filed).
2. Names of principal management/production people.

A beginning statement might be something like this:

> *AAA Productions is a California limited-liability company formed for the development and production of Hispanic-themed films as well as the employment of Hispanic actors in primary roles. Over the next four years, the Company plans to produce three independently financed feature films with budgets between $2 million and $7 million. During recent years, the movie market has become more open to stories about ethnic groups. Films with Hispanic themes have led the way and proved that there is a market.*

Not only has the writer said what films the company intends to make, but he has also identified a specific goal that is both professional and personal. The company's "principal purpose" describes its mission statement. It is closely tied to the personal beliefs and desires of members of the company.

What?

Mysteries do not work, except in scripts. The readers of your business plan want a straightforward summary of your intentions. Saying that you will make films without a discussion of content is not enough. What specifically do you plan to do? In the Company section of the business plan include a short recap of your film(s). You will explain the individual projects in more detail later in the Film(s) section. You should summarize all the areas that your plan covers, such as the following:

1. Films.
2. Budgets.
3. Types of functions (development, production, and distribution) in which you will be involved.

Rationality must intercede here. What you want to do and what you are most likely to get done may be two different things. In one of the piles of business plans from outside sources at my office, for example, a group stated that it planned to make 10 to 12 feature films a year with average budgets between $8 and $15 million. This undertaking is laudable even for a large, integrated production company like Relativity Media or The Weinstein Company, but it may be questionable for a brand new company due to the quantity of resources—both money and people— involved. For this brand-new company, it was a foolish goal. No one in the company had ever made a film before. Even if someone had, consider the effort. The films would require more than $100 million in production costs alone in the first year, not to say anything about finding the staff, cast, and crew to make them. Is this an investment that you would view as "reasonable" for your hard-earned money?

Of course, people beat the odds every day. If entrepreneurs believed in the word "impossible," there would be no progress in the world. Nevertheless, you should weigh the scope of your venture against the experience of the people involved in it. For a new company, aiming to produce one low-to-moderately budgeted film in the first year makes the odds of receiving funding a little better.

I always tell new, less experienced clients to make one first, then form a company. Since I make more money if they do a company with lots of films to forecast, there must be a good reason for that advice!

Experience producing or directing television programs, commercials, documentaries, music videos, and industrials is better than no experience at all; however, feature films are different in terms of time and budget. Being circumspect about the size of the feature budget in relation to your experience not only will impress investors but also will keep you from overextending your abilities.

With a one-film plan, you need only to look ahead five years (one for production, time for distribution, and two to three for revenue of most of the revenue stream.). If you are starting a multifilm company, however, you must consider where your company will be five years hence. Analyze everything you plan to be doing over that time. If you plan to go into book publishing in year four (I'm not recommending it), that goal needs to be part of your plan. Even plans to sell the company in five years must be mentioned. All of this is part of your projected bottom line. Although you may not know all the specifics, the size, scope, and type of your planned projects need to be stated.

Even if your company has been in business for a long time or if the principals have considerable experience, never assume that readers have an intimate knowledge of your business. If your genre is the Western, for example, you might write something like this: *We plan to produce Western films in which the Indians are the heroes.*

Treating the Indians as the heroes who they often were may attract a rich aficionado of American history to fund the film. The current status of Westerns is described in your Markets section (Chapter 4). Do not go into exhaustive detail. You will do that later. Remember that it is important in this document to keep the malarkey factor to a minimum. That does not mean that you cannot put in a little positive public relations, but leave your press clippings for the Appendix.

When?

In describing your project or company, you may have already stated how and when you began functioning as a company. You may have a great deal more to say, however. The majority of companies run by independent filmmakers are start-ups. If your company has only just begun, there may be a limited amount of information to provide. Be clear about the current situation, whatever it is. You may still be someone else's employee, for example.

Starting Steps

You have already taken the first step of starting a business—translating the entrepreneur's vision into a concrete plan of action. Next comes the practical process of actually setting up shop. Go ahead and file forms that may be necessary for your type of company, have an address (even if it is your home or a post office box), and print business cards. To digress for a moment, I urge everyone to have a business card. I have found that writers or people with below-the-line jobs tend not to have one. Always have your name, a contact phone, and an email address available to give to anyone you meet. It is crucial once you have the desire to start your own company (and its name is filed in the correct way) to have a business card.

You must create all those minutiae that say to prospective investors, "This person knows what he is doing." Note the following checklist:

- Define the job descriptions of the production team.
- Determine the location and cost of offices.
- Have your stationery and business cards printed.
- Set up phones and a fax machine for easy communication.
- Arrange for professional guidance from an attorney and an accountant.
- Introduce yourself to your banker and set up a checking account.

A more important step is choosing your legal form of business. There is no one form that is best for everyone:

1. A *sole proprietorship* is owned by one person. It is easy to initiate and faces little regulation. The individual owner has all the control but all the responsibility as well. It is the normal state of doing business for consultants and others who mostly work alone.

2. A *partnership* is a business with two or more co-owners. The LLC is a common form of partnership for independent filmmakers. It is an operating agreement for one person or between you and your production/management partners that you register with your state. This LLC, however, should not be confused with an Investor Offering, which also may be called an LLC (see Chapter 9).

If you already have a company, you probably will want to register a new LLC, which will be in partnership with the funders. For example, Business Strategies is my company. Karen and I decide to make films together. We will set up a new entity (Movie Money Pictures, LLC) for that purpose. MMP, LLC will then be the main (general) partner with the investors in the Investor Offering. That way all the profits due to the filmmakers will flow to the joint company, rather than Business Strategies or Karen's original company. It always is important to keep the accounting separate.

Suppose that you have had legal problems money in the past. Don't be coy. Obviously, you need other people's money for some reason. Most investors will insist on full disclosure. They need to know the depth of the problems to overcome. If you have leftover equity owners from a previous incarnation or have imprudently spent money on cars, confess now. In the business plan, the sin of omission is as serious as the sin of commission.

You may find yourself in another situation. What if a company of the same name or a company that you bought for this purpose was in some other line of business before you bought it? The name is established, but the business has not yet functioned as an entertainment entity. On the other hand, you may have bought an operating film company that has been unsuccessful. Both circumstances add assets and credibility to your company. Do not attempt to give the impression that you had anything to do with building the assets that remain the original company; on the other hand, be sure to explain any problems that may have occurred under previous owners. .

Do not be afraid to state the facts. Investors want to know what they are getting into. Besides, being candid has its own rewards. People with money tend to know other people with money. Even if one prospect is not interested, his friend may be. If there is anything negative to know, an investor probably will find out eventually anyway, and you will lose not only an investor but also the chance for him to recommend you to someone else. When I wrote the first edition, people were not on the Internet. It was a small world then, and the Net has made it even smaller. Once you start getting a negative rap, the word spreads quickly.

Where?

Potential investors want to know where you are going to sell your films. Although "worldwide" is a good thought, you should be more specific. If you are making your first independent film, it is not likely to have a $25-million budget. (If it does, please reconsider. Your company is not Fox Searchlight yet.)

There are many different things to choose from when starting a film company. I strongly suggest sticking to films in the beginning. However, some people want to make films for the broadcast media, direct-to-home video, or create their own distribution division for theatrical. This may hinder raising money when you do not have a significant track record. Remember that the Company section is an introductory statement, not a thesis. A short summary, such as the following one, is all you need.

The company's objectives are to:

- Develop and produce a film that will resonate with both domestic and foreign audience.
- Maintain strong management control over production to obtain the best quality.
- Pursue independent production financing in order to make the best possible deals with distributors, thereby maximizing returns to the investors.

How?

Up to this point, you have essentially outlined everything your company proposes to accomplish. In the rest of the business plan, you will describe each step in detail. Chapter 3, "The Films," is a continuation of the *what*. It is an in-depth study of each of your projects. Chapters 4 through 10 and 12 describe the *how*. This is the central plot of your business plan. How do you fit into the industry? How will you identify your place in the market? How do distribution and financing work, and how will you pursue each one?

MANAGEMENT AND ORGANIZATION

Conclude the Company section of your business plan with a brief description of your production team and its key members. This means writing just a paragraph or two for each. Save the six- or seven-page résumé for the Appendix. How many people you put in this section depends on the strength of the production team.

Generally, you only want to include people above-the-line—producer, executive producer, director, writer, coproducer, assistant producer, and editor. Unless they are producing the film, I put the bios of actors in the Film section. Track records also are important. Although they are normally considered to be below-the-line, I include the cinematographer, if they have notable experience. If I have a well-known musician or music producer as music supervisor, I will include them.

If you have never made a film, find someone who has and sign that person up. If you don't know anyone, network through film groups in your area or at film festivals and markets to connect with someone. You also can write to people whose previous work makes you think that they would love your film. Try to be rational here. Don't spend 10 years waiting for Kevin Costner or Kathryn Bigelow to respond.

Track records in other businesses are also important. I just finished a business plan for which one partner has extensive financing experience. I couldn't convince him to let me put his bio in a one-film plan. Even though the filmmaker has experience, this person's business experience definitely would make an investor feel comfortable.

The following is an example:

> *Production Team:*
> *Self Consumed, Director and Screenwriter*
> *Self Consumed will be writing and directing our first two films. Last year he directed the romantic comedy short film,* Louise Loves. *It was well received at several film festivals and won the critics' award at the Mainline Film Festival. His fifth*

*feature screenplay is in development at Crazed Consultant
Films. Consumed has directed commercials for 15 years.
In addition, he has done promotions for the Big Time cable
system.*

Simply Marvelous, Producer

*Simply Marvelous worked with MNY Co. in both acquisitions
and production. Among the films that she was responsible
for are* Cat Cries at Sunset, Phantom of La Loggia, *and*
Dreaded Consultants IV. *Previous to working in the film
industry, she served as Vice President of Production at APQ
Industries.*

Frieda Financial, Executive Producer

*Frieda financial brings to XXX varied business and entertainment
experience, including five years' experience in motion picture
finance with the Add 'Em Up accounting firm. Previously,
Financial worked in corporate planning for the health care
industry.*

Make these descriptions long enough to include the essential information, but the less important details should go elsewhere. For example, Mr. Consumed's commercials and the companies for whom he worked can be listed on a résumé in the Appendix. For the sake of your readers' sanity, however, do not create a 10-page listing of all of a director's commercials, even in the Appendix.

Catch-22 Experience

What do you do when no one in the company has any experience? Tread very carefully. My advice is to attach someone who does. Why would any investor believe that you can make a film with no previous experience and no help?

The amount of skill expected is related to the budget as well as the genre of the planned film. Suppose you have decided to make a $10-million film for your first venture. You have written a script and have partnered with people with financial or retail backgrounds, but no direct knowledge of or experience with film. Would you take $10 million out of your own pocket for this?

In certain circumstances, you can use the ploy of discussing below-the-line attachments of merit. Some clients of mine, for example, happened to have an Academy Award–nominated cinematographer or an Emmy-winning composer committed to their projects. It was to their benefit to include this type of experience in the production team descriptions.

Be careful how you do this, though. You want to avoid making the production of your films look like a committee effort. One wannabe producer came to me with a plan for a first movie, with himself as executive producer. He planned to start with a $20-million film and felt that running the computer system at a production company was appropriate film experience. His explanation read as follows:

> *So and So has 25 years' experience working with computer systems, 10 of them at X & X Production Company. So and So is the producer and has an experienced crew ready to work with him. These technicians have a combined experience of 105 years in the film business. If So and So has any questions, they will be able to help him.*

This is a dangerous trap. The expectation that your inexperience will be covered by other people working in various crew positions may backfire. The old saying, "A camel is a horse designed by a committee," is applicable here. The producer is the manager of the business and must make the final decisions; therefore, the person in this position must have knowledge on which to draw. If you don't have it, hire a producer who does. Investors expect to see people in charge who have more than a vague idea of what they are doing. When describing their experience, some people elaborate on the truth to a fault. When applying for a job of any kind, it is frequently tempting to stretch your bio a bit, if not to make it up out of whole cloth. Think carefully before you do this. Filmmakers often put their most creative efforts into writing the management summaries.

Compare the following real biography to the "elaborated" version that follows:

> *Real biography:* Leonard Levison worked as an assistant
> to the associate producer on *The Bell Rings*. Before that,
> Levison was a production assistant on four films at Great
> Movies Studios. He began his film career as gopher at the
> studio.
> *"Elaborated" business plan version:* Leonard Levison produced
> the film *The Bell Rings*. Prior to this project, he produced

Heavier Than Thou, The Poker Chip Always Falls, and two other films at Great Movies Studios. He began his film career as a coproducer on various films.

Harmless public relations "puffery," you say? This overstatement is similar to the inflated income some people put down on a home loan application. You might assume that this is just the way things are done, but this action can come back to haunt you. A Los Angeles entertainment attorney told me about a court case in which the fictional management biographies of the filmmakers were the investor's sole reason for suing when a film lost money. He said that he "bet on people" and only read the management portion of the Company section of the business plan.

Try to be objective about the film or films that you are creating. If you are making a very low-budget film, experience with short films may be enough. On the other hand, it is less likely that an investor will give money to totally inexperienced filmmakers with a five-film slate. No situation, as I have said, is impossible. The safer you can make the downside (chance of losing money) for the investors, however, the likelier it is that they will write you a check. No matter how emotionally involved an individual investor might be in the project, there is usually an objective, green-eyeshade type sitting nearby, trying to make your plan fit her idea of a "reasonable" investment.

A Word about Partnerships

In forming a company to make either a single film or many, you may want to take on one or more partners. The usual makeup is two or three people who co-own a company and work full time in it. Each one is personally liable for the others. It is quite common for good friends to become partners. Because of the relationships involved, however, many people doing business with friends often do not take the same care that they would take with total strangers.

Handshakes are only an invitation to work together. No matter what the affinity with one another, agreements between people must be signed contracts. Over the years, I have had countless partners come to discuss the business plan without first making their own agreement. In many cases, this has resulted in the project not starting—or worse, being stopped once they have paid—because the people involved had not made their own formal agreement. Once they are faced with making a formal agreement for the purposes of the plan, someone doesn't like the original handshake agreement. Or people don't agree on the details of the original agreement for which there are no notes. Even if there are emails, nothing has been signed, and a change of mind over who will get what is not unusual. I have even been told that I made the potential forecast sound so good that the writer who was on a work-for-hire contract was demanding a percentage.

A good partnership requires the presence of two contradictory elements. First, you and your partners must be very much alike so that your goals and objectives mesh. On the other hand, you must be very unlike and complementary in terms of expertise. Often, one partner is more cautious and the other more adventurous. Whether to form a partnership can be a difficult decision. As in many other situations, the best step is to list on paper the advantages and disadvantages of a partnership and see how it looks to you.

The following are examples of such lists. First, the advantages of entering into a partnership:

1. I will have a measure of safety because it takes two to make any decision.
2. I will avoid the unremitting and lonely responsibility of doing everything by myself.
3. I will have a partner with skills that are different than my own.
4. I will have someone to share crises with.

Here are some reasons not to enter into a partnership:

1. My share of the profits will be a lot less.
2. I will not have total control.
3. I will have to share recognition at the Academy Awards.
4. My partner's poor judgment could hurt me and the film.

ASSESSING YOUR STRENGTHS AND WEAKNESSES

Casting an unbiased eye over your plans is always hard for entrepreneurs. A strong desire for everything to work often clouds your vision. Evaluating the strengths and weaknesses of your film(s) in the beginning, however, will save time, turmoil, and money later. You might be able to describe the strengths of your company as follows:

- Associates of the company possess unique skills or experience.
- We have special relationships with distributors or other professionals or companies in related fields.
- Unique aspects of this business that will help us are ....

On the reverse side of the ledger are your company's weaknesses. Be honest with yourself when identifying your company's failings. This exercise saves many companies from later failure. By converting the strength statements to negative statements, you can spot problems. Write them down on a piece of paper to review:

1. No one in this company possesses unique skills or experience.
2. Our films have no distinctive characteristics that set them apart from others in the marketplace.
3. We have no special relationships with distributors or other professionals in the entertainment industry.

Being good in one area of business does not guarantee success in another. For example, suppose that an entrepreneur from one area of entertainment, such as commercials, decides to go into theatricals, an area in which he has no experience. Although he knows how to manage a profitable business, feature filmmaking has its own unique set of concerns. The business requires larger sums of money per project than do commercials and involves greater risks in terms of market.

In addition, running a company as opposed to being a studio producer or an independent working on one film at a time requires different skills. Successful executives often rush into new businesses without preparing properly. Used to calling all the shots, they may have trouble delegating authority or may hire lower-level development personnel rather than experienced producers in order to maintain control. The producer can counter these weaknesses by studying the new industry first and hiring seasoned film people. Running through this exercise will help you in two ways. First, you will locate the holes in the dike so that you can plug them before any leaks occur. Second, you can use it to assess how much confidence you or anyone else can have in your organization. In addition, pointing out the obvious to readers never hurts. You should not make readers work to see the good points. As to weaknesses, most investors are sophisticated executives and will see the problems themselves. If you do not mention how you will overcome the obstacles your company faces, the investor may question your ability to understand them. Being frank may help your cause rather than hurt it.

LESS IS MORE

The Company section of your business plan not only summarizes the essential facts about your company but also is an introduction to the rest of the business plan. It should be short and to the point. Prospective investors want to know the basics, which will be described in exhaustive detail throughout the rest of your proposal. Many readers of this book's previous editions have told me that the phrase that was most important in writing their own plans was "less is more."

3

The Film: The Investor Needs the Whole Story

Who the hell wants to hear actors talk?
—HARRY M. WARNER, WARNER BROS., 1927

PROJECT SCOPE

The focus of this chapter is narrative theatrical films. While the industry is going through many technological changes, who knew a silent film could return and make money? Whether you are making one film or a slate of films, this chapter looks at what needs to be addressed in terms of the film's synopsis and its attachments. It demonstrates how to describe them and explains not only the amount of information that you need to include, but also what you should leave out.

As of this edition, discussion of feature documentaries, animated films, and large format (IMAX and other giant screen films) has been moved to Chapter 12, "Breaking the Rules." The "nontraditional" films, those that don't go out theatrically but are distributed through various ancillary and new technology methods (iPhones, iPads, other smartphones, and so on), as well as short films will be discussed in Chapter 7, "Distribution: Nontheatrical and the Wild West."

Whether you are making one film or a slate of films, this chapter looks at what needs to be addressed about a film. It demonstrates how to describe it and explains not only the amount of information that you need to include but also what you should leave out.

The Right to Know

As your partner, the investor has a right to know what activities are contemplated in order to make an informed decision. In a one-film plan, you should have a full script and budget before creating the business plan. In doing a company plan with films planned over more than one year, you may not have all the scripts. Undoubtedly, you know more about some films than others; some of you may not even have specific projects yet. You may have a script to shoot next year, but may not have a clue about the script for a film planned four years down the road. Nor can you know what delays may occur along the way. You need to know at least what type of films you plan to make and the estimated budgets. It is less important to be psychic than to be as accurate as possible in terms of intentions and timing. If circumstances alter the original plan, everyone involved will reevaluate it.

Several years ago, a young man came to me with a proposal to create a highly specialized series of films. He planned to sell them in a narrowly segmented market. The plan contained much discussion about the future success of his company, but the only description of the projects was the word "films." He estimated that millions of people would go to see these unspecified films. Being the curious type, I asked him what kinds of films he planned to make. His answer was, "Good ones." I pressed on, trying to elicit more information. After all, he guaranteed that millions would clamor to see these films. He replied, "I'm not going to tell anybody anything. They might steal the idea. Besides, it's no one's business; all they need to know is that it's a good investment."

Don't laugh too loudly. This story is only one of many, and this young man's attitude is not unusual. "Films," as you may have realized by now, is not a sufficient description. Putting yourself in the investor's shoes, how would this strike you? You would probably insist on knowing the content of these incredible films, which belonged to this guaranteed market, and how the films were going to pay back your investors.

There are certainly a couple of valid reasons why a filmmaker (or any other entrepreneur) might worry about revealing the details of a proposed project: (1) no identifiable plans exist or (2) someone might steal the idea. Although theft of concept is not an unknown phenomenon, there is a difference between not telling the general public all about your plans and refusing to tell a potential money source. Prudent filmmakers refrain from describing script details in a loud voice at the local coffee shop or at a crowded party; they also resist the temptation to ask seven or eight friends to read their projects. However, the prudent do give the right people enough information to prove the advisability of the investment.

Success in any business revolves around the product. In film, where all forward motion to the goal is content driven, the story is crucial. To sell your projects, remember the refrain, "Story, story, story." Hype has a place also, but it must take a back seat in the context of this plan. The trick is to do some jazzy selling around a solid idea. All the public relations in the world will not save a bad film. From Chapter 2, "The Company," you know that the first goal for the business plan is to identify your future course of action. The second is to show investors how profitable a film will be. There is no way to forecast your success without specific ideas to evaluate. Does this mean that you must have all your scripts, directors, and stars in tow? Not necessarily, but you do need to have a framework. At the very least, for example, you want to know that you are going to produce X budgets and Y genres over a Z-year period. You must provide enough information to estimate revenues and give the investor a chance to agree or disagree with your forecast.

In this section, you are telling the whole story of the film in one or two pages, endings included. In addition, you are describing what attachments to the film factually exist. Fantasies may play an important part in scriptwriting, but using wish lists in this document can present a problem. Confusing the issue by citing a cast that has never heard of the project or books you do not own or have not optioned may give investors the wrong idea. Whether you create a false impression by accident or on purpose, the result is the same. Investors negotiate contracts based on the information you provide. If they find out that you have not been truthful, they can withdraw their money. Worst case scenario—they can sue you.

FILMS

When describing your film projects, the objective is to tell the whole story within one to two pages with a minimum of extra prose. You should disclose each film's assets (components that may add commercial value to the project) as well as any nonmonetary values that are important to the types of films you want to make.

Show and Tell

The trick is to tell enough to engage readers but not so much that you risk losing them. As we go through the different elements of this section, we will attempt to draw a line between sufficient content and excessive wordiness. Readers who must wade through pages of information that is hard to follow will just go to sleep.

Writers of scripts, books, and other literary pieces have a tendency when writing nonfiction to create a stream of consciousness that is hard to follow. Fiction requires emotional and subjective content that will draw readers into the fictional world. Business writing—and nonfiction of any kind—requires simplicity and directness. Dr. Linda Seger, noted author of books on screenwriting, says:

> Screenwriting is about being indirect; proposal writing is about being direct. While the object of good fiction writing is to be subtle, hide exposition, and present many ideas indirectly, good proposal writing insures that the audience is getting the information clearly and consciously.

This is the reason why some genius invented the Appendix. In the business plan, it contains details that may be outside the formula of simple and direct information. As you proceed through the following sections, you will get a clearer picture of what this means. There are no official rules as to how much information you ought to include; but bring your common sense into play; and always try to be alert to the reader's point *of view*.

Scripts

Disclose enough material about each script so that readers understand its value. A synopsis is the usual format. For mot films, you can tell the essentials of the story in a page and indicate the genre of the film.

A student once questioned whether or not to include the title of his script. He feared that someone would steal it, because it was innovative and catchy. The chances that someone will finance a film for which you won't give a title are slim. More often, writers fear that someone will pirate their ideas rather than their titles. Nevertheless, you can't copyright either one of them.

The first step to take to protect yourself from possible theft of your story is to copyright your project. Most writers register their scripts with the Writers Guild of America. An even better procedure is to file for registration with the Library of Congress in Washington, DC. Once you have done this, you can prove that your story existed as of a particular date, and you can feel free to give it to others. Keep in mind that registration does not prevent theft; it just helps you prove ownership in the event of theft. Unfortunately, you cannot copyright ideas themselves. Michael Donaldson, in his book *Clearance and Copyright*, says:

> *Copyright law only protects "expression of an idea that is fixed in a tangible form." This means that written words are protectable; the ideas behind them are not. You can't copy something that is just an idea in the air.*

You also cannot copyright titles. Well-known book titles, such as *The Hunger Games*, will have been trademarked. However, there are other reasons your title can change. Distributors often reserve the right to change it, particularly, if they feel it will be confused with another film. If you go through the Motion Picture Association of America process, you may come into conflict with having your title approved. Please don't email me that you have seen multiple films with the same title. The point is that you want to check the situation for your own film—another good reason for working with a film attorney.

Title: *Boys Who Wreak Havoc*
Four teenage boys decide to take over a small Wisconsin town. They kidnap the minister's daughter as a bargaining tool in their effort to make one of their members the mayor. Their attempt to control the population unites the townspeople, who, although previously selfish in their individual pursuits, come together to take back their town. The girl is saved without bloodshed, and peace reigns.

This paragraph does not tell enough about the story to give the reader a true idea of everything that is in the film. Several sample plot synopses have been included on Focal's Companion Website for the book. Be sure to read them.

You want to include the entire story line within one page and the ending of the film. You are not trying to get investors to go to the film. If they have money involved, they will go anyway. They need to have enough information so that they do not misconstrue the type of film you plan to make. If the girl is raped or there is a nude scene, be sure to mention it. Failing to mention a scene that affects the nature of the film because you think potential investors might not like it is a sin of omission. If, for example, you let your investor assume that you were making a PG-13–rated film although you know that it will be R-rated, your money source can object and demand his money back.

What if you do not have a specific script or you have one budgeted script but want to do a slate? State this up front. Raising money for one film, you need to have a budget to tell the investor. Even without all the scripts in hand, however, you can define your projects in terms of budget size and genres. You may be looking for development money to obtain scripts. Concentrate on what you know about your project. You must tell investors at least the size of the films that you plan to make.

One way to describe this situation is as follows:

We are planning to make three films with family themes over the next five years, ranging in size from $1 million to $5 million. The initial $50,000 will allow the Company to develop scripts and to option stories from other writers.

This scenario is not as tempting to investors as the first one, but it is doable. For investors, providing money for development is always a greater risk than providing money for well-planned projects. The danger for the investor is that the producer may never find the right project and begin production. Or an agreement made with the source of production money may further dilute the initial investor's position. However, if you have some experience and a credible team, try for the development money. Rather than writing a full business plan, you can choose to have an attorney write a proposal for development money. It will specify how much money the investors will be paid when production money is raised and what points they will receive in the eventual production.

Suppose that you know neither the subject of your films nor the size of their budgets. In one plan, the company stated: "The producers plan to make low-budget features with the formula that has proved most profitable both in theatrical and video releases … scripts in this area are plentiful." Seems a little vague, doesn't it? Aren't you curious to know what these proven formulas are?

Typically, the information in a proposal of this type is not enough. The right mix of ingredients is always a balancing act, but you probably would have to be a known filmmaker with an impressive track record to get away with this proposal. Even for an experienced moviemaker, this pitch would be hard to sell. Most people want to see specifics to which they can attach a value, either monetary or personal. Anyone with a modicum of business sense understands that handing out money to someone with no real plans except "to make a film" would appear to be foolish.

No doubt you can find an exception to this rule somewhere. Perhaps you've heard about an eager young filmmaker who, with his toothy smile and youthful enthusiasm, convinced a jaded deal-maker to hand over money. Nothing is impossible, but the odds are against it happening. This scenario sounds too much like movie fiction and not enough like real life.

At this point, you may also want to think about the potential audience for your flick. It does not hurt to add a qualifying sentence to your plot synopsis—for example, "Films about Wisconsin, such as *Walter from Wisconsin* and *Cheeseheads Reign Supreme*, have been popular lately. We plan to capitalize on this phenomenon." On the other hand, you may be shooting the film in Wisconsin and raising your money there. In that case, add "Director Buffy Angel was born and raised in Milwaukee, where the film will be shot." However, save the discussion of the distribution and financial ramifications of your films for later sections of the plan. If your readers follow custom, they would have read the Financing section before this one anyway. It is easiest for readers to follow your plan if you group all of the project descriptions together and do not digress with long discussions on other subjects.

ATTACHMENTS AND THEIR VALUES

In this balancing act, any person, place, or thing that adds value to the script is important. You want to give your project every chance to see the light of day, so recount any attachment with a perceptible value. Here are five examples of attachments: (1) options, (2) books, (3) stars, (4) director, and (5) dollars. Notice that your favorable opinion is not one of the choices.

Options

An option is a written agreement giving the producer exclusive rights to a project over some specific length of time. If the option is exclusive, it ensures that no one else can make the project while the producer holds the option. Obviously, if you are the writer, it is your project. However, if you are representing other writers' scripts as part of your package, you must declare the ownership status. Representing films as your own when they are not is clearly a no-no.

Not only the script itself but also the subject may need an option. If you are dealing with true stories of living people (or deceased persons whose estates own the representation of their likeness and life), you may need to seek permission to do the story. Getting the option, or "rights," after the fact can be a costly process.

You do not want to be in the position of having a deal on the table for a film and having to go back to obtain the rights to it. After the fact, the subject can and often will deny having given verbal permission. If you have not done your homework, it is the subject's right to stop the production, which sometimes leads to an expensive payoff or a court injunction.

Books

A published book adds value to a film in several ways. The sales history adds clout to your project, the specialized market it represents provides a ready-made audience, and the book usually furnishes additional ways to hype the film. Unless it is your book and copyright, the first step is—you guessed it—an option. The cost of the option depends, again, on the person you are dealing with and the relative fame of the book. It would be useless to even try to give you prices. As soon as the ink is dry in this book, the market would have changed. In truth, a book option, like a script option, can cost anywhere from nothing to millions of dollars.

An author (or the representatives of an estate) may have a subjective reason for you to make the book into a film and be very generous in making an agreement with you. On the other hand, if money is the primary focus, the author will drive as hard a bargain as possible. This area is one of the few in which your sparkling manner can have a concrete impact. On occasion, deals have been done because the author liked the filmmaker and wanted to see the project get made. Passion for the project counts for a lot in negotiating with authors. One way to be sure that you cannot use the book, however, is to refrain from seeking the rights to it.

Options can be obtained for a reasonable price if the timing and people involved are right. For example, two producers bought the rights for a paperback mystery novel plus the author's next two books for a few thousand dollars. No one else had approached the author, and the books were not the type to make the best-seller lists. Nevertheless, the author had a large audience among mystery fans. With no competitive bidders, the producers were able to make a good deal.

Another producer optioned several books of women's stories. The books had a large following, but the subject was still "soft" at major studios. She couldn't get the deals that she wanted and the films deserved. After Best Picture nominees *Black Swan* and *Winter's Bone* (2010) and *The Help* (2011), as well as *Bridesmaids*, *Hanna*, and *Soul Surfer* were released to critical acclaim and/or significant box office results, studios and independent companies were falling all over themselves to make similar deals. It's all in the timing. A change in the attitude of the trendmakers (studio executives, agents, and distributors) increased the value of the producer's optioned books.

Being able to read manuscripts before they are published gives you an advantage over other filmmakers. Agents have access to unpublished manuscripts all the time. If you happen to know about a book that is about to be published by an unknown author and you can strike a deal prior to publication, it may work to your advantage financially.

Real-Life Stories

As documentaries and films based on true stories have become more popular and successful at the box office, it is important to understand that all the options talked about above apply. Many times over the years, people have approached me to write a business plan for a film about a famous athlete or someone else in the news. When I have asked if they have an option on the story, the reply often has been, "He told me to go ahead." Not good enough. You must get the agreement in writing. It is best to have an attorney draw up the agreement but, at least, have something written that is signed by both of you. The same goes for stories about nonhumans.

If you want to make a film about the horse that wins the Kentucky Derby, talk to the people involved and get their agreement in writing. How many people have to give their permission to be portrayed in the film is best discussed with an attorney. As happens with partners, more than one client has had a verbal agreement for a free option with the subject of their biographical film only to have money demanded before a formal agreement was signed.

Stars and Other Fantasy People

Attaching star actors, star directors, and famous producers is the fantasy of many independent filmmakers. Having Brad Pitt, Ryan Reynolds, or Denzel Washington in your $500,000 film might be a recurrent dream of yours, but, unfortunately, their salaries include several more zeros. Nevertheless, you can have attachments that add value to your project, as long as they are real. No wish lists.

With lower budgets, "bankable" stars (the actors whose names ensure a certain level of box office revenue when the film opens) are probably not an option, but you still can have a name that interests an investor. The value of the name is often in the eye of the beholder. Foreign buyers may put value on names that are only a moderate attraction on a U.S. movie marquee.

Directors who command high salaries will also be out of the reach of very low-budget filmmakers. As the budget gets higher, the experience of the director becomes more important. Emphasize your director's previous experience, but do not fabricate it. If you are planning a $15 million film and your director has never helmed a feature film, the inexperience may be a hindrance in obtaining financing but possibly could be damaging to complete a good film on budget. You want the director to be able to handle the film and, especially, the actors. In addition, experienced actors often are unwilling to work with an unseasoned director, and investors become more nervous about spending their money.

All the elements in a film are relative to one another. Because the producer has the major responsibility for keeping the budget on track, previous experience with feature films is important. In independent filmmaking, the producer is often the only connection between investors and their money. Once the cash has gone into the film's bank account, investors must depend on the producer to protect its use. Not only does the producer watch the money, but she also has to have enough clout with the director to stop him from going over budget. Always keep in mind that this process is a balancing act of all the different elements.

Money

"Well," you say, "of course, money adds value." It seems redundant but really is not. Clearly, hard cash for development and production has a straightforward relationship to your project, but what about any partial funds attached to your project? For some reason, newer producers do not think to mention them as part of their project's description, but they should. If any money at all is attached to your project, announce it here. If you have paid money for any option, include that information in the details about the option. Keep in mind that it always impresses investors that you have put your own money into securing an option.

All of the elements in a film are relative to one another. Two years ago, I was asked for an advice by a producer who had been having trouble raising money for several years. He had a totally unknown cast that would cost little money, a director with no feature experience, a simple plot with few locations and a $15 million budget. I suggested that he should lower the budget for which there seemed to be no reasonable explanation, except that he wanted to film in 3D. He didn't like the advice, and he still hasn't raised the money.

You will discuss it at greater length in the Financing section. Remember that all attachments are of value to the film and belong in this section. You want to depict any ingredients of this mix that will positively influence someone to make your film. In addition to hard cash, you should mention any coproduction agreements, below-the-line deals, negative pickups, or presales. But make sure you have your deals in writing before putting them in the business plan.

BUDGET

For prospective investors to evaluate your films completely, they need to know the size of the budget. Again, we have two types of films: those with complete scripts and those that are just a gleam in the producer's eye. When real scripts exist, real budgets should exist as well.

To save money, many filmmakers pass a tuning fork over their script and say, "One million dollars." Do not just make up a figure. Anyone who contemplates financing your film will take this number seriously. So should you.

Many independent films have been delayed because the money ran out during either principal photography or post-production. The investors have said, "You told me $800,000, so that is all you are getting." Studios often have reserves for a certain amount of budget overruns; equity investors do not.

Some filmmakers develop only the two top sheets of the budget—this is just one step ahead of the tuning fork method—and figure out the complete cost later. However, you should calculate the total cost now to save explanations later. Estimating the cost of the general categories (cast, location, wardrobe, and so on) can be very dangerous, no matter how experienced you are. Break down the script. Production managers, line producers, and unit production managers often work freelance. Be sure to hire one who has experience with budgeting independent films, however. Calculate the entire amount and be careful to have enough money. It is always better to keep your budget forecast a little high rather than cutting it too close to the bone.

When describing your film in the Executive Summary and Company section, you should simply state the size of the budget along with its attachments. A paragraph or two on the entire project will be sufficient. Consider the following example:

> *This film has a $2-million budget, based on filming in Cincinnati. Susie Starstruck and Norman Goodlooking are set to star in the film. Ms. Starstruck has been featured in* The Gangbusters *and* Return of the Moths. *Mr. Goodlooking has appeared in several movies of the week. Herman Tyrant, the director, has made two low-budget films (*Be My Love *and* Girls Don't Sing) *and has previous experience in commercials. The film has partial financing of $100,000 for development from an equity investor.*

In this paragraph, the writer has explained the essentials. Here we learn the size of the budget, the location (much of the cost in this example is predicated on the film being shot in a right-to-work state), and the experience of the lead actors and director. One investor already has an equity position, but all of the sales markets are available. Note that the writer has saved any discussion on the implications of adding another equity investor for the negotiation. All relevant information belongs to the Investor Offering (see Chapter 9), which is always written by an attorney, not the filmmaker.

A Word About Incentives

Always seek the entire budget of your film without deleting the potential value of incentives. In most cases, this money is not guaranteed and is dispensed only after the film has been made. You first have to raise the entire budget and make the film, before incentives can be considered.

Do not worry about repetition; it is part of the building-block formula. You give an overview of the film. Then, in the Distribution and Financing sections, you go into greater detail about pertinent elements.

What if you do not have a full script or any actors and you have little or no experience? Do not lose heart. You can still explain what you are planning to do. Look at this example:

> *The ABC Company plans to make four films over the next five years. The first two films will be low budget ($250,000 and $1 million), and will deal with coming-of-age themes. Both films are in the treatment stage, and the director, Fearless Author, will write the screenplays. Mr. Author wrote and directed four short films, two of which have won awards at film festivals. Mr. Experienced Producer, whose films include* Growing Up? *and* Life Is a Flower, *has given us a letter of intent agreeing to serve as Executive Producer. The third and fourth films will be in the $3- to $5-million range. Mr. New Producer will produce these films after serving as Co-Producer on the first two. Neither treatments nor scripts exist for the third and fourth films. They will be in development during the first two years.*

Common sense will tell you that this package has less substance than the first one. It may be harder to find financing, but not impossible. If you find yourself in a similar situation, all you can do is try to create as many advantages for yourself as possible. The worst approach you can take is to say, "We are nobody with no plans. We plan to find no one experienced in anything, but we want your money anyway." It's true that no one is going to be this truthful, but on many proposals, it is not difficult to read these words between the lines. You have to learn to make realistic compromises to reach your goals. And above all, don't lie.

Too Much Can Be Harmful

One of the biggest nightmares that financial folks have is to receive a 10-pound business plan that includes every piece of paper in the producer's desk. Your goal is to have people read your proposal; therefore, you want to give them enough information without making the plan too heavy to lift. Suppose you have a complete budget for each of your projects. Do not put them anywhere in this business plan. An interested party will ask for them soon enough and you can have the dubious thrill of explaining every last nickel. If you have a strong desire to show detail, you can put the top sheets of the budgets in your Appendix for perusal at the reader's convenience.

The same goes for the biographies of the stars, director, producer, and anyone else involved with your projects. A few paragraphs describing each principal's background is sufficient. The three-page bios do not need to be in the body of the plan. If you feel strongly that someone will have a burning need for this information, the Appendix is the place for it.

Don't make potential investors guess about the applicable credits by including newspaper reviews in your business plan. Summarize the essentials. If you are bursting at the seams with your wonderful reviews, you know where they go—the Appendix.

As far as I am concerned, photocopies of any kind should be forbidden by law from appearing in business plans. When you are trying to separate investors from their money, a well-typed, neat page counts; it shows that you care enough to give them the very best.

One finished plan given to me a few years ago weighed in at two pounds. Thrown in with the appropriate and readable text were nine pages detailing every industrial and commercial film that the director made. Later sections included photocopies of numerous charts and articles from various publications. The investor was presumably supposed to wade through all this paper and reach a conclusion. Not wise. By filling your plan with extraneous paper, you might appear to be covering up an absence of fact, or you might give the impression that you do not understand the proposal yourself. Personal impressions are intangible, but they count. Always keep in mind that the human beings who read your treatise will have human failings. Once they are distracted or annoyed, their attention may be lost and your package may be tossed in the "forget it" pile. Some rules are made to be broken, but the one about brevity and clarity is not.

START SMALL AND THINK BIG

Since the first edition of this book, business strategies have worked with filmmakers with all kinds of experience, from none to 40 years. Trying to have a start-up company with more than one film is difficult. Often clients want to do films, distribution, video games, and music—all at the same time. My advice is to start small and expand as the company becomes successful. If it is your first film (or all your previous experience is short films), make one film. After that film is finished and released, then put together a plan for a company with several films. If you already are experienced and insist on handling your own distribution, I recommend adding an experienced distribution executive rather than all the expenses of a division. Either way you go, don't start out with that much overhead.

Harvey and Bob Weinstein of The Weinstein Company (who many clients want to emulate) started Miramax in the 1960s as a small domestic distributor of videos. They produced their first feature film in 1986. Many successful years later, the company became the proverbial "800-pound gorilla" in the indie world. (See Chapter 4 for more on the brothers and their emergence from the Disney fold as The Weinstein Company.) The point is that they started small and grew to multiple films per year and assorted ancillary divisions through making profits over time.

For a new company, you need to have focus. A business plan is great, with the operative word being "plan."

4

The Industry: The Facts and Nothing But

The cinema is an invention without a future.
—LOUIS LUMIÈRE

A BIT OF HISTORY

Moving images had existed before. Shadows created by holding various types of objects (puppets, hands, and carved models) before a light were seen on screens all over the world. This type of entertainment, which most likely originated in Asia with puppets, was also popular in Europe and the United States. Then in 1877, photographer Eadweard Muybridge helped former California Governor Leland Stanford settle a bet by using a series of cameras to capture consecutive images of a racehorse in motion. Little did he know.

William Friese-Greene obtained the first patent on a moving image camera in England in 1889. Next came Thomas Alva Edison with his kinetograph in 1890, and shortly thereafter, the motion picture industry was born. Edison is widely credited with inventing the first camera that would photograph moving images in the 1890s. Even he did not have a monopoly on moving pictures for long. Since Edison didn't take out any patents in Europe, the door was open for the Lumière brothers to create the cinematograph, another early form of moving image camera, in Paris in the 1890s. Little theaters sprang up as soon as the technology to project moving pictures appeared. In 1903, Edison exhibited the first narrative film, *The Great Train Robbery*. Seeing this film presumably inspired Carl Laemmle to open a nickelodeon, and thus, the founder of

Universal Studios became one of the first "independents" in the film business. Edison and the equipment manufacturers banded together to control the patents that existed for photographing, developing, and printing movies. Laemmle decided to ignore them and go into independent production. After several long trials, Laemmle won the first movie industry antitrust suit and formed Independent Moving Pictures Company of America. He was one of several trailblazers who formed start-up companies that would eventually become major studios. As is true in many industries, the radical upstarts who brought change eventually became the conservative guardians of the status quo.

Looking at history is essential for putting your own company in perspective. Each industry has its own periods of growth, stagnation, and change. As this cycling occurs, companies move in and out of the system. Not much has changed since the early 1900s. Major studios are still trying to call the shots for the film industry, and thousands of small producers and directors are constantly swimming against the tide.

IDENTIFYING YOUR INDUSTRY SEGMENT

Industry analysis is important for two reasons. First, it tests your knowledge of how the system functions and operates. Second, it reassures potential partners and associates that you understand the environment within which the company must function. As noted earlier, no company works in a vacuum. Each is a part of a broader collection of companies, large and small, that make the same or similar products or deliver the same or similar services. The independent filmmaker (you) and the multinational conglomerate (most studios) operate in the same general ballpark.

Film production is somewhat different when looked at from the varied viewpoints of craftspeople, accountants, and producers. All of these people are part of the film industry, but they represent different aspects of it. Likewise, the sales specifications and methods for companies are different not only from each other but also from the act of production. Clearly, you are not going to make a movie without cameras, but the ones you may use are changing. Now we have the Red (digital) camera, while other films still are being shot in 35 mm. The business operations of the companies that make equipment are seriously being impacted. The Eastman Kodak Company, founded by George Eastman who put his first camera in the hands of consumers in 1888, filed for Chapter 11 bankruptcy in 2012.

When writing the Industry section of your business plan, narrow your discussion of motion pictures to the process of production of a film and focus on the continuum from box office to the *ancillary* (secondary) markets. Within this framework, you must also differentiate among various types of movies. Producing the $140-million *Captain America* or the $170-million three-dimension (3D) *Hugo* is not the same as making the $800,000 *Winter's Bone* or the $2.5-million *Courageous*. A film that requires extensive computer-generated special effects is different from one with a character-driven plot. Each has specific production, marketing, and distribution challenges, and they have to be handled in different ways. Once you characterize the industry as a whole, you will discuss the area that applies specifically to your product.

In your discussion of the motion picture industry, remember that nontheatrical distribution—that is, Blu-ray/DVD, free television/cable, pay-per-view, the Internet, and domestic and foreign television—are part of the secondary revenue system for films. Each one is an industry in itself. However, they all affect your business plan in terms of their potential as a revenue source.

Suppose that you plan to start a company that will supply movies specifically for cable or the home video market. Or you plan to mix these products with producing theatrical films. You will need to create separate industry descriptions for each type of film. This book focuses on theatrically distributed films and how all the other revenue sources make up the total of each film. When films bypass theatrical and are sent directly to other media platforms, you have a problem with forecasting for investors. Currently, there are not databases to use. Chapter 6, "The Markets, Part II," discusses distribution methods that fit this description.

A Little Knowledge Can Be Dangerous

You can only guess what misinformation and false assumptions about the film industry the readers of your business plan will have. Just the words *film* and *marketing* evoke all sorts of images. Your prospective investors might be financial wizards who have made a ton of money in other businesses, but they will probably be uneducated in the finer workings of film production, distribution, and marketing. One of the biggest problems with new film investors, for example, is that they may expect you to have a contract signed by the star or a distribution agreement. They do not know that money may have to be in escrow to sign the star or that the distribution deal will probably be better once you have a finished film, or, at least, are well into production. Therefore, it is necessary to take investors by the hand and explain the film business to them.

You must always assume that the investors have no previous knowledge of this industry. Things are changing and moving all the time, so you must take the time to be sure that everyone involved has the same facts. It is essential that your narrative show how the industry as a whole works, where you fit into that picture, and how the segment of independent film operates. Even entrepreneurs with film backgrounds may need some help. People within the film business may know how one segment works, but not another. As noted in Chapter 3, "The Films," it can be tricky moving from working for a studio or large production company to being an independent filmmaker. The studio is a protected environment. The precise job of a studio producer is quite simple: Make the film. Other specialists within the studio system concentrate on the marketing, distribution, and overall financial strategies. Therefore, a producer working with a studio movie does not necessarily have to be concerned with the business of the industry as a whole. Likewise, if you are a filmmaker in another country, your local industry may function somewhat differently. Foreign entertainment and movie executives may also be naive about the ins and outs of the American film industry.

A Snapshot of the Industry

The total North American box office in 2011 was $10.2 billion. The share for independent films was $3.4 billion or 34 percent of the 2011 total. Revenues for North American independent films from all worldwide revenue sources for 2011 are estimated as more than $8 billion. Worldwide box office revenues totaled $32.6 billion in 2011. Projections for 2013 are for the overall filmed entertainment market to reach $45.1 billion in the United States and $102.2 billion worldwide. Once dominated by the studio system, movie production has shifted to reflect the increasingly viable economic models for independent film. The success of independent films has been helped by the number of new production and smaller distribution companies emerging into the marketplace every day, as well as the growing interest of major U.S. studios in acting as distributors in this market. Also, there has been a rise in the number of screens available for independent films.

Investment in film becomes an even more attractive prospect as financial uncertainty mounts in the wake of Wall Street bail-outs and international stock market slides. Widely recognized as a "recession-proof" business, the entertainment industry has his-torically prospered even during periods of decreased discretionary income. Although the North American box office was down four percent in 2011, it is up 14 percent year-to-date. "In mature markets such as the United States, the business can be more cyclical in the short term, driven by product supply and distribution patterns. In the long term, however, domestic revenues continue to grow...2012 looks to be another growth year," National Association of Theater Owners (NATO) President John Fithian said. Senator Christopher Dodd, Chairman and CEO of the Motion Picture Association of America (MPAA), stated at the December 2011 Asia Pacific Screen Awards, "I am proud to report that the film industry remains a key driver of economic growth around the globe."

As you go through this chapter, think about what your prospective investor wants to know. When you write the Industry section of your business plan, answer the following questions:

- How healthy is the industry?
- How does the film industry work?
- What is the future of the industry?
- What role will my film play in the industry?

MOTION PICTURE PRODUCTION AND THE STUDIOS

The history of Universal Studios shows an interesting change of own-ership among foreign conglomerates. In 1990, Japanese conglomerate Matsushita Electric Industrial Co. bought MCA Inc., the parent com-pany of Universal Pictures. After five years of turmoil and disappoint-ing results, they sold MCA/Universal to Canada's Seagram in 1994, which sold it to French communications/water company Vivendi in 2000. In 2003, Vivendi sold Universal Pictures to American mainstay

General Electric. In 2011, cable television company Comcast bought 51 percent of the company, which is now called NBCUniversal. Some foreign companies have hired consultants to do in-depth analyses of certain U.S. films in order to understand what box office and distribution mean in this country.

Another interesting case study is MGM. The once-prominent brand was taken private in 2005 by a consortium of private investors including Sony Corporation of America. After a year, the contract to distribute only Sony films ended and MGM started functioning as an independent distributor with a recent return to funding films. Then, in 2011, the company was rescued from bankruptcy by a new group of private investors and is being run as an independent company by Spyglass Entertainment Co-Chairmen, Roger Birnbaum and Gary Barber. The company cofinances many of its films with studios but also makes its own independent films.

Originally, there were the "Big Six" studio dynasties: Warner Brothers (part of Time Warner, Inc.), Twentieth Century Fox (now owned by Rupert Murdoch), Paramount (now owned by Viacom), Universal (now NBCUniversal), Metro-Goldwyn-Mayer (now MGM), and Columbia Pictures (now Sony Pictures Entertainment). After the Big Six came the Walt Disney Company. Together, these studios are referred to as "the Majors." (Note: A good source for the early days of Hollywood is *The Moguls: Hollywood's Merchants of Myth* by Norman Zierold.) In most cases, the Majors own their own production facilities and have a worldwide distribution organization. With a large corporate hierarchy making production decisions and a large amount of corporate debt to service, the studios aim most of their films at mass audiences. Although the individual power of each has changed over the years, these studios still set the standard for the larger films.

Until the introduction and development of television for mass consumption in the 1950s, these few studios were responsible for the largest segment of entertainment available to the public. The advent of another major medium, television, changed the face of the industry and lessened the studios' grip on the entertainment market. At the same time, a series of Supreme Court decisions forced the studios to disengage from open ownership of movie theaters. The appearance of video in the 1970s changed the balance once again. Digitally recorded movies, which are the next big paradigm shift, are discussed at the end of this chapter.

How It Works

Today's motion picture industry is a constantly changing and multifaceted business that consists of two principal activities: production and distribution. Production, described in this section, involves the developing, financing, and making of motion pictures. Any overview of this complex process necessarily involves simplification. The following is a brief explanation of how the film business operates.

The classic "studio" picture would typically cost more than $10 million in 1993. Or, conversely, seldom could you independently finance above that figure, unless you were a well-known international filmmaker like Ron Howard or Martin Scorsese. Now, there isn't a real threshold, as independent companies like DreamWorks and Lionsgate are capable of financing movies in the multimillions, thanks to hedge funds and foreign investments. Still, many high-budget films need the backup that a studio can give them. Occasionally, the studio will take a chance on a low-budget film (from their perspective, $20 million) that may not have a broad appeal. However, the studio can spread that risk over 10 to 15 films. Currently, they prefer "tentpole" films; budgets for a single film of this type, like *Pirates of the Caribbean: On Stranger Tides*, may top $250 million.

The typical independent investor, on the other hand, has to sink or swim with just one film. It is certainly true that independently financed films made by experienced producers and with budgets in the mid-range of $20 to $40 million are being bankrolled by production companies with consortiums of foreign investors. For one entity to take that kind of risk on a single film, however, is not the rule. Besides the production budget, the Print and Advertising (P&A) cost also has to be recouped for a film to break even.

There are four typical steps in the production of a motion picture: development, pre-production, production, and post-production. During development and pre-production, a writer may be engaged to write a screenplay or a screenplay may be acquired and rewritten. Certain creative personnel, including a director and various technical personnel, are hired; shooting schedules and locations are planned; and other steps necessary to prepare the motion picture for principal photography are completed. At a studio, a film usually begins in one of two ways. The first method starts with a concept (story idea) from a studio executive, a known writer, or a producer who makes the well-known "30-second pitch." The concept goes into development, and the producers hire scriptwriters. Many executives prefer to work this way. In the second method, a script or book is presented to the studio by an agent or an attorney for the producer and is put into development. The script is polished and the budget determined. The nature of the deal made depends, of course, on the attachments that came with the concept or script. Note that the inception of development does not guarantee production, because the studio has many projects on the lot at one time. A project may be changed significantly or even canceled during development.

The next step in the process is pre-production. If talent was not obtained during development, commitments are sought during pre-production. The process is usually more intensive because the project has probably been *greenlit* (given funding to start production). The craftspeople (the *below-the-line* personnel) are hired, and contracts are finalized and signed. Because of many lawsuits over the past 20 years over "handshake deals" that seem to indicate otherwise, producers need to strive to have all their contracts in place before filming begin.

Production commences when principal photography begins and generally continues for a period of not more than three months, although major cast members may not be used for the entire period. Once a film has reached this stage, the studio is unlikely to shut down the production. Even if the picture goes over budget, the studio will usually find a way to complete it. In post-production, the film is edited, which involves transferring the original filmed material to digital media in order to work easily with the images. In addition, a score is mixed with dialogue, and sound effects are synchronized into the final picture, and, in some cases, special effects are added. The expenses associated with this four-step process for creating and finishing a film are referred to as its *negative costs*. A master is then manufactured for duplication of release prints for theatrical distribution and exhibition, but expenses for prints and advertising for the film are categorized as *P&A* and are not part of the negative costs of the production. Although post-production can last from six to nine months, continuing technological developments have changed the time frame for arriving at a master print of the film.

Tracking the Studio Dollar

Revenues are derived from the exhibition of ⌐
the world in theaters and through various
Studios have their own in-house marketing and ⌐
for the worldwide licensing of their products. Be
expenses of a film—development, pre-productio.
post-production, and distribution—are controlled by ⌐ ⌐rate
body, the accounting is extremely complex.

Much has been written about the pros and cons of nurturing a
film through the studio system. From the standpoint of a profit participant, studio accounting is often a curious process. One producer
has likened the process of studio filmmaking to taking a cab to
work, letting it go, and having it come back at night with the meter
still running. On the other hand, the studios make a big investment.
They provide the money to make the film, and they naturally seek
to maximize their return.

If your film is marketed and distributed by a studio, how much
of each ticket sale can you expect to receive? Table 4.1 provides a
general overview of what happens when a finished film is sent to
an exhibitor. The table traces the $10.00 that a viewer pays to see a
film. On average, half of that money stays with the theater owner,
and half is returned to the distribution arm of the studio. It is possible for studios to get a better deal, but a 50 percent share is most
common. The split is based on box office revenue only; the exhibitor keeps all the revenue from popcorn, candy, and soft drinks.
For all intents and purposes, the distribution division of a studio

TABLE 4.1

Tracking the Studio Dollar

Your Ticket	$10.00
Exhibitor Share (50%)	$5.00
Studio Share (50%)	$5.00
Studio Share (50%—See Above)	$5.00
Minus Distribution Fee (50% of $5.00)	$2.50
	$2.50
Minus Overhead Fee (12% of $5.00)	$0.60
Amount Left to Apply Toward Film Negative (38% of $5.00)—	$1.90
Does Not Include Interest Charges	

Note: This example is based on average results. An individual film may differ in actual percentages.

like a separate company in terms of its handling of your
You are charged a distribution fee, generally 40 to 60 percent
(we're using a 50 percent average), for the division's efforts in marketing the film. Because the studio controls the project, it decides
the amount of this fee. In Table 4.1, the sample distribution fee
shown is 50 percent of the studio's share of the ticket sale, or $5.00,
leaving 50 percent of the box office revenues still in the revenue
stream. Next comes the hardest number to estimate: the film's share
of the studio's overhead. *Overhead* is all of the studio's fixed costs—
that is, the money the studio spends that is not directly chargeable
to a particular film. The salaries for management, secretaries, com-
missary employees, maintenance staff, accountants, and all other
employees who service the entire company are included in overhead. A percentage system (usually based on revenues) is used to
determine a particular film's share of overhead expenses.

It should be noted that the studios did not make up this system;
it is a standard business practice. At all companies, the non-revenue-
producing departments are "costed" against the revenue-producing
departments, determining the profit line of individual divisions. A
department's revenue is taken as a percentage of the total company
revenue. That percentage is used to determine how much of the
total overhead cost the individual department needs to absorb.

In Table 4.1, a fixed percentage is used to determine the overhead fee. Note that it is a percentage of the total rentals that come
back to the studio. Thus, the 12 percent fee is taken from the $5.00,
rather than from the amount left after the distribution fee has been
subtracted. In other words, when it is useful, the distribution division is considered to be a separate company to which you are paying money rather than a division of the studio. Using that logic, you
should be charged 12 percent of $2.50 ($.30) rather than $5.00 ($.60),
but, alas, it doesn't work that way.

Now you are down to a return of $1.90 or 38 percent of the
original $5.00, to help pay off the negative cost. During produc-
tion, the studio treats the money spent on the negative cost as a
loan and charges you bank rates for the money (prime rate plus
one to three percent of points). That interest is added to the negative cost of your film, creating an additional amount above your
negative cost to be paid before a positive net profit is reached. We
have yet to touch on the idea of stars and directors receiving gross
points, which is a percentage of the studio's gross dollar (e.g., the
$5.00 studio share of the total box office dollar in Table 4.1). Even if

the points are paid on "first dollar," the reference is only to studio share. If it has several gross point participants, it is not unusual for a box office hit to show a net loss for the bottom line.

Studio Pros and Cons

When deciding whether to be independent or to make a film within the studio system, a filmmaker has serious options to weigh. The studio provides an arena for healthy budgets and offers plenty of staff to use as a resource during the entire process, from development through post-production. Unless an extreme budget overrun occurs, the producer and director do not have to worry about running out of funds. In addition, the amount of product being produced at the studio gives the executives tremendous clout with agents and stars. The studio has a mass distribution system that is capable of putting a film on more than 4,000 screens for the opening weekend if the budget and theme warrant it. *Harry Potter and the Deathly Hollows, Part 2*, for example, opened on 4,375 screens. However, I should mention that a very large independent company can have the same clout. Lionsgate opened *The Hunger Games* on 3,916 screens and increased the release to 4,127 screens the following week. Finally, the producer or director of a studio film need not know anything about business beyond the budget of the film. All of the other business activities are conducted by experienced personnel at the studio.

On the other hand, the studio has total control over the filmmaking process. Should studio executives choose to exercise this option, they can fire and hire anyone they wish. Once the project enters the studio system, the studio may hire additional writers and the original screenwriters may not even see their names listed under that category on the screen. The Writers Guild can arbitrate and award a "story by" credit to the original writer, but the screenwriting credit may remain with the later writers. Generally, the studio gets final cut privileges as well. No matter who you are or how you are attached to a project, once the film gets to the studio, you can be negotiated to a lower position or off the project altogether. The studio is the investor, and it calls the shots. If you are a new producer, the probability is high that studio executives will want their own producer on the project. Those who want to understand more about the studio system should watch fictional treatments of it, such as Christopher Guest's film *The Big Picture*,

Robert Altman's *The Player*, Jeff Nathanson's *The Last Shot*, or the "Aquaman" segments in HBO's series *Entourage*. Even though Guest's film was made in 1989, nothing has changed but the names. I also suggest reading some insightful books on the subject from true insiders, such as William Goldman's *Adventures in the Screen Trade* and sequel *Which Lie Did I Tell?: More Adventures in the Screen Trade*, Dawn Steel's *They Can Kill You but They Can't Eat You*, and Lynda Obst's *Hello, He Lied*. The studios are filled with major and minor executives in place between the corporate office and film production. There are executive vice-presidents, senior vice-presidents, and plain old vice-presidents. Your picture can be greenlit by one executive, then go into turnaround with her replacement. The process of getting decisions made is a hazardous journey, and the maxim "No one gets in trouble by saying no" proves to be true more often than not.

MOTION PICTURE PRODUCTION AND THE INDEPENDENTS

What do we actually mean by the term *independent*? Defining "independent film" depends on whether you want to include or exclude. Filmmakers often want to ascribe exclusionary creative definitions to the term. When you go into the market to raise money from investors (both domestic and foreign), however, being inclusive is much more useful. If you can tell potential investors that the North American box office for independent films in 2011 was $3.4 billion, they are more likely to want a piece of the action. The traditional definition of independent is a film that finds its production financing outside of the U.S. studios and that is free of studio creative control. The filmmaker obtains the negative cost from other sources. This is the definition of independent film used in this book, regardless of who the distributor is. Likewise, the Independent Film and Television Alliance defines an independent film as one made or distributed by "those companies and individuals apart from the major studios that assume the majority of the financial risk for a production and control its exploitation in the majority of the world." In the end, esoteric discussions don't really matter. We all have our own agendas. If you want to find financing for your film, however, I suggest embracing the broadest definition of the term.

When four Best Picture Oscar nominations went to independent films in 1997, reporters suddenly decided that the distributor was the defining element of a film. Not so. A realignment of companies that began in 1993 caused the structure of the industry to change over and over as audiences and technology have continually evolved. A surge in relatively "mega" profits from low-budget films encouraged the establishment of "independent" divisions at the studios. By acquiring or creating these divisions, the studios handled more films made by producers using financing from other sources. Disney, for example, purchased Miramax Films, maintaining it as an autonomous division. New Line Cinema (and its then specialty division, Fine Line Pictures) and Castle Rock (director Rob Reiner's company) became part of Turner Broadcasting along with Turner Pictures, which in turn was absorbed by Warner Bros. Universal and Polygram (80 percent owned by Philips N.V.) formed Gramercy Pictures, which was so successful that Polygram Filmed Entertainment (PFE) bought back Universal's share in 1995, only to be bought itself by Seagram-owned Universal. Eventually, Seagram sold October Films (one of the original indies), Gramercy Pictures, and remaining PFE assets to Barry Diller's new USA Networks, and those three names disappeared into history. Sony Pictures acquired Orion Classics, the only profitable segment of the original Orion Pictures, to form Sony Classics. Twentieth Century Fox formed Fox Searchlight. Metromedia, which owned Orion, bought the Samuel Goldwyn Company, and eventually was itself bought by MGM. Not to be left out of the specialty film biz, Paramount launched Paramount Classics in 1998 (reorganized as part of Paramount Vantage in 2006), and in 2003, Warner Bros. formed a specialty film division, Warner Independent Pictures. Between 2009 and 2011, most of the studio specialty divisions were absorbed and became merely labels.

In 2003, Good Machine, a longtime producer and distributor of independent films, became part of Universal as Focus Features. The company's partners split between going to Universal and staying independent as Good Machine International. Focus operated autonomously from Universal and was given a budget for production and development of movies by its parent company. Universal, in turn, used Focus as a source of revenue and to find new talent. In 2008, Focus was absorbed into the studio. By the definition used in this book, then, the films produced by Focus would no longer be considered independent; however, it continues to operate as an autonomous division along with Working Title Films.

Then there is DreamWorks SKG. Formed in 1994 by Steven Spielberg, David Geffen, and Jeffrey Katzenberg, the company was variously called a studio, an independent, and—my personal favorite—an independent studio. In the last quarter of 2005, Paramount bought the DreamWorks live-action titles and their 60-title library plus worldwide rights to distribute the films from DreamWorks Animation (spun off as a separate company in 2004) for between $1.5 and $1.6 billion. Paramount then sold the library to third-party equity investors, retaining a minority interest and the right to buy it back at a future date. Spielberg could greenlight a film budgeted up to $90 million, which caused Business Strategies to count films solely financed by DreamWorks as independent. In October 2008, DreamWorks sought a divorce from Paramount and is once again a standalone production company starting life a new as DreamWorks Studios. This means that it is a very large, vertically integrated company that makes independent films. (In the strange lexicon of Hollywood, it is referred to once again as "independent studio.") Although the studio started with investments upward of $1 million from Reliance and investment companies, it was immediately hit by the 2009 downturn with mixed results. As this edition is being written, DreamWorks looks like it may have a big uptrend with the 2011 Oscar-nominated box office blockbuster *The Help.*

In-house specialty divisions provided their parent companies with many advantages. As part of an integrated company, specialty divisions have been able to give the studios the skill to acquire and distribute a different kind of film, while the studio is able to provide greater ancillary opportunities for appropriate low- to moderate-budget films through their built-in distribution networks. Specialty labels have proven themselves assets in more literal ways as well. At one point, Time Warner planned to sell New Line for $1 billion (Turner paid $600 million for the company in 1993) to reduce the parent company's debt load. New Line's founder Robert Shaye and the other principals had always made their own production decisions, even as part of Turner Pictures. In the summer of 1997, New Line secured a nonrecourse (i.e., parent company is not held responsible) $400-million loan through a consortium of foreign banks to provide self-sufficient production financing for New Line Cinema. Making their own films meant that New Line kept much more of their revenue than they would have if they had been a division of Warner Bros. Everyone liked this situation until the release of *The Lord of the Rings: Fellowship of the Ring*, the first film of the trilogy, earned $1.1 billion worldwide, and all three films went on to earn $3.5 billion. In 2007, New Line was taken in-house and made merely a studio label by Warner Bros., which also swallowed up Bob Berney's Picturehouse and Warner Independent Pictures. Former New Line Cinema chiefs Robert Shaye and Michael Lynne formed Unique Features, a new independent company that plans to produce two to three titles a year. Paramount changed Paramount Vantage from a specialty division to merely a brand name. And Relativity Media bought genre division Rogue Pictures from Universal Pictures for $150 million. Looking at the label as not just a movie brand; Relativity partnered with the Hard Rock Hotel and Casino in Las Vegas to launch a clothing line that targets 15- to 25-year olds with hoodies, T-shirts, and hats that will be featured in Rogue's films and a social networking site, *www.RogueLife.com*, to promote the label's films and products. The hotel also will rename its music venue as the Rogue Joint and use it to host film premieres and screenings. As this edition is going to press, the only studio specialty divisions operating independently are Sony Classics, Focus Features, and Working Title Films. The studios do have distribution deals with independent companies, such as Joel Silver's Dark Castle Pictures and DreamWorks Animation.

As always, new indie production companies have appeared in the last three years. Red Granite Pictures, launched in 2010, got off to a good start with 2011's *Friends with Kids* as its first film. Indian Paintbrush has among its films *Young Adult*, *Jeff Who Lives At Home*, and *Like Crazy*. Guns and Roses guitarist Slash started Slasher Film in 2012. XYZ Film is an L.A.-based foreign sales representative that has begun producing films in both the United States and other countries. *The Raid: Redemption*, released in 2012, is an Indonesian film. These are just a few. To give you a good list, this book would need to be a loose leaf, as companies come and go as film results and economic conditions dictate.

If a film remains independently funded, the prime definition of being an "independent" has been met, no matter which studio distributor's logo is tacked onto it. It is up to you, the reader, to track what has happened in the meantime. My advice is to spring for the cost of http://www.proimdb.com. It will be a big help.

How It Works

An independent film goes through the same production process as a studio film from development to post-production. In this case, however, development and pre-production may involve only one or two people, and the entrepreneur, whether producer or director, maintains control over the final product. For the purpose of this discussion, we will assume that the entrepreneur at the helm of an independent film is the producer.

The independent producer is the manager of a small business enterprise. She must have business acumen for dealing with the investors, the money, and all the contracts involved during and after filming. The producer is totally responsible from inception to sale of the film; she must have enough savvy and charisma to win the confidence of the director, talent, agents, attorneys, distributors, and anyone else involved in the film's business dealings. There are a myriad of details the producer must concentrate on every day. Funding sources require regular financial reports, and production problems crop up on a daily basis, even with the best laid plans. Traditionally, the fortunes of independent filmmakers have cycled up and down from year to year. For the past few years, they have been consistently up. In the late 1980s, with the success of such films as *Dirty Dancing* (made for under $5 million, it earned more than $100 million worldwide) and *Look Who's Talking* (made for less than $10 million, it earned more than $200 million), the studios tried to distribute small films. With minimum releasing budgets of $5 million, however, they didn't have the experience or patience to let a small film find its market. Studios eventually lost interest in producing small films, and individual filmmakers and small independent companies took back their territory.

In the early 1990s, *The Crying Game* and *Four Weddings and a Funeral* began a new era for independent filmmakers and distributors. Many companies started with the success of a single film and its sequels. Carolco built its reputation with the *Rambo* films, and New Line achieved prominence and clout with the *Nightmare on Elm Street* series.

Other companies have been built on the partnership of a single director and a producer, or of a group of production executives, who consistently create high-quality, money-making films. For example, Harvey and Bob Weinstein created Miramax in the eighties as a video company. Eventually, the company became the 800-pound gorilla by wresting Oscar Best Picture wins away from studio films. In 1993, The Walt Disney Company purchased the company but let it operate essentially independently. In 2005, the Weinsteins negotiated a divorce from Disney but lost the use of their Miramax label and much of the catalog. The Weinstein brothers then created The Weinstein Company, raising $490-million equity in only a few months. Eventually, Disney sold the Miramax label and catalog to private investors. As a newly independent company, Miramax and the Weinsteins work together on many films.

Then there are smaller independent producers, from the individual making a first film to small- or medium-size companies that produce multiple films each year. The smaller production companies usually raise money for one film at a time, although they may have many projects in different phases of development. Many independent companies are owned or controlled by a creative person, such as a writer–director or writer–producer, in combination with a financial partner or a group. These independents usually make low-budget pictures in the $50,000- to $5-million range. *Like Crazy* and *Kevin Hart: Laugh at My Pain*—made for $250,000 and $750,000, respectively— are at the lower end of the range, with the former often called "no-budget" and the latter "very low." When a film rises above the clouds, a small company is suddenly catapulted to star status. In 1999, *The Blair Witch Project* made Artisan Entertainment a distribution force to contend with, and in 2002, *My Big Fat Greek Wedding* was a hit for IFC Films (now owned by Rainbow Media) and gave Gold Circle Films higher status as a domestic independent producer and distributor. In 2008, Summit Entertainment, which heretofore had been a foreign sales company, earned more than $400 million with its first production, *Twilight*, making the company a major independent player. In 2011, however, the company merged with Lionsgate. A reason to keep track of these changes is always to know who the players are. Several of my clients had projects working their way through the management hierarchy at Summit when the Lionsgate deal occurred. They had to wait for the inevitable termination of executives in duplicate jobs, then locate who now had their project. In the worst-case scenario, of course, a project that had been championed by a mid-level executive was sent back to the filmmaker by the next person in the same position.

Tracking the Independent Dollar

Before trying to look at the independent film industry as a separate segment, it is helpful to have a general view of how the money flows. This information is probably the single most important factor that you will need to describe to potential investors. I don't insert this table in plans, as each one has its own forecasts. However, it does serve as a general comparison to the studio system.

Table 4.2 is a simplified example of where the money comes from and where it goes. The figures given are for a fictional film and do not reflect the results of any specific film. In this discussion, the distributor is at the top of the "producer food chain," as all revenues come back to the distribution company first. The distributor's expenses (*P&A*) and fees (percentage of all revenue plus miscellaneous fees) come before the "total revenue to producer/investor" line, which is the *net profit*.

TABLE 4.2
Tracking the Independent Dollar (in millions)

REVENGE OF THE CRAZED CONSULTANT*

Domestic Box Office Gross	10.00
Exhibitor Share of Box Office (50%)	5.00
Distributor Share of Box Office (50%)	5.00
REVENUE	
Domestic	
Theatrical Rentals (50% of Total Box Office)	5.00
Home Video and Television/Cable	11.00
Domestic Revenue Total	16.00
Foreign	7.50
TOTAL DISTRIBUTOR GROSS REVENUE	23.50
LESS:	
Budget	3.00
Print and Advertising	4.00
TOTAL COSTS	7.00
GROSS INCOME	16.50
Distributor's Fees (35% of Gross Revenue)	8.22
NET PRODUCER/INVESTOR INCOME BEFORE TAXES	8.28

---

*This is a fictional film.

The box office receipts for independent films are divided into exhibitor and distributor shares, just as they are for studio films (see Table 4.1). Here, the average split between distributor and exhibitor is 50/50. This is an average figure for the total, although on a weekly basis the split may differ. In the example in Table 4.2, of the $10 million in total U.S. box office, the distributor receives $5 million in rentals. This $5 million from the U.S. theatrical rentals represents only a portion of the total revenues flowing back to the distributor. Other revenues added to this sum as they flow in, generally over a period of two years, include domestic ancillaries (home video, which currently encompasses DVD, Blu-ray, and digital sources, plus television, cable, etc.) and foreign (theatrical and ancillary). Whether VOD is included in available figures is not clear.

Technology is rapidly changing, and as it does, the revenue stream for films changes, too. As you may already know, in 2007, the production of VHS tapes ended, although there was still minimal revenue from sales of tapes in 2008. Blu-ray was just beginning to make inroads when the economic collapse temporarily halted its progress. As of mid-2012, DVD is still with us, Blu-ray is growing again, and downloaded films are included in the home video total. However, Microsoft Corporation has announced that their Windows 8, slated for release in late 2012, will not support DVD or Blu-ray discs, signaling the increasing dominance of streaming and downloadable media formats in the home entertainment marketplace.

Film production costs and distribution fees are paid out as money flows in. From the first revenues, the P&A (known as the "first money out") are paid off. In this example, it is assumed that the P&A cost is covered by the distributor. Then, generally, the negative cost of the film is paid back to the investor. In recent years, filmmakers have paid back from 110 to 120 percent of the budget to investors as an incentive. The distributor takes 35 percent or less of the worldwide revenue as his fee (35 percent is used in forecasting when no distribution deal exists), and the producer and the investor divide the remaining money.

Pros and Cons

Independent filmmaking offers many advantages. The filmmaker has total control of the script and filming. It is usually the director's film to make and edit. Some filmmakers want to both direct and produce their movies; this can be like working two 36-hour shifts within one 24-hour period. It is probably advisable to have a director who directs and a separate producer who produces, as this provides a system of checks and balances during production that approximates many of the pluses of the studio system. Nevertheless, the filmmaker is able to make these decisions for himself. And if he wants to distribute as well, preserving his cut and using his marketing plan, that is another option—not necessarily a good one, as distribution is a specialty in itself, but still an option.

The disadvantages in independent filmmaking are the corollary opposites of the studio advantages. Because there is no cast of characters to fall back on for advice, the producer must have experience or find someone who does. Either you will be the producer and run your production or you will have to hire a producer. Before you hire anyone, you should understand how movies are made and how the financing works. Whether risking $50,000 or $50 million, an investor wants to feel that your company is capable of safeguarding his money. Someone must have the knowledge and the authority to make a final decision. Even if the money comes out of the producer's or the director's own pocket, it is essential to have the required technical and business knowledge before starting.

Money is hard to find. The popular saying is "If it was easy, everyone would be doing it." Here in Hollywoodland, we get the impression that everyone is. However, that isn't true in other parts of the country and world. Budgets must be calculated as precisely as possible in the beginning, because independent investors may not have the same deep pockets as the studios. Even if you find your own Megan Ellison (Annapurna Pictures) or Jeff Skoll (Participant Productions) with significant dollars to invest, that person expects you to know the cost of the film. The breakdown of the script determines the budget. When you present a budget to an investor, you promise that this is a reasonable estimate of what it will cost to make what is on the page and that you will stay within that budget. The investor agrees only on the specified amount of money. The producer has an obligation to the investor to make sure that the movie does not run over the budget. Trying to go back to investors for more money after the initial infusion of cash usually doesn't work.

PRODUCTION AND EXHIBITION FACTS AND FIGURES

The North American (United States and Canada) box office reached $10.2 billion in revenues in 2011, according to the MPAA. The independent share of this box office was $3.4 billion, or 34 percent, as calculated by Business Strategies. The worldwide box office was $32.6 billion. Although U.S. theatrical distribution is still the first choice for any feature-length film, international markets are gaining even greater strength than they had before. New to the picture are VOD releases. Films are beginning to be released *day-and-date*—in other words, VOD and theatrical on the same day.

Separating the gross dollars into studio and independent shares is another matter. Although databases often include films distributed by specialty divisions of the studios as studio films, being acquired does not change the independent status of the film. In order to estimate the total for independent films, we keep our own database tracking films by financing source and control of production.

Theatrical Exhibition

At the end of 2011, there were 42,390 theater screens (including drive-in screens) in North America with approximately 39,641 in the United States. In the early part of the decade, the companies with multiscreen venues went through bankruptcies and mergers. Despite many ups and downs, such as the advent of the multichannel cable universe and the growth of the home video market, theatrical distribution has continued to prosper.

Film revenues from all other sources are driven by theatrical distribution. For pictures that skip the theatrical circuit and go directly into foreign markets, home video, television, or the Internet, revenues are not likely to be as high as those for films with a history of U.S. box office revenues and promotion. The U.S. theatrical release of a film usually ends between three and five months. The average for both studio and independent films before going into home video generally is four months, although this is slowly becoming closer to three. As with other generally accepted standards, this one is undergoing changes. While studio films begin with a "wide" opening on thousands of screens, independent films start more slowly and build. Rentals will decline toward the end of an independent film's run, but they may very well increase during the first few months. It is not unusual for a smaller film to gain theaters as it becomes more popular.

Social media has had a big impact on distribution. For independent films, it allows the word to spread faster the first weekend, and successful films to expand more rapidly. For potential studio blockbuster films that depend on a big opening, friends tweeting bad reviews on Friday night can now kill the weekend for the film.

Despite some common opinions from distributors, the exhibitor's basic desire is to see people sitting in the theater seats. There has been a lot of discussion about the strong-arm tactics that the major studios supposedly use to keep screens reserved for their use. (This is sometimes referred to as *block booking*.) Exhibitors, however, have always maintained that they will show any film that they think their customers will pay to see. Depending on the location of the individual theater or the chain, local pressures or activities may play a part in the distributor's decision. Not all pictures are appropriate for all theaters.

Time and time again, independent films that have good *buzz* (prerelease notices by reviewers, festival acclaim, and good public relations) and favorable word of mouth from audiences not only survive but also flourish. *The Visitor* is a good example. It started out in a small number of theaters and cities. As audiences liked the film and told their friends about it, the movie was given wider release in chain theaters in more cities. Of course, good publicity gimmicks help. People still ask me if 1999s *The Blair Witch Project* is a real story; I have even been accused of lying when I say that it is utterly fictional, a "mockumentary" no more real than *Borat* or *Paranormal Activity 1-3*.

DIGITAL AND 3D

Digital

Digital film is rapidly changing the film industry. While there were 324 digital screens in the United States at the end of 2005 and 5,474 in 2008, there were 25,621 in 2011—13,001 digital non-3D and 12,620 3D—according to the *IHS Screen Digest*. At the 2012 Cinemacon convention, NATO Chief John Fithian said, "About two-thirds of all screens now have digital projectors, and the transition—as well as the demise of celluloid prints—could be complete by the end of 2013." He also urged theater owners to check out exhibitors promoting the next stages in the evolution of digital cinema: faster frame rates and laser projection.

On June 5, 2000, Twentieth Century Fox became the first company to transmit a movie over the Internet from a Hollywood studio to a theater across the country. Well, to be more exact, it originated in Burbank, California, and went over a secure Internet-based network to an audience at the Supercomm trade show in Atlanta. (Trivia buffs, take note: The film was the animated space opera *Titan A.E.*)

As we roll rapidly through the twelfth year of the 21st century, filmmakers keep calling me about the $30,000 digital film they are going to shoot on their low-cost digital camera that will look like a $10-million film and be distributed on 3,000 screens. Probably not likely on both counts. What is missing in those expectations? For one thing, the filmmaker's expertise at putting production quality on the screen. That aside, there still is a question about low-budget digital films. It is likely an estimated 1,000 specialty theaters will not be upgraded to digital any time soon due to the expense. The conversion costs to "d-cinema" screens are considerable; each digital projector is $150,000, along with the more than $20,000 per screen required for the computer that stores and feeds the movies. Studios and distributors have been willing to work with the big chain exhibitors to share or even bear the expenses; however, they aren't concerned about smaller venues.

For most independent filmmakers, it still will be a long haul to the celluloid-free future. Despite the reported number of screens and the number of digital films sent to film festivals, we have yet to find a successful independent film that was distributed in digital format alone. Include money in your budget to convert to 35 mm for exhibition. Don't assume that the distributor wants to do it. Look at it from his viewpoint. If the distributor is planning on releasing 10 to 20 films a year, and it runs $55,000 or more per film for a quality upgrade from digital to 35 mm, then he is likely to opt for a film that is already in a 35 mm format. "But," you say, "my film will be so exceptional, he will offer to put up the money." It is within the realm of possibility, but I wouldn't want the distribution of my film to rest on that contingency. Or you may say, "I'll wait until the distributor wants the film, and then I'll raise the money for the upgrade." Although this is not out of the question, don't just assume you will be able to raise the money. Those pesky investors again. Whether it is one investor or several in an offering, you have to go back to those people for the additional $50,000. Will they go for it? Maybe yes or no. If they don't, then you may be stuck. If you raise the money from additional sources, you still have to get the agreement of the original investors. After all, you are changing the amount of money they will receive from your blockbuster film.

Then there is the question of quality. When technology experts from the studios are on festival or market panels, they always point out that audiences don't care how you make the film; they care how it looks. In a conversation shortly before the 2009 National Association of Broadcasters in Las Vegas, a Kodak rep told me that experienced filmmakers still prefer to shoot on 35 mm, edit digitally, and then return the movie to 35 mm for the final print. If you can really make your ultra-low-budget digital film have the look of a $5-or $10-million film, go for it. But be honest with yourself.

3D

This section would reasonably be titled "Everything old is new again." Readers over 60 will remember this technology's first incarnations in 1952 to 1954, with films like *House of Wax* (the first with stereoscopic sound) and *It Came from Outer Space*. It faded in the late 1950s but had a revival in the early 1980s when the large-format IMAX screens offered their early docs in 3Ds. Studios and other production companies discovered 3D in the past four or five years as the "new format" that will revolutionize the film industry. Thanks to improvements in technology, filmmakers can deliver a better product.

It appears that 3D is here to stay. According to a study conducted by Opinion Research Corp., "consumers are savvy in selecting what movies to watch in 3D. They look at it as a more fun, exciting and valuable experience." However, how many films that audience will continue to pay a premium for each year to come remains to be seen.

Exhibitors are moving ahead converting screens to 3D. In 2011, there were 13,695 (39 percent of the total) digital 3D screens in North America, 11,642 in Europe, 8,116 in the Asian/Pacific area, and 2,026 in Latin America. In the United States, studios have been footing the bill for audiences' 3D glasses to help push 3D conversion along. As of May 2012, Sony stopped paying for glasses, which cost $5.0 to $10.0 million for a major release. If other studios follow suit, either the cost for tickets will rise or moviegoers will have to buy their own.

FUTURE TRENDS

For six editions of this book, digital and digital 3D were the future. Now they are here. More revolutionary changes in the manner in which motion pictures are produced and distributed are now sweeping the industry, especially for independent films. Web-based companies like Movielink (owned by Blockbuster), Amazon's Video on Demand (VOD), CinemaNow, and Apple's iTunes Store are selling films and other entertainment programming for download on the Internet, and websites such as Netflix and Hulu (through Hulu Plus) stream filmed entertainment to home viewers as rentals. New devices for personal viewing of films (including Xbox, Wii, video iPod, iPhone, and iPad) are gaining ground in the marketplace, expanding the potential revenues from home video and other forms of selling programming for viewing. On a local newscast, I recently saw a demonstration of a wristwatch on which you can make phone calls and see text. Will short films be next?

WHAT DO YOU TELL INVESTORS?

All business plans should include a general explanation of the industry and how it works. No matter what your budget, investors need to know how both the studio and the independent sectors work. Your business plan should also assure investors that this is a healthy industry. You will find conflicting opinions; it is your choice what information to use. Whatever you tell the investor, be able to back it up with facts. As long as your rationale makes sense, your investor will feel secure that you know what you are talking about. That doesn't mean he will write the check, but at least he will trust you.

Tables and Graphs

A picture may be worth a thousand words, but 20 pictures are not necessarily worth 20,000 words. The introduction of user-friendly computer software brought a new look to business plans. Unfortunately, many people have gone picture crazy. They include tables and graphs where words might be better. Graphs made up about three-fourths of one company's business plan that I saw. The graphs were very well done and to a certain extent did tell a story. The proposal, put together by an experienced consultant, was gorgeous and impressive—for what it was. But what was it? Imagine watching a silent film without the subtitles. You know what action is taking place, and you even have some vague idea of the story, but you don't know exactly who the characters are, what the plot is, or whether the ending is a happy one. Similarly, including a lot of graphs for the sake of making your proposal "look nice" has a point of diminishing returns.

There are certainly benefits to using tables and graphs, but there are no absolute rules about their use. One key rule for writing screenplays, however, does apply. Ask yourself what relation your tables and graphs have to what investors need to know. For example, you could include a graph that shows the history of admissions per capita in the United States since 1950, but this might raise a red flag. Readers might suspect that you are trying to hide a lack of relevant research. You would only be fooling yourself. Investors looking for useful information will notice that it isn't there. You will raise another red flag if you include multiple tables and graphs that are not accompanied by explanations. Graphic representations are not supposed to be self-explanatory; they are used to make the explanation more easily understood. There are two possible results: (1) the reader will be confused or (2) the reader will think that you are confused. You might well be asked to explain your data. Won't that be exciting?

5

The Markets: The Spin

Never treat your audience as customers, always as partners.
—ACTOR JIMMY STEWART

You may view the 7.02 billion people in the world as potential moviegoers, but very few filmmakers expected to sell tickets to all of them—that is, until *Jurassic Park* pushed the box office frontier farther than ever before in 1993. It earned more than $750 million worldwide. You didn't need to speak English or know anything about biology to enjoy this film. It had something for everyone who was old enough to watch it. Then, in 1998, *Titanic* racked up $1.7 billion worldwide.

On the independent side, the three films of *The Lord of the Rings* trilogy, released between 2001 and 2003, earned more than $3 billion worldwide. Then through 2011, the seven *Saw* films earned more than $1.4 billion in total revenue.

What does this mean to you the independent? While studios are emphasizing tentpole films, there remains a very large theatrical ballpark in which independents can play. The indie home runs being hit in this century have opened the game to many more players.

On the financing side, everything has gone through a strange transformation. With the change in the economic climate since 2008–2009, many hedge and real estate funds have failed. While the hedge funds were more interested in large, integrated production companies real estate investors have been partnering with individual filmmakers. As we will discuss in Chapter 13, "Other People's Money," not all these investors seek the same film package. Whether your film's budget is $400,000 or $40 million and whether it has newbie actors or stars, you need to research the market for your film and explain it for your investors.

The market comprises all those people who are going to buy tickets. In this chapter, we will be looking at the potential popularity of the themes and styles your films represent. To some extent, we also will look at marketing, but do not confuse these two concepts. Marketing involves selling your idea not only to the investor but also to the distributor and audience. Here, we will focus on selling to the investor through the business plan, but we will also touch on current forms of self-marketing; the distributor is dealt with in Chapter 7. To make terms somewhat more confusing, this book also refers to "the markets," such as the American Film Market and Cannes, the two largest international marketplaces where production and distribution deals are closed.

In the previous section of your business plan, the Industry section, you defined the industry as a whole and independent film as a segment of it. Now, in the Market section, you will build on that definition by further dividing your industry segment. Your segment may not be as global in size as "everyone," but it has its own value. You will also take the projects that you described in the earlier Film section and use their components to pinpoint your market. This analysis gives you a base for later estimating those very important gross revenues.

MARKET SEGMENT

Your market segment, or niche, consists of the type of person out of the total moviegoing population who is likely to rush out to see your film the first weekend, as well as secondary target groups that will be interested. You need to identify, for yourself and those reading your proposal, the size and population characteristics of this segment. By devising a snapshot of your film's likely audience, you will be able to determine the film's ability, first, to survive and, second, to succeed. Who are the end users of your film—that is, the ticket buyers—and how many of them are there likely to be? Before you worry about marketing strategies and distribution channels, create a picture of the potential size of your market's population. How can you do this? Very carefully. But do not worry. It is easier than you think; it just takes work. You do not need to have inside information or to live in Los Angeles to do this. Research is your tool.

Having divided the industry into studio and independent, you now need to divide your segment into smaller pieces. In looking at this piece of the market, ask yourself these questions:

- How large a population segment is likely to see my film?
- What size budget is reasonable vis-à-vis the size of this segment?

Defining Your Segment

Filmmakers would like to appeal to everyone, and some independent films reach a mainstream goal. For the most part, though, an independent film will attract moviegoers from one or two identifiable segments of the audience. To understand how to focus your investor's expectations (and your own), you will have to do a little research. You do not have to be an expert, but investigation will help make you and your investor wiser and wealthier.

The profile of your target market in terms of audience might include the following:

- Main film genres into which your film would fit—comedy, action, thriller, horror, drama, romance.
- Special formats—documentary, animation, large format.
- Underlying themes—inspirational, young adult, magical realism (*Beasts of the Southern Wild, Pan's Labyrinth*).
- Affinity groups—ethnic, urban, religious, sports.
- Age and sex groups.
- Similar budget parameters.

To Pigeonhole or Not To Pigeonhole

Your identification of the target audience for your film begins when you select the genre of the film. The term *genre* can be very confusing. Some people appear to use the term to refer to cheap and formulaic, as in "it is a genre film." One client of mine was upset that I was cheapening her films by using the term *genre*. For the business plans I write, it is used to refer to films that can be grouped together by plot, settings, and/or themes. Genre doesn't refer to how well you made the film or the amount of the budget. You could probably use the word *category*, but it doesn't have the same movie feel.

As a genre, horror films, for example, are generally movies that scare you for some reason and have lots of blood and gore. In the Internet Movie Database (http://www.imdb.com), there are almost 3,400 theatrical horror films from 2007 to mid-2012, ranging from the no-budget *Paranormal Activity* to the higher-budgeted *One Missed Call*. These films have different premises (sci-fi creatures, blood and gore, childhood nightmares) and appeal to different audience segments. The former will appeal to teenage moviegoers as an initial audience, while the over-35 group is more likely to be drawn to the latter. In the end, though, both of them are still horror films.

Genres can be big or small. Drama is considered the most pervasive genre but is inclusive of many films. The next most popular genre by number of films produced is usually comedy. Both of these genres include films that often carry descriptive adjectives, such as *family*, *romantic*, or *dark*, to further narrow the category. Then we have thriller and action/adventure, which are unique genres. Defining the genre of a particular film doesn't have to be difficult. Very few films are just one genre or theme. A filmmaker wants to use everything that fits the film, which sometimes can be a large number of the main genres. For example, *One For the Money* is described as an action, comedy, crime, romance, and thriller. What isn't included in that general description is the *"female protagonist."* This genre is growing as the audience, both men and women, have become used to women heading films that aren't classified as "chick flicks."

There are also filmmakers who are linked with specific genres and who have become their own genre. Saying a movie will be a Quentin Tarantino, Judd Apatow, Kirby Dick, Tyler Perry, or Hayao Miyazaki film creates a frame of reference for the particular experience moviegoers will have. Woody Allen is so identified with comedy romance by an older audience that *Midnight in Paris* in 2011 grossed much better than films in recent years that his dramas.

You can even have a producer genre. For example, an Avi and Danny Lerner film would immediately be envisioned as a recent *Rambo* or *The Expendables*. If a producer or production company is identified with a particular type of experience, the audience tends to pick the film based on that track record rather than anything else. If you feel that your style is akin to a particular director's niche, you can draw from that audience.

Why bother identifying the genre for your film? Many writers and directors believe that categorizing their films is not only meaningless but also, in some cases, demeaning. There are always filmmakers who say, "My picture is different and can't be compared to any other films." This entrepreneurial attitude is the same in all industries. Nonetheless, all films can be compared, and you do have competition. By giving your investors these frames of reference, you are able to identify the groups of moviegoers to whom the film might appeal and explain the genesis of your projections. One of the challenges you face with your business plan is being understood. You must be certain that you convey your meaning correctly to investors. It is important, therefore, that you define your terms so that everyone is on the same page.

Art Versus Specialty

For 25 years, I have participated in discussions on whether independent films are by definition *art films*, and, if they are, what an art film is. In one such discussion, one person claimed that Federico Fellini and art films were one and the same. Someone else said that they "explain human foibles in an intellectual way." Another suggested that the term had nothing to do with a film's subject. Various people still insist to me that *The Blair Witch Project* was a commercial film and, therefore, by definition, not art or specialty. The terms are not mutually exclusive.

As far back as the first edition of this book production and distribution companies have preferred the term *specialty* for their films rather than *art-house* and with good reason. *Art* may bring to mind a very narrow image of a type of film. Many would assume the film to be an inaccessible film only for the intellectually intense. *Specialty*, on the other hand, is a broader term without these negative connotations. Until you define it, there may be no frame of reference for the investor. Creating a definitive description that everyone agrees with would be impossible. In writing your business plan, you have to find whatever phrases and film references best convey your meaning.

I have been involved with proposals for companies that the client intended to be like the Weinstein Company (a lot of people seem to think they are the Weinstein brothers), Lionsgate, or Sony Classics. What did we start with? We used those companies to define the genre. For example, you could write the following as your introduction:

> *We define the specialty market by the types of films acquired by Lionsgate Releasing and Sony Pictures Classics. Our films have a sensitivity of story and a delicate balance of characters that require unique handling. Therefore, our audience will be the same people who saw* Gods and Monsters, Monster's Ball, *and* Real Women Have Curves.

These pictures may have nothing in common in story or overall theme, but they are used to present a backdrop for the discussion; they give readers something to relate to. Of course, Lionsgate and Sony Classics do not have a lock on specialty films. Which companies you use for comparison depends on your feeling about their products and your reasons for making it.

An important aspect of specialty films is their distribution (and, consequently, revenue) potential. In recent years, the scope of specialty films has widened tremendously. Typically, a specialty film may open on 1 to 15 screens and expand to more screens as revenues become available. On the other hand, if the distributor has enough money and faith, a small independent film can play on many screens. *Little Miss Sunshine* opened on seven screens domestically and played on 1,602 at its widest distribution. *Juno* opened on seven screens, and due to its extraordinary success, it was on 2,534 screens at its widest point of distribution.

Genre History

When describing the history of the Western genre, for example, you do not need to go back to Hopalong Cassidy (ask your grandmother). For the most part, your primary reference period should be the past five to six years. Some genres, such as action/adventure or comedy, are always going strong. They are always popular in one form or another. This is not the case with other genres, however.

Take horror again, for example. This genre, once popular, languished in the ultra-low-budget, direct-to-video, and direct-to-foreign world until the release of *Scream* in 1996. (Note: The first DVD wasn't released until 1997, and the format didn't outstrip VHS releases until 2003.) Until *Scream*, the general wisdom was that horror films were not worth putting any money into; therefore, it was hard to get the investment community interested in the genre.

Timing is everything. Now production money is available everywhere not only for the traditional scary film (*Hostel 1* and *2*, *Saw 1* through *5*, *Halloween*) but also for variations on the theme, such as the *Scary Movie* franchise (comedy/horror) and *The Devil Inside* (mockumentary). Suppose you wanted to make a horror film before any of the above films were released. How would you convince someone that your film would be successful? There are several techniques you could use:

1. *Emphasize other elements: Devil* is a horror/mystery/thriller in which five people trapped in an elevator are killed, one by one, an alcoholic detective and rescuers work to free them. Do bad things happen for a reason?
2. *Redefine the genre: Twilight* is a teenage Romeo and Juliet vampire story. Moving to a small town to live with her father, Bella meets the mysterious and beautiful Edward. The two fall unconditionally in love with each other. Even learning that he is a vampire does not deter her passion. How will they resolve this unnatural relationship?
3. *Override the horror genre altogether: Shaun of the Dead* has the zombies playing comic foils to Shaun, even while eating and killing people.
4. *Use the cycle theory:* The three (so far) *Paranormal Activity* films are mockumentary/horror stories with found footage.

More about Cycles

The argument used in the last technique is not a spurious one. The popularity of a particular genre often rises and falls in cycles. For example, continuing our examination of horror films, this genre made up 24 percent of the product at the 1989 American Film Market, fell to less than 3 percent of the total in 1993 (interestingly, the genre fell out of favor in the book industry at the same time), and rose back to an estimated 20 percent by 2011.

A successful film often inspires a number of similar films that try to capitalize on the popularity of the original. *Film noir* is a term coined by French movie critics to describe American crime dramas in the 1940s. After a brief reappearance of the genre in 1962 with the original *Cape Fear*, the genre's real resurgence began in the 1990s with Martin Scorsese's *Cape Fear* remake in 1991 followed by, among others, *The Usual Suspects* in 1994. It encouraged a proliferation of updated film noirs (the darkly lit look of the 1940s films contributed to the term), such as *Fargo, Lost Highway, Devil in a Blue Dress, The Underneath, Exotica, L.A. Confidential, No Country For Old Men, The Town, The Dark Knight, Brooklyn's Finest,* and *Winter's Bone.* These films broadened the boundaries of the genre beyond the detective thriller to represent a way of looking at the world through a dark mirror reflecting the shadowy underside of life. (Note that, being purists about the term *film noir,* the Internet Movie Database (proimdb.com) uses the term "Neo-Noir" to refer to the post-1950.)

Considering the length of time from development to release, the market may be glutted with a particular type of film for two or three years. When this happens, the audience may reach a saturation point and simply stop going to see films of that genre for a while. Then someone comes along with a well-crafted film that makes money, and the cycle begins again.

Special Niche/Affiliated Groups

Certain groups of films initially appeal to a small segment of the population and then grow, often to the surprise of the filmmakers, to become crossover films. *Y tu mamá también* is an example of a film in Spanish that initially was targeted to an older, Hispanic/Latino audience and attracted a significant number of teenage Anglo filmgoers. The high cost structures of the studios inhibit their ability to exploit smaller, underdeveloped markets, but independent filmmakers have the ability to take chances. They can make a low-budget or even a "no-budget" film to play to a tiny initial market. If the film and its theme catch on, the audience grows, and the film crosses over to a larger portion of the public, introducing that genre to a new group. Subsequent films of that type then draw on the larger audience. When the first edition of this book was published, it appeared to be big news that African-American filmmakers could draw a wide audience. Throughout the rest of the 1990s, gay and lesbian films came to the fore, capped by the Oscar wins of 2005's *Brokeback Mountain* and *Capote.* By 2010, *The Kids Are All Right* was talked about more as a film about family relations than that the family was headed by a Lesbian couple.

Until 2000, the Walt Disney Company seemed to have a lock on family films. It was almost impossible for independents to break into that category. Now Hollywood seems to have discovered that not R-rated films but G- and PG-rated films are its next best thing. The industry makes its biggest profits from G- and PG-rated movies, according to many analysts' reports, and plans to fill the nation's screens in the next few years with even more princesses, monsters, talking animals, bright school kids, and scrappy ballplayers. The independent film *My Dog Skip* was part of the family film renaissance in 2000. This was followed by Dimension's *Spy Kids*, a breakout hit with a U.S. box office of $113 million that inspired a sequel and a flock of imitators. Feeding the burgeoning family film market through 2011 were such films as *Spy Kids 3* and *4D, Akeelah and the Bee, Are We Done Yet?, The World of Arriety,* and *Soul Surfers.* John Fithian has said, "Family values are OK. Family values sell tickets."

What originally I categorized as "faith-based" films, I now identify as "inspirational" films. One of the popular film genres of the past 12 years, inspirational films cover elements of good versus evil, redemption, and the eternal questions of who we are and why we are here. In the past few years, films such as *The Passion of the Christ, The Pianist,* the *Tyler Perry* films, *What the Bleep Do We Know?,* and even *March of the Penguins* alerted production companies and distributors that there is a major market for inspirational films.

Now that this larger genre has been defined, faith-based films fit into it nicely as a subset, including the many films that are likely to appeal to the large Christian audience. For example, *Facing the Giants, End of the Spear, Fireproof,* and *Courageous* specifically espouse Christian values, even though they may contain some questionable elements. The tagline for *Facing the Giants*—"Never give up. Never back down. Never lose faith."—is a good example. At *Variety*'s "Faith and Values Movie Conference" in 2012 Grace Hill Media's Jonathan Bock, who worked on campaigns for *The Vow, War Horse* and *Act of Valor,* said, "On any given weekend, forty-three percent of the country are in church, with two-thirds attending once a month. When you're talking about an audience that big, you're talking a broad spectrum of movie tastes, Hollywood has a tendency to view Christians in political terms, and the audience is much more than that." My admonition to my faith-inspired filmmaker clients is to make a film that has a subtle message and doesn't announce an agenda (i.e., sermonize). Producer Samuel Goldwyn has often been quoted as saying, "If you want to send a message, call Western Union" (ask your grandmother again). Or, as Paul Haggis, director of *Crash,* said, "Film is an emotional medium, not an intellectual medium, so you have to move people. You can't just lecture them."

Inspirational films appeal both to people who are philosophically curious or generally spiritual in addition to people who adhere to specific religious and spiritual groups. As the filmmakers of the popular film *What the Bleep Do We Know?* stated on their website, "There are a great number of mystical traditions and spiritual practices, many paths that lead people to wholeness and peace of mind." With this type of film, you may be describing different groupings of target audiences. For example, for one such film, I included yoga groups and "cultural creatives" in the target market. Or you may have a film that shows someone overcoming great odds that will inspire a few filmgoers to change their lives.

Another large group to look is the *Latino/Hispanic* audience. While the terms tend to be used interchangeable, a Latino client has suggested that I use the word *Hispanic* to describe the entire market. Films that appeal to this audience also have been considered a "new market" for the past 10 years. The latest census reveals that of the 50.5 million Hispanics in the United States. While only 16 percent of the population, they were 24 percent of frequent moviegoers in 2011. On top of that, Latino adults are nearly twice as likely as the total adult population to see a movie on opening weekend and are, on average, 10 years younger than the population as a whole, making them prime movie consumers. Despite buying about 22 percent of all movie tickets, however, Hispanics are a relatively untapped group in terms of film marketing. These moviegoers are concentrated in the trend-setting major markets that make or break Hollywood releases.

The success of Latin American imports is bringing more attention and investment to U.S. filmmakers who want to make films with Hispanic/Latino themes, but, at this point, it is still hard for these films to go beyond very limited distribution. Jack Foley, President of Distribution at Focus Features, told *The New York Times*, "The Latino market in the United States is not changing. Latinos most enjoy English-language Hollywood entertainment. They want escapism and entertainment, exactly as the majority of American moviegoers demand." Films like his company's Spanish-language feature *The Motorcycle Diaries* and Fox Searchlight's *La misma luna* (released in the United States as *Under the Same Moon*), as well as Lionsgate's *Ladrón que roba a Ladrón* and *amores perros* worked in the limited independent specialty market and did well overall financially. Films from U.S. filmmakers, such as *Frida*, *Real Women Have Curves*, and *Tortilla Soup*, also have helped awaken what has been termed the *sleeping giant* of the Hispanic market. However, both the imports and the U.S.-made films have failed to attract the broad, multiethnic, Spanish-speaking population in the United States. Still, they have the attention of the power brokers—investors and distributors. That is what counts.

Sports movies are going to attract people who are interested in not only specific games, but sports in general. I have done business plans for football, baseball, basketball, and soccer. For each of those, you use films of any sport to show the genre. In this section of the business plan, you are not confined by similar budgets. Your goal is to how that there is an audience for sports films. For a plan that I wrote in 2010, I used *The Blind Side, Miracle, The Rookie, Coach Carter, Glory Road, We Are Marshall*, and *Invincible* as examples. In a separate sentence, I mentioned the "classics" *Hoosiers* and *Rudy*, as baby boomers are a big part of the audience. In this case, I did not use their box office results. You still only want to use revenues from the past five years plus the current year.

Who Is Going to See This Film?

Demographics are an important subsection. Do you know the age and sex of the person most likely to see your film? Market research properly belongs in the hands of the person doing the actual marketing (probably the distributor), but you can estimate the appeal of your potential market based on its age groups. For example, for years we accepted the term "family" as referring to G-and PG-rated films. Now we have started referring to many films as "family-friendly," which allows PG-13 to be included.

Teen films are targeted toward an affluent and sizable group. The run the gamut from *High School Musical 1* through *3*, and *How She Move* to slacker/stoner films, such as *Superbad, That My Boy*, and the *Harold and Kumar* films. Teenage movies are traditionally released at the beginning of the summer, when schools are out and teens have a lot of time to go to the theater. While the often have gone to the same movie more than once with various groups of friends, it is likely that their additional viewings may via the assortment of ancillary sources available.

Studios are particularly eager to make films for the teen and young adult market—usually defined as people between the ages of 12 and 24. No longer the single largest audience block, they made up 22 percent of moviegoers in 2011, according to the *2011 Theatrical Market Statistics Report* of the Motion Picture Association of America (MPAA), while filmgoers 40 and over made up 39 percent of the audience. The crossover group of the audiences (ages 25–39) made up 24 percent. These admissions measurements change from year to year; therefore, you will want to check the MPAA's website (http://www.mpaa.org) for current information. In 2011, the National Association of Theater Owners (NATO), which collects these data for the MPAA, either counted everyone under 12 or just assumed that the other 15 percent were ages 2 to 11. Unfortunately, that range is too wide to use.

For the preteens (often referred to as the "tweens"), who are ages 8 or 9 to 12 depending on who is counting, I use marketing statistics. This group is 20 million-plus strong and has a buying power of $43 billion. The *Hannah Montana*, Jonas Brothers, and Justin Bieber films and concerts owe much to this group.

Be careful to use as wide a market as you have. For example, I have had students say that a film is for women ages 35 to 45. If women are the first group that is going to be attracted, then use the broader categories of 25 and under or 25 and older. Don't leave out the grandmas. We oldies still like to have fun. As I was writing this edition, the movie *Magic Mike* was released. Despite a moderate budget of $7 million, it grossed $40 million the first weekend. If you had been putting together a business plan for this film which you knew was going to be R-rated, my suggestion would be to use women aged 18 and over. The MPAA stats in 2011 showed that 75 percent of moviegoers were over the age of 17, and women were 51 percent of all moviegoers. The actual results for *Mike*, according to *The Wall Street Journal*, were that females made up 73 percent of the audience and those under the age of 35 made up 57 percent of the audience. That is your primary group that will make up the first weekend audience. Was everyone who went over the age of 18? I doubt it. However, when looking ahead to the audience you want to predict data for which you have backup.

On the other hand, don't discount men. When *The Help* was released, everyone assumed it was simply a "chick flick." Exit interviews done with the audience indicated that men began going by themselves by the end of the first weekend. Welcome to the new media era. Good buzz travels faster.

In addition, the old four-quadrant system that the studios like to use is no longer viable. The system says that a film will attract exclusively young boys, young girls, older men, and older women. It is clear now that the sexes and age groups do not necessarily restrict themselves to one kind of film.

Production Cost

When writing a business plan, you need to find as many ways to support your argument as possible. A valid comparison for films concerns the amount of the production (negative) cost. In some cases, the cost is additional confirmation for your assertions; in other instances, it may be your only argument. There are as many configurations of a film's budget as there are producers. No two situations are ever alike. So, we will review the most common cases and let you extrapolate from there.

Case 1: Similar Films, Similar Budgets

Your films should be able to make equivalent or better revenues as films that share a genre or theme with yours and cost about what you're budgeting for your film. When preparing your proposal, the first step is to read every interview with the filmmakers that you can find. You will usually be able to find information on how they made their pictures work—creating a production budget, finding a distributor, and getting by on a low budget. The market is more open for a small film to be successful than it has ever been. The potential for having a breakout film increases with the release of each successful film.

Case 2: Similar Films, Higher Budgets

If your film has a story or theme similar to that of others but will be made with a significantly higher budget, you can point out that better attachments are likely to help bring in more revenue. If you have a well-known director who will draw some attention, be sure to mention that it is another Arthur Artiste picture. For a film with a budget of up to $1 or $2 million, both the director and the stars can be unknown; the film will rely totally on its story and quality. For a larger film, story and quality will still matter, but name value will mean even more.

Case 3: Different Films, Moderate Budgets

There may be a ceiling on the ability of niche films to grab the market. One strategy in this case is to start with moderate budgets that have mainstream potential. For this example, we will assume that you will start with a $5-million movie and move up to a much broader market. Always keep your genre in mind in addition to all the factors mentioned in Case 2.

There are many variations to putting together your comparative films and your explanations of the markets for your film. The point is that you should build on what exists. No matter what your niche market—and it may be a specialized one that has not really been explored yet—the same principles apply. Take the experience of similar films and use it to your advantage.

Even with these three cases, a discussion of the success of similarly budgeted films is in order. For example, I created a business plan for the producers of a $7-million gay/lesbian romantic comedy several years ago. Since there were no gay/lesbian films made within the $3- to $14-million budget range to use for comparison at that time, I created tables of other romantic and comedy films.

Detailed tables showing the actual results of other films with similar budgets belong in the Financing section of your plan. Here, however, you can use the summary information to build a story. Gather comparative market information to prove the size and extent of the audience for your film.

What if you do not know the budgets of the films you are going to make? Your case will be much weaker, but you can still develop a rationale. Showing the results of films with various budgets will help. The other elements of your company, as described in Chapter 3, "The Films," can bring more credence to your proposal. If you have well-known directors or actors committed to your projects, you can use their previous films to describe a segment of the market.

What if you have someone else's budget for a $2-million film? Don't use it. Your film will have characteristics that don't match that budget and needs a knowledgeable person, such as your friendly production manager, line producer, or unit production manager (UPM), to create its budget. Make sure you are right before going to investors. At the end of the day, you have to work within this budget.

Incentives

With the proliferation of state incentives, filmmakers have been tempted to subtract the total that they "hope" to get from the state. While states will approve a film for their incentives, in most cases, the money is not guaranteed. At the end of filming, you will be sending in a Certified Public Accountant (CPA) report on expenses which will be gone over by their CPA. That person will then certify what amount of money you will get. To make the film, however, you need to raise the entire amount of your budget. Any amount that is paid back by the state later will make both you and your investors very happy.

MARKETING STRATEGY

Marketing strategy is usually defined as the techniques used to make the end user aware of a product. In film, you have more than one potential end user, more than one person who might queue up to the box office to buy a ticket. There is also an intermediate end user: the money person. The ticket buyer will not read your business plan. Instead, your marketing is aimed at those who might provide the financing to make those ticket purchases possible. First, we'll look at your own strategies for getting the film made. Then, we'll look at some of the marketing tactics that distributors and producers may use for the film.

Experts often talk about the four Ps of marketing: product, price, place, and promotion. We have already touched on the first three in this section. In the Markets section of your business plan, you don't want to forget promotion. However, do not confuse what you will do and what the distributor will do.

Market Research

As cognizant as investors or distributors might be about the emergence of a particular market, they may not know its true scope. One step in promoting your projects is to obtain as much market research data as possible to bolster your contentions. Whether you are raising money for one film or a group of them, gathering data on the feasibility of your concept is important. Part of that information is contained in your description of the market segment. However, you can go a step farther and get real facts and figures.

There are many formal and informal ways to gather information. Many of them are right in your own backyard. You can gain a lot of knowledge with a minimum of time and effort if you know how. Granted, some of these tricks of the trade are easier the closer you are to Hollywood or New York, but with the proliferation of events to which "Hollywoodites" travel and the proliferation of resources on the Internet, being from another city is not a good excuse for failing to do adequate research. Your task may be a little harder, but you can still accomplish it.

Reading—A Lost Art

The most difficult idea to get across to many filmmakers is that they need to become voracious readers. Many creative folks are too busy doing their own thing to take time out to read. Even seasoned professionals say, "But I don't have time." This is a big mistake. There is a lot of information available to you if you will take the time and trouble to find it.

Much of the information in industry websites is free. In those with box office data, you may hit a pay wall; but that is free on http://www.boxofficemojo.com. Likewise, you can read a great deal of the *Hollywood Reporter* (http://www.hollywoodreporter .com) for free. Those longtime papers, however, have begun to be replaced by totally free news services. For overall entertainment news, I recommend subscribing to the daily news release of http://www.deadline.com and http://www.thewrap.com. I also subscribe to http://www.screendaily.com to keep track of European and Asian news. Even though there are some articles that require the paid subscription, there is still a large amount of free information. The website's home page also has a section called "The Web Today," which has links to articles on websites in the United Kingdom, the United States, and other countries. A hint about for pay sites: even if you log on and just read the first paragraph of stories, you will have enhanced your knowledge of the industry.

Since the last edition of the book, the only film-centered daily trade paper still available in print is *Variety*. *The Hollywood Reporter* is available in a weekly magazine. If you are a film student, you may be able to find those publications in your library. *Screen International* which may have a weekly publication in the United Kingdom is not available in the United States.

The trades have the news articles that tell you who is ⟨ what with whom and how much it is going to cost. If you follow these sources carefully, you can pull out enough data to fill in the minimum financial information for any package. Nestled among the press releases and gossip are facts on the production costs of films and descriptions of how the producers found their financing. In addition, the trades also publish lists of films in production, pre-production, and development. From the production columns, you can learn what genres of films are being made and with what types of casts. Some of the pre-production material is real and some is fantasy, but it gives you a fair idea of what people want to produce. You can list your films in the development columns free of charge. Many filmmakers have gotten contacts with production companies and distributors that way. Placing announcements also gives private investors a chance to hear about you. Many people with the ability to finance films choose to remain incognito; otherwise, they would be deluged with unwanted phone calls or scripts. Some do read the trades, however, and it gives them the opportunity to contact producers whose stories interest them. Admittedly, this may be a long shot, but it does not cost you anything, and it gets your name out there. And if you see anything that looks just like your film, don't worry. You will make a better film! One interesting quirk about Hollywood, and this is probably true of other places as well, is that people have more respect for names they recognize than for those that are unfamiliar. They will not necessarily remember where they saw or heard your name, but familiarity results in returned phone calls. Therefore, any opportunity to get your name in print is helpful.

Another benefit of reading the trades is that you learn who the movers and shakers are. Take the case of Robert Rodriguez, writer/ director of the reportedly $7,000 miracle film, *El Mariachi*. He did not know any agents or other film contacts in Los Angeles, but he saw the name of Robert Newman, an agent at ICM (one of the three largest talent agencies in the entertainment business), in the trade papers and sent him the film as a sample director's reel. Newman took it to Columbia Pictures. Rodriguez went on to make *Spy Kids* 1 through 3 as well as *Sin City*, among others. Now people have to know his name!

Besides the industry publications, you can find a lot of information in regular monthly magazines that have no direct connection to the film industry. Let's look at just a small sampling of magazines. Interviews with producers or directors of independent films and articles with business statistics were published recently in such nonentertainment publications as *The New York Times, Vanity Fair, Time, Newsweek,* and *Forbes.* Local daily newspapers and *USA Today*, a national daily, also carry interviews in their entertainment and business sections. The proliferation of sites on the Internet has made this information far more accessible and, in many cases, free.

Where's the Data?

As mentioned above, you can find box office totals on Box Office Mojo. For total worldwide data, however, I recommend Baseline (baselineresearch.com). You will find different areas, such as studio systems, script shark, and inhollywood. However, I recommend going directly to the "Film Revenue and Cost Estimate" (FRCE) at (baselineintel .com) in order to access the per film data that the company sells. There are various levels of subscriptions. With the extended FRCE, besides the domestic and foreign box office and budget, you get will get both domestic and foreign home videos and domestic prints and ads. Why should you spend the money? Besides the fact that you don't want to make it up, you need a credible reference to give investors. When you are asking other people to fund your film, making up data is a very bad idea; and using only the North American box office doesn't give a good picture of how well a film performed.

Libraries

The entire marketing research section originally was titled "Libraries and Computer Sources." Times have changed. Even I do most of my research on the Internet. Like reading, however, another lost art appears to be the ability to do research in a library. If you are a student, you have free access to information that can't be found—or at least can't be found for free—on the Internet. In addition to the film school libraries, your local library may subscribe to data services that will help.

Networking

My first Sundance Film Festival was also my first entertainment industry event. Until then, I had worked in "real business," creating business plans and corporate strategies. Although I had mixed and mingled at meetings before, I had never tried to "work a town." I knew no one and had a general feeling of nausea as I got off the plane. On the shuttle to Park City, Utah, everyone was silent. Finally, I asked a gentleman sitting behind me if it was his first trip. He and his friend turned out to be film commissioners. We chatted the rest of the way. That night I went with them to the opening night gathering and met more people. The next day, I chatted with those people and learned a lot about how they had financed their films and other salient information. Had I not spoken to the first two people, I might never have met the rest. The concept of networking this way can be very scary, but you can do it. Being friendly is a way not only to gather information, but also to make yourself known to others.

Why do you want to network? Your best sources of information may come from attending seminars, college classes, luncheons, industry meetings, festivals, and markets. Besides listening to whatever public speaking occurs, you should go up and introduce yourself to the speakers and mix with the other people in the room. You don't have to be in Los Angeles or New York. Many states and cities have festivals and other meetings. Take advantage of whatever is in your area. Always check with your local film commissioner to learn about events in your area.

There is no better source of information for you than other independent filmmakers. Whenever you have a chance to meet filmmakers, grill them for advice and facts. People like to talk about their experiences and, especially, their successes. (If this were not the case, I would not be able to get well-known filmmakers to talk to my classes and seminars.) You will learn more from someone who has done what you are interested in doing than from all the books in the world.

Promoting Yourself and Your Projects

We make our own opportunities, as every overnight success will tell you. By doing all that market research, you have prepared yourself for two things:

1. Quantifying your market segment.
2. Approaching others with your project.

At the beginning of this chapter, we talked about the market segment and how it is time to focus on marketing yourself and your project. As noted before, your goal is to find the money or links to the money. There are entire books that focus on this subject, so I am providing you with just the basic information.

Arm Yourself with Ammunition

As a good promoter, there are certain materials you can prepare before seeking out contacts. Business cards, sales sheets, press kits, and director's reels are among the promotional materials you might use. Some filmmakers have even made a short version of their film, often on their websites, for promotion. For first-time filmmakers with no other footage to show, making a short video of yourself talking about the virtues of your film may be the way to go.

Whether your aim is to sell a single film or to obtain financing for your company's group of films, the first step is to evoke interest. Making contacts is your objective, wherever you are. Earlier we talked about networking as a means of gathering information. Another purpose is to unearth those money sources, wherever they are.

People with like interests tend to congregate in the same places; therefore, entertainment-related gatherings are your most likely place for success.

Film Markets

Knowing how to attend and network at film markets is critical. You do not want to be carrying around business plans, handing them to everyone who says, "I can get you a deal." That is why you bother with the materials described earlier. Those are the items you hand to people initially. Common sense will stand you in good stead in attending markets. There is no trick to meeting and greeting, no secret handshakes or passwords. (Just get out there and shake hands!) When you attend a market, remember that a distributor's goal in being there is not to meet you; it is to sell product. Here are guidelines for you to follow:

- *Be prepared*: Bring your short-term promotional materials and bone up on who is who before you go. Let your fingers do some walking through the trades.

- *Be aware*: Distribution companies usually focus on certain types of films. Look at their posters and at the items listed in their market catalogs. Try to match your films to their inventory. After all, the distributor is your shortest route to those foreign buyers and presales.
- *Be inquisitive*: Ask questions of everyone you meet—in an office, in the lobby, on the street. Try to discover the person's qualifications before spilling your guts about your plans and projects, however.
- *Be considerate*: In introducing yourself to distributors, pick slack times. Very early in the day and at the end of the day are best. Whenever you reach a distributor's display room, notice if buyers are there. If they are, go back later.
- *Be succinct*: Keep the discussion short and sweet. Your objective is to get a meeting at a later time. You want your "prey" to feel relaxed and be attentive. Try for a meeting at the distributor's office.
- *Be dubious*: Lots of people are milling around screenings, hotel lobbies, and expo halls pretending to be something they are not. It may be a big rush for someone to tell you that they were the "real" investor behind *The Visitor* (when they had nothing to do with it) and are interested in financing your film for $2 million (when they have no money). Listen carefully, take cards, and try to verify the facts afterward. Do not give your scripts or proposals to anyone unless you can validate their credentials.

There is more detail about pitching in Chapter 13, "Other People's Money."

Advice from a Filmmaker

Joe Majestic formed Majestic World Entertainment in 2007 as a film, multimedia development, and distribution company. Previous to that, in 2003, he co-founded the Ilya Salkind Company, where he served as Vice President of Production. He was a contributing architect of the company's initial slate of film and television properties. In 2008, he partnered in Monterrey Pictures Entertainment. He left that company in 2009 to focus on film development and sales as President of Majestic. In 2011, he also founded film and television production company Hurricane Film Partners, LLC. Having worked with Joe as a consultant since 2003, I asked him to lend his advice on both attending and being an exhibitor at the American Film Market. In addition, check the market's website at http://www.ifta-online.org/afm/ for its section "How to Work the AFM."

LL: How did you first start working the market?
Joe: I first attended the AFM with a visitor's badge. I suggest that filmmakers go ahead and get a badge, go around the film market, get all the materials, and network. It took me five years of having a badge full time as an attendee, because I didn't have a mentor or work with a distribution company. I had to learn by trial and error.

LL: Who are the companies that rent offices in the Loews during the market?
Joe: Any production or distribution company that wants to sell products to the more than 1,500 accredited buyers that come from countries around the world can obtain office space at the AFM.

LL: What are some of the activities you suggest for filmmakers attending for the first time?
Joe: People don't realize what a valuable tool the market is. Make a plan. I have seen many filmmakers waste their time by not scheduling their days. Do research. Get the attendee guide that comes with your badge. It tells you which companies are in each room. Then get the special AFM edition of *Variety* or the *Hollywood Reporter* that lists what each company is selling. Individual companies often have specific genres they sell, and you want to know who would be the most likely company to be interested in your film. You also can look them up on the Internet.

LL: How do you approach the distributors?
Joe: They are unlikely to speak to you on day one or two or on the last day when they are packing up. Spend the first couple of days gathering information. The middle to near the end is best, as the market tends to be slower. They will talk to you if you have a project and are seriously packaging it. Ask their advice. They will give it, because they need product.

LL: Can you just walk into an office?
Joe: Filmmakers think they can go in all the offices just because they have a badge. Technically, you should be invited. Remember that their

main goal is to sell to buyers who will have appointments. Try to contact sellers in advance. If you have an appointment, the exhibitor can give you a guest pass to the office floors. You won't be allowed onto any of those floors without either a badge or pass. If you don't have an appointment in advance, ask the office assistant for one. That person will probably say, "Contact us after the market." Try to hold out for a meeting at the market. Be clear. Say that you are packaging your film project and give a specific genre ad budget. Don't get expansive with mixed genre descriptions. Ask them what talent they would like to see attached to the film. If people look too busy, try for at least a brief introduction. If not, call them after the market. Say something like, "Congratulations on your great AFM. I went by your office several times, and you were too busy. I'd like to send you information on my film _____ budgeted at _____. I have found that it is better to call before sending an email and/or materials."

LL: Why are you meeting them?
Joe: You probably will be looking for a distributor to either help you do presales on a film to be made or to obtain a distribution guarantee to help you raise money from other sources.

LL: What made you decide to pay for office space?
Joe: My company, Majestic World Entertainment, had several projects to rep for sales. Having learned how the market works, it was time. I already had worked with Hector Grob of Monando Film Distribution, who has 25 years in film distribution going back to working with the Salkinds on the *Superman* movies. I met him while working with Ilya, and whenever he was in town during AFM, I spent time at the market with him. It is important to work with someone who has experience in selling at international markets. If you are interested in being a sales representative, try to meet other sellers and buyers when you are initially at the market. Everyone has a badge. You can talk to people in elevators, on the terrace, at the pool, or at the bar in the lobby.

LL: What should I do if I need to hire someone with market experience?
Joe: The staff at AFM is extremely helpful. They will guide you through the details of obtaining and setting up an office and recommend people to work with you. You need a good assistant to set up meetings and work the phones.

LL: How many films do you need to have for sale?
Joe: You could have one film, although more is better. We were selling three horror films for our clients. General wisdom is that you should have no more than ten films.

LL: What materials should you have to give to buyers?
Joe: 1. Similar to the list above, the three most important pieces of information are cast, budget, and genre. Male actors are most important in obtaining foreign financing. Know what your actors are worth vis-à-vis your budget. Don't get an actor who was worth $250,000 last year and is now worth $25,000. As I said before, be specific about the genre. Don't say "sci-fi action drama." Just say, "action." There is also "contained action," which is a low-budget action film.
2. Promo teaser. You don't need a scene from the actual movie. Shoot a short one-and-a-half- to two-minute section from the script. You need a visual for buyers, since it isn't a radio show. We had promos for all our films. Also, quality counts. You can have unknown actors and inexpensive surroundings, but the look of your two minutes has to be good. We did presales as a result of the whole package. In addition, we already had talent attached. That isn't a requirement, but attached talent gives your project more value.

LL: How do presales work?
Joe: Generally, the buyer gives you twenty percent down of the price they are paying for their specific territory and the rest on delivery of the film. You should have all the legal documents available for this transaction. Have them drawn up by an entertainment attorney familiar with distribution and markets. Don't write your own. Your attorney will probably be available for meetings also. Usually, an attorney with clients at the market will be there himself.

LL: Is it important to have someone in your office who speaks multiple languages?
Joe: No. It is nice, but the buyers will always have someone who speaks English. They are buying from you and want your product.

LL: I know that you previously went to Cannes. Is there additional advice for that market?

Joe: Cannes is very expensive. The offices are twice as much, and all other expenses are three to four times more expensive than going to AFM. If a film project isn't completely packaged with a first-class promo, don't spend the money. Don't go there just to get experience.

LL: Assuming you have the project and promo, are there ways to save money?
Joe: American filmmakers can become members of the American Pavilion. You will have a headquarters and exhibition space, although you won't have an office. You will be able to go to the various Cannes offices and network. The Pavilion provides an array of business services, seminars, networking events, and parties. More networking is done at parties in Cannes than at AFM. For the parties given by major companies, you need to be invited, of course. The best parties are at the beginning of both markets. Other countries have pavilions also. They are all lined up together.

SOCIAL MEDIA AND SELF-MARKETING

An important component for any film, especially the opening weekend of the film, is word-of-mouth. Without incurring additional costs, it is possible for a filmmaker to implement a marketing strategy that is complementary to that of the distributor. Or, in the absence of having a distributor, create word-of-mouth. You can get a "buzz" by contacting grassroots organizations with a process referred to as *viral marketing*. Many special-interest groups have email lists and will be happy to send out information on a film that attracts them. It is a strategy that encourages individuals to pass on an email or video marketing message to others, creating the potential for exponential growth in the message's exposure. The people on their lists then send the email on to other individuals and organizations, and the marketing message is spread exponentially. Don't forget to include your hometown newspapers in this activity. An important component for any film, especially the opening weekend of the film, is word-of-mouth.

For some inspirational films, it may also be appropriate to schedule free showings in a church, synagogue, or other spiritual gathering place. By having such screenings, which often are free to the participants, you create word-of-mouth before a film opens on local screens. For other films, you can promote the film on websites devoted to the genre. For example, there are quite a few sites devoted to horror films. When you think about the "affiliate groups," make them aware that your films will open. For example, in a business plan that had a story about a writer, I added: "Particularly relevant to [name deleted] are the hundreds of writer's groups that meet live and/or online. In the age of the Internet, they all have email lists."

Facebook, LinkedIn, and Twitter, along with other social media sites, are used every day for this purpose. No matter how big a site is and fast it has grown when I am writing this edition, it can fall out of favor with consumers just as fast. Do you remember Friendster? Remember when MySpace was an unbeatable force? None are immune to change.

Self-marketing is an area in which it is good to think outside the box. Explore what is best for your film. Remember, however, that anything you describe in your business plan is a type of promise to the investor. Do not say that you will do something for which you have to spend money that you don't have. Never, every use the word "guarantee."

The entire discussion of Social Media and Self-marketing that I currently use in business plans can be found in Chapter 11, "The Sample Business Plan." Much of it is boilerplate; however, I update and tweak it depending on what is happening in the industry and the genre of the film. Be sure that you do the same.

6

Distribution: Theatrical and the Changing Landscape

Marketing your film is much more stressful than making it.
—ANURAG KASHYAP, DIRECTOR, *BMW: BOMBAY'S MOST WANTED*

We all know that the film home video/ancillary business is going through a major paradigm shift. The question still exists—where is it going and how soon? Theoretically, everything will be streamed and downloaded some day; but that specific day is unknown. Before the audience can buy a movie ticket, rent a disc, or order a digital download, the movie has to get off the filmmaker's desk and into the movie theaters. This method of circulation is called *distribution*. Simply put, it is the business of selling the film to various media.

This chapter looks at distribution strategies in general, glances briefly at studio distribution, and examines independent distribution in more depth. Nevertheless, it is not intended to replace the many books on film distribution that you can read for more detailed knowledge. While we will look at types of deals, I am not a distributor or a lawyer. When making any deal, you need one of each.

WHAT IS DISTRIBUTION?

When writing your business plan, you will need to explain the distribution system in general. As with other elements of the plan, you should proceed on the assumption that your reader does not know how the system works. Wrong assumptions on either side could block the progress of your films.

The "rights" of a film stem from the ownership of the copyright, which endows the legal use of the film to the copyright holder. Having secured a formal copyright, the producer contractually licenses, or rents, the film to a distributor for a specific length of time. The producer can relinquish all control of the film by shifting the entire copyright to the distributor in perpetuity, or she can license a specific right such as domestic, foreign, home video (DVD/Blu-ray, streaming), television/cable, satellite, tablet, cell phone, and wrist watch (or any other device brought to market since the book was published) to the distributor for a specific length of time. In return, the distributor collects the rental monies or ancillary fees and remits the producer's share.

The following is from a sample domestic distribution contract. Although it is boilerplate (the starting point for negotiations), the following section is not likely to change. Pay attention to the phrase in parenthesis.

> *The "Rights" consist of the sole and exclusive right, license, and privilege under copyright (including all extended and renewal terms thereof) to distribute, exhibit, market, reissue, advertise, publicize, and otherwise exploit the Picture and the literary material upon which they are based, the picture, sound, music and all other physical elements thereof, and trailers in any and all media and by any and all means (whether now known or hereafter developed, discovered, invented, or created) throughout the Territory.*

WHAT IS A DISTRIBUTOR?

Long before Carl Laemmle produced his first maverick film, middlemen existed (as did agents, attorneys, and litigation). These intermediaries bought low and sold high even then. Among the most maligned of all entrepreneurs, middlemen are still harshly criticized for doing their job.

History does not tell us when the term *distributor* began to be used. All industries have intermediaries. In other industries, they buy inventory at discount prices, add a price markup, and resell at a higher price. In this sense, these intermediaries are considered just another one of the channels for getting the product to the market. Unlike film distributors, they are not involved in making artistic decisions about the product, changing the name for better marketing, or obtaining premanufacturing financing.

Motion picture distributors also are middlemen, and they are a curious lot. They are viewed either as people of tremendous skill, nourishing the growth of business, or as flimflam artists reaping obscene profits. Like politicians, distributors are sometimes seen as a necessary evil. On the other hand, they perform an important function without which the average filmmaker would not thrive.

Distributors have tremendous power, and in independent film, their impact is magnified. Studios normally have committees and different levels of people making a decision. In an independent distribution company, one person, with no one to answer to, may determine the entire course of your film. The distributor has the ability to influence script changes, casting decisions, final edits, and marketing strategies; in addition, distributors often are intimately involved in the financing of the film.

They have this power by virtue of the distribution agreement. The specifics of the distribution deal and the timing of all money disbursements depend on the agreement that is finally negotiated. As a new filmmaker, you have little or no leverage for changing this agreement. Even an experienced filmmaker seldom can exact any substantive changes in the standard contract. One can debate fees. In the end, however, even though each deal is different, the basic contents stay the same. The distributor must be a salesperson, an entrepreneur, a skillful negotiator, and a raconteur and must have a sixth sense about matching the buyer with the product.

Armed with the rights, distributors go about the business of relicensing the film to the various media. The U.S. theatrical box office is the backbone in the chain of revenues for a film. All ancillary results theoretically are driven by the domestic theatrical release. Some products are designed to skip that step and go directly to home video or foreign markets, but the value of a film in any other media and territories is generally greater with a good theatrical release. Even a small theatrical release can increase the value to buyers of an otherwise unknown film.

STUDIO DISTRIBUTION

How It Works

The major studios (and the larger production companies) each have their own distribution divisions. They not only release their own films, but also occasionally acquire other films. All the marketing and other distribution decisions are made in-house. The distribution division sends out promotional and advertising materials, arranges screenings of films, and makes deals with domestic and foreign distributors. Because of their size and the box office capability of their films, the studios naturally have a lot of clout in getting their films onto theater screens.

When it comes to foreign markets, studios have offices around the world, either singly or with other studios, to distribute their films in other countries. Often, a studio will partner with a local distributor and the release will bear the names of both companies. The studio always retains the copyright, which it licenses to the foreign distributor for a specific length of time.

Based on the share formulas we saw in Table 4.1 that the studio's distribution arm receives its share of the box office grosses from the exhibitor and passes them through the in-house accounting system. The studio charges distribution fees back against the film as if its distribution division were a separate company. These fees can range from 45 to 65 percent of the total film rentals. In addition, the studio takes the entire fixed cost of the distribution division (overhead) and applies a portion of it to each film. Overhead fees pay for running the division and cover expenses that are not covered by other fees. Before the accountants are done, the studio will also take a portion of the overhead from the production side of the studio and add it to the total cost of the film.

The formula in Table 4.1 in Chapter 4 shows a "net profit" model for a studio film. Each studio has a standard method in its contracts for determining revenues, expenses, and profits. These formulas are nearly impossible to change, even by influential filmmakers. Typically, the producer is paid a percentage of the net profits in addition to receiving a salary. With studio films, it is fair to say that the chances of the net profit being greater than zero are rarer than with independent films. The studios have more films to cross-collateralize (using the profits from one film to offset the losses from another) and more places to bury unreasonable costs, although many contracts now prohibit films from being cross-collateralized.

The Advantages

There are many advantages to studio distribution. The studio has the ability to put 4,000-plus prints of a film in circulation on the opening weekend. Its own channels of publicity and advertising are manifold. The studio has the financial resources to inundate television and the press with ads, and it has significant clout in getting placements for producers, directors, and actors on early-morning and late-night national interview television shows. For example, the Walt Disney Company owns its eponymous cable network (consisting of ESPN, ABC Family Channel, Disney Channel, Toon Disney, and SOAPNet), the ABC network (talk shows, such as *The View* and *Jimmy Kimmel*), as well as the ABC television stations. In addition, the studio is able to negotiate a deal with its own affiliate at a value on paper that is less than free market value.

As noted earlier, the studios have been able to monopolize the chain movie theaters in the past. Some have moved back into theater ownership. Be that as it may, with the success of independent films, exhibitors insist that they do not bow to studio pressure. They can only afford to have films in their houses that fill theater seats. If the audience does not come to see a particular film, the exhibitor must look for another that will be more popular. Consequently, more screens become available to independent films. As small films have received acclaim, they have continually one into wider distribution (for example, expanding from 500 to 1,200 theaters) and gotten bookings in major chains that would not have played them previously.

INDEPENDENT DISTRIBUTION

The Players, They are a-Changin'

In 1994, neither this author nor Bob Dylan, or probably even Harvey Weinstein for that matter, could have foreseen what would be going on now. Many would-be seers at that time thought the independents would disappear, even though the first edition of this book said that it wasn't true. The intervening years have shown a total change in which studios tried to emulate the success of independents with lower-budgeted films.

The Majors acquired independent companies and made them into specialty divisions as the quickest way into the lower-budget market. Most of the specialty divisions of the studios—Focus Features, Paramount Vantage (the former Paramount Classics is a division), and Warner Independent Pictures—eventually were closed and/or became labels. Warner Bros. absorbed Picturehouse and New Line with Picturehouse disappearing and New Line becoming merely a studio brand. Fox Searchlight is no longer independent producer. Sony Classics remains the lone specialty division with autonomous control over its product. Still an independent film picked up for distribution by a studio remains a film that was independently made. Meanwhile, new independent companies continued to appear.

Independent Companies

Similar to our definition for independent films, the independent distributor is one that releases a film independent of one of the major studios. As we know, studios and their divisions pick up indie films. Some larger companies, such as DreamWorks and DreamWorks Animation, have had distribution deals with studios. There are a myriad of other companies, both U.S. based and foreign based with a U.S. office, that distribute films.

Even independent companies that are highly capitalized and making successful films come and go. In the 1990s, Artisan Entertainment is a good example. At the same time that they were buying October Films in 1997, a consortium headed by investment firms Bain Capital and Richland, Gordon and Company bought Live Entertainment, which had one of the largest independent film libraries (2,000 titles) in the world, for $93 million. The new company became Artisan Entertainment. Then Boston-based Audax Group along with other investment companies bought a controlling share. Artisan slowly grew until 1999, when the success of *The Blair Witch Project* single-handedly moved the company into the front ranks of independent distribution. At that time, Bain was interested in purchasing Trimark Pictures (originally the motion picture arm of one-time video major Vidmark), but the sale did not happen. Meanwhile, an investor purchased Cinepix Film Properties and changed the name to Lionsgate Films. In 2000, Lionsgate bought Trimark Pictures for approximately $50 million. At least two of Artisan's investors wanted to cash out, and in a bidding war, Lionsgate bought the company. Lionsgate bought Summit Entertainment in 2001. With the merging of the distribution divisions, one potential acquirer of independent films was taken off the market.

Why do you care about all these financial machinations? First of all, you should know the history and personnel of the company with which you want to do business. How have they acted in the past? Are they likely to be dealmakers who are more interested in selling the company for a profit than being distributors for your film, or are they hands-on film lovers who are likely to be around for the long haul? Remember that the length of time that a company takes to negotiate a merger or buyout can hurt any film in its library. My favorite film from Sundance 2000, *Songcatcher*, was acquired by Trimark. By the time the Lionsgate/Trimark merger was complete, the film was in the library of the new company, which may not have had the same regard for its potential success as the original buyers. In addition, the film's resulting release in June 2001 may have been too late for the buzz press from its Sundance screenings to be meaningful.

THINKFilm, which had become a notable producer and distributor of documentaries and other films, became a victim, along with the U.K.'s Capitol Films, of their parent company's financial troubles, Pergasus Entertainment Group. Also gone are Fox/ Walden Media, which was shuttered and absorbed into Twentieth Century Fox, longtime indie New Yorker Films, and Rogue, which was repurposed by Relativity Media. In 2010, FilmDistrict was formed. It is still in business, but Bob Berney—arguably the smartest indie marketer of the last three decades—is no longer involved.

Among some of the companies new to theatrical distribution are the new producers, such as Megan Ellison's Annapurna Pictures and Joe Drake's Good Universe, African-American Film Festival Releasing Movement, FilmDistrict, Red Granite Pictures, Red Flag Releasing, Open Road films (formed by AMC Entertainment and Regal Entertainment), and Talking Drum Entertainment. Other indie distributors are Anchor Bay, Peach Arch Entertainment, Oscilloscope Pictures, Music Box Films, Gold Circle Films, IDP/ Samuel Goldwyn, Magnolia Pictures (and its offshoot for genre films, Magnet Releasing), Palm Pictures, Zeitgeist Films, Roadside Attractions, Rocky Mountain Pictures, and First Run. This list is not meant to include everyone. I always say that I should put the date (July 2012) on the list, as there will be companies being formed, purchased, or just giving up the ghost by the time you read this book. It is particularly important during the current economic challenges. The overall picture for the past 20 years has continued to be true. As one company merges, becomes a studio brand, or just disappears altogether, others quickly come in to fill the distribution void. Did someone say independent distributors were dead? They did, but they were wrong.

Do your own research to see who is doing what. Since the land-scape is constantly changing in this dynamic industry, the indepen-dent filmmaker must function in a fluid environment. The small independent of today could be the Weinstein Company of tomor-row. It is also important to keep in mind that some companies specialize. For example, Eros Entertainment and Yash Raj Films spe-cialize in distributing films from India in the United States. Strand Releasing and Regent Releasing specialize in the distribution of gay- and lesbian-themed films. Interestingly, in 2008, Regent also made a point of expanding into foreign-language films. According to Regent co-founder Stephen Jarchow, "Gay and lesbian people represent one third of the audience that goes to foreign movies. They are three times more likely to go and see a foreign-language film." He also pointed out that a small independent distributor considers a film that gener-ates $2 million to $3 million at the box office to be a success.

Always look at how your potential distributor tends to dis-tribute a film. The larger producer-distributors, such as Lionsgate or the Weinstein Company, have the ability to put a film on 1,000-plus screens. Of course, that doesn't mean they will. On the other hand, some of the smaller companies prefer to put a film on only one to three theatrical screens as a prelude to a home video. It is always important to have an attorney carefully read your contract. Some filmmakers have found that, after being picked up at a festi-val, their contract didn't require a theatrical release.

Too Many Films?

The theatrical marketplace is crowded. In 2011, studio members of the Motion Picture Association of America (MPAA) and their sub-sidiaries released 141 films and nonmembers released another 469. That 610 total "includes all titles that opened in 2011 that earned any domestic box office in the year," according to Rentrak Corporation's *Box Office Essentials*. Checking my database of independent film revenues for 2011 and taking out films released by studios (47), I came up with the same 469 number. However, those other 47 films are counted in my annual independent film box office total. As you recall, the definition does not include what company distributes a film but the sources of financing and control of production.

The idea that too many filmmakers are making too many bad films and have a 90 to 99 percent chance of failure has been around since I entered the business in 1988 and surely before. Every year Sundance and other large festivals have more than 3,000 films entered. Clearly, there are many more films made than will ever see the light of day in a theater or make back their production costs. We don't even know the profit/loss results for all the films distributed. For one thing, we don't even have an estimated budget for many of the smaller films released. In addition, we can track all the potential revenue sources. Will this information stop you from making a film? Probably not.

How It Works

Watching an independent distributor bring a film to its audience is seeing a true master of multitasking at work. More than just a functionary for getting your picture out, the independent distributor can perform one or more additional roles, including participating in creative decisions and contributing to the film's financial resources. For most independent filmmakers, the independent distributor is the only game in town and deserves an extensive look.

Domestic Versus Foreign

The domestic territory generally comprises just the United States, but it might also be considered to include Canada and, many times, Puerto Rico and other Caribbean islands. Many of the independent distributors consider the United States and Canada to be one North American package and prefer not to have them separated beforehand. For one thing, the distributor may have output deals with Canada. If the opportunity for Canadian financing arises, therefore, producers must be careful. If the Canadian investors are going to take some or all of the Canadian territory for themselves, the producer might have a problem finding a distributor for the U.S. market.

Domestic rights refer not only to theatrical distribution but also to all other media, such as DVD, cable, and the Internet. A producer who secures an advance from one of these media for production financing makes the deal a little less attractive to the distributor, because the rights have been fractionalized, or split up. Any source of future revenue taken out of the potential money pie before a distributor is found makes an eventual distribution deal tougher for the producer to close. Most distributors make a substantial investment in print and advertising (P&A) costs. Although they may recoup these amounts from the theatrical marketplace, it is not likely to cover their distribution fees. Therefore, they prefer that other revenue sources be available to them.

Being a domestic distributor may mean that a company does not sell foreign rights itself. However, no rule says that a domestic distributor cannot venture into foreign waters. While distributors at the festivals used to pick up films for North American distribution only, they often now include all English-speaking territories. Or they pick up worldwide rights and sell off the other territories to subdistributors.

There are also U.S.-based distributors that specialize in foreign only. These companies deal with networks of subdistributors all around the world. It is sometimes confusing for producers to distinguish between a distributor and a foreign sales agent. If a distribution company is granted the rights to the film for the foreign markets, that company, whether it is 1 person or 20, is the distributor. The company may be referred to as a foreign sales agent also. There is no fundamental difference, just one of semantics. Independent Film and Television Alliance publishes an annual directory of their members. In addition, there are sources on the Web.

Internet rights are a question. How big this business will become is still unknown. What you have to know is that you do not want to license your film to anyone on the Internet before you have a contract with traditional domestic and international distributors. Whether or not they will do anything with those rights, the distributors want them available. Of course, that doesn't mean you have to include those rights. Generally, the producer retains ownership of the copyright and only grants someone a percentage of the receipts for obtaining distribution contracts for a particular territory and/or medium. A typical term for granted rights is seven years, although some distributors will want 10 years.

To Video On Demand or Not

With the growth of new releasing platforms, the paradigm for releasing is changing. For example, a day-and-date release on Video on Demand (VOD) at the same time as a theatrical release or even before it is starting to gain traction. There has been a lot of discussion about *Margin Call*'s $4 million VOD revenue total, as reported by distributor Magnolia Pictures. While other anecdotal reports on VOD have been made, there isn't enough data to make predictions for investors. There are too many factors we don't know and unanswered questions about the new media distribution systems. For example, how much does this type of pretheatrical release affect the box office revenue? For the same number of audience views, are we exchanging the price of the ticket for the lesser revenue from a download? Magnolia Pictures co-owner Mark Cuban told thewrap.com in December 2011, "In reality, for most independent movies, VOD will be far and away the largest source of revenue in the future...more than theatrical and far more than streaming." The opposite opinion came from Tom Bernard, Co-President of Sony Pictures Classics, who told thewrap.com at the same time, "It's a more complicated situation than what Mark Cuban is trying to sell. If your movie can play through all the windows that start with the theatrical release, nine times out of 10 it will be much more successful than the VOD/theater box office."

The important concept in all of this is the word "future." Cuban's future isn't here yet. I don't feel it will be here for the next four to five years. Whether or not I am right, currently, we have to hope that films receive at least a small theatrical release before going to the aftermarket. Of course, a big theatrical release is always better!

A Deal Is a Deal

What is a typical deal? There is no such animal; no two deals are ever exactly the same. Distributors will take as much as they can get, and it is the producer's job to give away as little as possible. Do not under any circumstances enter into one of these agreements without the advice of an entertainment attorney experienced in film. Some distributors will try to get you to sign an agreement before their fees are specified or without any agreement for theatrical distribution. Their business is to be persuasive, and they are good at it. The attorney knows what needs to be in the agreement before you sign it. She can be equally persuasive.

The attorney's film experience is important. When I was first advising filmmakers, I would tell them to get an entertainment attorney. Sometimes they would find someone who worked in another area of entertainment but not film. Distribution deals in this business are different from other areas of the entertainment industry, however, and you want your attorney to be familiar with it. The other mistake that filmmakers often make is using their father's corporate attorney to negotiate their film contract. The filmmaker has to pay for the attorney's learning curve (lawyers charge by the hour) and ends up with a bad deal, or, worst case, no deal at all.

The distributor's fees vary from territory to territory or medium. This amount can be as low as 15 percent (for a "hired gun") or as high as 50 percent of the revenues from the film. Although most contracts treat domestic and foreign revenues separately, general wisdom says that the overall average for an indie distributor's fees is 35 percent or under. Take time to add up the total fees. If they come to more than 35 percent, you probably don't want to sign. How much the distributor wants to take depends on the company's participation in the entire film package. The distributor may do the following:

- Get a finished picture.
- Provide P&A money.
- Be rented.
- Raise equity or presale financing.
- Provide a minimum guarantee.
- Pay an advance.

There are no hard-and-fast rules. A lot depends on how much risk the distribution company is taking, whether or not it puts in production money, and how badly it wants the film. The amount of risk is primarily related to the amount of money the distribution company pays out of its pocket. The more upfront expenses it has to assume, the greater the percentage of incoming revenues it will seek. These percentages apply only to the revenues generated by the distributor's own deals; if that company is only making foreign sales for you, then it takes a percentage of foreign revenues only.

Do not assume knowledge about another film's agreement and promise the same deal to your investor. Often clients want me to give examples of purchase prices in their business plans. In that case, it is important to note for the investors that the prices announced in the press may be advances against future revenue streams or total buyout prices with no further remuneration to the filmmakers and their investors. For example, an article may say that a film was picked up for $8 million. However, there may be a small or no advance, with the rest contingent on a percentage of the U.S. box office. If the box office is low, then the producers and investors will never see the full $8 million. Always remember the words of John Pierson, a longtime filmmaker and producer's rep, who said, "Get it up front. That's your bond."

The good news is that, with the caveat noted above, there are good stories to tell as a hook for the investors. Sometimes a producer, director, or producer's representative will give useful financial details in an interview. At the 2004, the $400,000 *Napoleon Dynamite* was offered $3 to $4 million in advance with a guarantee of a 1,200-screen release. At the 2005 fest, Paramount paid a total of $9 million for *Hustle & Flow*, which was budgeted at $3.5 million. Then the big prize went to *Little Miss Sunshine* which sold for $10.5 million in 2006. However, the brakes were put on buying sprees in 2009 and 2010 after several big purchases with upfront fees of $8 to $10 million in 2007 and 2008 failed to deliver profits. The business, along with the rest of the world, was going through the beginning of a recession.

Surprisingly, distributors did a total 180 and went on a buying frenzy in 2011. The number of films picked up by the last day of the festival was 51, including 20 picked up after the films were announced but prior to the start of the festival. In comparison, the total in 2010 was 29 and 30 in 2009. The economy appeared to be picking up, distributor's inventories were low and/or they just plain liked the films. The Weinstein Company paid $6 to $7 million for *Our Idiot Brother*, and Fox Searchlight offered $4 million for *Homework*.

Buyers evidently continued to believe in the strength of the indie market at the 2012 Sundance. This year's total of 39 sales was the second highest in the last six years. The biggest change for 2012 was caution in terms of price. All buyers kept the purse strings a bitter tighter remembering that the 2011 Sundance films that failed to light up the box office. The highest price reported was $6 million for *The Sessions* (Fox Searchlight), but the majority were between $1 and $3 million. Perhaps of more significance was an increase in the number of films announced as day-and-date for theatrical and VOD.

Print and Ad Money

The first step in distributing a film used to be printing copies made from the master negative. If you are buying this book in 2015, you could be saying "What is a print?" The answer is that at one time all films were shipped to theaters on reels of film stock. A high-profile studio film opening on as many as 3,000 to 4,000 screens in multiple markets (a "wide" release) could have an initial marketing expense of $3.5 million to $6 million, accompanied by a very high advertising program. The smaller independent distributors would start with anywhere from 1 to 50 prints and move the prints from city to city.

The business has been going through a changeover between screens that play the 35-mm prints and those that accept digital, which makes a major difference in cost. The studios helped subsidize the conversion to digital of a majority of the theater screens and projectors. Fully outfitting a single screen with the necessary equipment costs a minimum of $70,000 with more for 3D. Middlemen called "integrators" helped with the cost and established a Virtual "Print" Fee (VPF) for each film played on a digital screen. For a studio, the $800 to $900 per engagement VPF is actually a saving compared to the number of prints they used to make. And, yes, they still refer to the digital copies as "prints." (Refer to an article by Ira Deutchman of Emerging Pictures in indiewire.com, March 8, 2012, for more details.)

By contrast, independent films typically have a "platform" release. In this case, the film is given a buildup by opening initially in a few regional or limited local theaters to build positive movie patron awareness throughout the country. The time between a limited opening and its release in the balance of the country may be several weeks. This kept the cost of striking 35-mm prints to a minimum. Using this strategy, smaller films can be successful at the box office with as few as two or three prints that are moved from theater to theater. In the new digital system, each time the film hits a new screen, the fee mounts. With a successful film on an escalating number of screens, the distribution cost could run $1 and $2 million.

All screens have not been converted. The U. S. studios haven't had enthusiasm for smaller venues. The question is how many screens are left? In recent interviews, distributors have said that they can't get a good count. I have seen estimates that by the end of 2012 year over 80 percent of theaters in the United States will be digital. Recently, U.S. distributors have told me that there were at least 1,000 screens that have not been converted. In addition, various speakers at a European training program in Venice (Italy) in September 2012 said that 60 percent of Europe's screens were digital and that

80 percent of the screens in the "major" markets in European would be digital by the end of 2012. Concerns were voiced that distributors would stop handling 35-mm prints in 2013. Whatever the numbers, you know that many independent films still will be going to the nondigital screens.

Distributors plan their release schedules not only with certain target audiences in mind, but also with awareness of which theaters—specialty or multiplex—will draw that audience. If a film is going to a multiplex, there probably isn't a question about digital versus 35 mm. Each reader should follow the latest technical news on one of the many free Internet sites. With a two-year lag in being able to obtain distribution costs, in mid-2012, there is no way to know how the digital change has affected the print and ad costs. When the 2011 revenue and cost data become available, we may be able to get a feel for it.

Distributor's Fees

Many distributors encourage producers to provide the P&A money, because this limits their risk even more. Producers who do provide the P&A can negotiate a lower distribution fee, often ranging from 10 to 22.5 percent, with the most common fees being 15 to 17.5 percent. These deals—often informally called "rent-a-distributor" or "hired gun"—usually have an escalator clause to give the distributor an incentive. For example, the fee might be 15 percent until net revenues to the producer equal the cost of the film or some multiple of the cost of the film, at which time the distribution fees escalate to 17.5 percent. On the other hand, some distributors just negotiate a flat fee for working this way.

There are varied opinions as to whether it is practical for a producer to pay P&A costs. By putting up the money, the producer lessens the amount that the distributor will receive from the total revenues. On the other hand, many believe that the greater the distributor's share of the incoming revenues, the harder the company will work to maximize them. The producer may also be cast in the role of monitoring the value of the distribution process; without experience, how will you be able to judge? How to handle the P&A question is one issue you have to decide for yourself. In the end, however, having to ask an investor for several million dollars in addition to the production costs may help you decide to forgo this choice.

Distributor As Financier

Chapter 9, "Financing," discusses financing in detail, but let's look here at the situation that arises when the distribution company is the provider of funds. If the distribution company produces a minimum guarantee, it is taking on greater risk, and therefore the fees are higher. Sometimes the deal may give the distributor an equity participation in the film on the back end. The distribution fee is taken off the top, expense reimbursements are second, and then the revenues are split on some percentage basis. The distributor is now on the hook for providing a minimum amount of money no matter what the film does. If the company has provided a bankable guarantee for the producer, the distributor has to make good on the bank loan.

DISTRIBUTOR STRATEGIES

The marketing of the film to the general public is the distributor's job. He makes decisions regarding the representation of the film in terms of genre, the placement of advertisements in various media, the sales approach for exhibitors and foreign buyers, and the "hype" (word-of-mouth, promotional events, alliances with special-interest groups, and so on), all of which are critical to a film's success. Because marketing is part of the distribution company's area of expertise, it usually is unwilling to give the filmmaker a say in the sales strategy, the poster design, or how the film is portrayed.

This comes as a shock to many filmmakers, who assume that they are going to have significant input or even a vote on how the posters look and where the film is opened. Many producers and directors expect a studio to ignore them, but they are under the impression that small distributors run their businesses as cooperative ventures.

Look at this from the distributor's point of view. Too many people involved in the decision-making process could be a nightmare. Formulating a marketing plan by committee could result in the proverbial camel. Artistic people tend to feel that they know the best way to present their project. After all, it is their baby, and they know it more intimately than anyone else. And how hard could advertising really be?

Franklin Delano Roosevelt once said, "If I were starting life all over again, I would go into the advertising business; it has risen with ever-growing rapidity to the dignity of an art." We are all specialists, and marketing is the forte of the distributor. The filmmaker's task is to check out the distributor by researching other films the company has sold and the methods they used in the process. It is hoped that the distributor and the filmmaker will meet each other's standards and that a marriage will be made. Doing your own research to find the best distributor for you should head off a divorce later down the line.

What the Distributor Looks For

In acquiring a project, the distributor looks at many of the same elements discussed in Chapter 3, "The Films":

- Uniqueness of storyline.
- Genre.
- Ability of the cast members to attract audiences or buyers on their names alone.
- Past successes of the producers or director.
- Name tie-in from another medium, such as a best-selling novel.
- Special audience segment for the type, or genre, of film.
- Attached money.

Being able to sell a film involves a mix of elements, although the story is always the first concern. The people to whom the distributors sell must see something in the film that will appeal to their audiences. This varies from country to country and depends on the perspective of the buyer. No two buyers necessarily think the same. It is difficult to define why one distributor will buy a particular film, yet the distributor in the next room at the American Film Market (AFM) will not. It often boils down to a gut feeling—a notion that the distributor knows how to sell and profit from the movie. Every company operates in its own particular niche, but on any given day, some distributors are likely to find your film appealing.

As a producer, you cannot count on miracles or on someone's gut feelings, however. Your best bet is to make your product and your approach as strong as possible. The more components that you bring to the table with the film, the more ammunition your distributor has. Negotiating is their business, but they need something to bargain with.

To complicate your life even more, the definition of a saleable commodity can change from year to year or from market to market. While distributors are in the thick of the battle getting the latest information, the rest of us might be a year behind. This situation makes meeting and talking to distributors crucial. One year, when I was new to this business, I arrived at the AFM with a client to promote his already finished film. The director had convinced a well-known actress to do a 15-minute wraparound (inserting a well-known person into the film purely to make it more saleable). She had been popular at previous markets. Unfortunately, the most recent European market had seen a glut of films with this person, and when we arrived at AFM to make our pitch, there were yawns all around. The distributors knew she was old news, because it is their business. We had not thought to check beforehand to see if the star's popularity had changed.

Approaching a distribution company with a finished film has advantages. The distributor knows what you can do and how it will look on the screen. The company's risk level is lowered and its financial output is less. A finished film also puts you in a stronger negotiating position. Many distributors say that they prefer even partially completed films to scripts because they can see the film's quality.

Festivals are another way to secure distribution. If you can get your film accepted at one of the primary festivals (Sundance, Tribeca, Toronto, and Cannes), you have a chance of attracting distribution. Individually, those festivals tend to attract more distributors than other festivals. Being at a competitive festival is good. You will find the psychology of the herd at work. If an audience likes a film or if one distributor becomes interested, all of a sudden a distributor feeding frenzy can start and prices will go up.

Methods for Releasing Films

Few people invent new release strategies; they just refine the old tried-and-true ones over time. Some are in fashion, and some are out of fashion. When I first started in the business, the late Peter Myers, then Senior Vice President of Twentieth Century

Fox Entertainment, told me that there were essentially two ways to distribute a film—fast and slow. That says it in a nutshell. All of the distribution books that you read (and you should learn as much as you can) will give names to procedures that are variations of fast and slow. I've added another speed, moderate, for our discussion.

Fast

The fastest way to release a film is to release it wide. Studios use this strategy for releasing many of their films by opening on thousands of screens simultaneously around the country. The wide release allows for a big opening weekend, which could have one of two outcomes.

First, suppose a lot of people go to see the film, like it, and tell their friends. Assume the film opens on 4,000-plus screens. The average mall theater seats around 500 people, and the film shows six times a day. You have 5 to 12 million people leaving the theater on a Saturday and telling their friends to see the film. The film develops excellent "legs," which means that it runs for a long time with good box office. The studios often use the results of the opening weekend as a measure of how much effort to put into promoting the film in the ensuing weeks.

For a tentpole film, there is often a worldwide opening to limit the possibility of piracy. In 2012, for example, The Amazing Spider-Man opened on 4,318 screens in North America earning $144.6 million. The same weekend it opened in 15 countries earning an additional $201.6 million for a total of $346.2 million. Keeping everything in perspective, the budget for the film was $230 million.

The second possible result of a big weekend is that the same people tweet to their friends while still watching the movie, "Terrible film. Stay home." (In the old days prior to March 2006, you didn't get that news until coffee on Monday.) The film doesn't have legs or doesn't get extensive promotion. However, it does have that crowd of people who came opening weekend to see the star. The studio can use that in whatever advertising they do to lure more moviegoers into the theaters, before they hear any bad word-of-mouth. The film *Bruno* is the poster child for such an event.

Moderate

There is no standard definition for this type. It used to be that a moderate opening for an indie film would be around 1,000 screens. Looking at films with budgets between $20 million and $60 million released in the first half of 2012, the average opening appears to be 2,500 screens. Films with budgets less than $10 million generally follow more of the old platform release pattern. The film starts in a 10 to 20 selected theaters and moves on in some sort of pattern. A particular film may work best in one market because of the makeup of the population or because the film was shot there. On the other hand, the distributor may use a pattern of 10 to 12 theaters across the country to get a feel for his next moves if the film is doing well.

Films with difficult themes or at least an unknown audience usually open in New York City or Los Angeles. The cosmopolitan nature and the size of the population in those cities are an advantage. With good reviews, a film will continue to move through the country in one of several fashions. It might move to contiguous states, open in successive theaters based on a certain schedule, or cascade into the markets that are most likely to produce revenue. Whatever method is used, the film will continue to open in more and more theaters. Eventually, the number of theaters will decrease, but the film will remain in distribution as long as it attracts audience. These methods have several advantages. They give unique films special handling, and they allow a popular genre, small-budget film to move at the limit of its advertising budget. For example, if your film has a Native American theme, you can open in a moderately large city that also has a significant Native American population, such as Seattle or Albuquerque. In this instance, the film plays to a special-interest audience in a town where the initial box office dollars probably will give you a good start.

The goal of moderate-speed distribution is to realize sizeable opening audience (relative to the budget and theme of the film) and good reviews and then use the money and reviews to continue distribution. Clearly, no one expects a $3 million film to sell $17 or $20 million in tickets during the first weekend. The distributor may start with a few screens and fund additional releases more out of the revenues from the first few theaters. Advertising works the same way. Ads in a major city newspaper can run anywhere from

$1,000 to $10,000. As a moderately budgeted film earns money, it finances the advertising in the cities to follow. For example, *Juno*, made for $7.5 million, opened on seven screens on December 5, 2007. In mid-December, it received nomination for both the Critics' Choice Award and for three Golden Globes. By December 25, the film was on more than 1,000 screens. When it arrived at the Academy Awards, the film had grossed over $130 million in the United States alone. By the end of its run, the film grossed over $200 million worldwide. Had the initial audience not liked *Juno*, it would have been pulled early and rereleased after the nominations.

Slow

The difference between slow- and moderate-speed distribution is not necessarily the type of sequencing but the budget of the distributor. A very small distribution company may be able to afford only one print. Therefore, the film will start in one theater and the distributor will "bicycle" it from theater to theater. Low-budget and "no-budget" films are promoted with this kind of marketing budget—exceedingly small. If a film attracts a larger audience than expected, they may sell the distribution rights to another independent with greater funds. I've seen a small company pick up a film at the Sundance festival and "flip" it to a larger company for a profit before the week is over.

"Four-walling" is another tactic that sometimes works with lower-budget films. In this case, the distributor rents a theater for a flat weekly fee and takes all the receipts. The gamble is that the total box office dollars will be significantly greater than the guaranteed minimum to the exhibitor. To double-check the receipts, you may have to stand at the box office and count the "house" as people buy tickets. Four-walling is used infrequently now, although occasionally a producer will self-distribute and revive this strategy.

Over the past six years, numerous alternative distributors have come into the market. Rather than mention the individual companies, many of whom may not be in business by the time you are reading the book, I'm just going to speak briefly about their methods. Companies will scour the various festivals looking for films that are not picked up. Some are trying direct-to-DVD at the same time that they do a small theatrical distribution. Whether you or the company pays for the distribution costs varies. They take the same rights retentions as traditional distributors, and there is no standard back end for the filmmaker. A for-hire company may give the filmmaker total control over where the film plays, how many screens it hits, marketing, and press screenings. In this case, there is a significant upfront cost to the filmmaker; however, you are still getting professional advice and guidance on what to do.

Self-Distribution

When no distributor wants your product, there is self-distribution. I generally advise clients against self-distribution. Many don't have enough (or often any) previous business expertise to understand the dynamics. Sometimes filmmakers have no choice. No distributor wants the film. The filmmaker wants to gain better ancillary deals by exhibiting the film in a few theaters. Occasionally, the distributor runs out of money and can't afford to live up to an agreement for theatrical distribution. Investors will be very upset if the film is never seen anywhere. However, even a small theatrical distribution usually will mollify them.

There are several ways to approach self-distribution. Many filmmakers will put extra money into their budgets for marketing. If any of these funds haven't been spent, they can be used to get the film out. If the film is appropriate for a specialty theater, you may be able to screen the film for very little cost during one of the theater's down times. Localized publicity, such as flyers or the theater's newsletter, may get enough people into the theater to interest another distributor in picking it up. Or the original distributor may suddenly find that money is available that hadn't been accessible before.

Be aware. The exhibitors have been in business a long time and are experienced negotiators. You are not. Trying to work with them yourself puts you at a disadvantage. They are going to offer you a deal that benefits them, not you. Distributors may be difficult, but they know what the best deal is and how to negotiate it. If you want to do this yourself, learn the rules first.

Do not confuse self-distribution with self-marketing as described in Chapter 5, "The Markets." When no one picked up *What the Bleep Do We Know?*, the film's investor paid for initial releasing. Once it was clear that there was a substantial audience for the film, the Samuel Goldwyn Company picked it up. The free screenings that were done for spiritual groups helped build word-of-mouth for the film. Putting it in theaters yourself costs money; there are many free ways to promote the film.

In 2012, Kevin Smith formed the Kevin Smith and SModcast Pictures Presents label to self-distribute his film *Red State*. The reported U.S. box office for the $4 million film was $1.1 million, although more will be known when the total revenues are reported by Baseline. Before you say that you want to do what he did, keep in mind that Smith, in addition to being a well-known, successful filmmaker for 17 years, had 1.8 million Twitter followers and 700,000 Facebook friends.

If you are determined from the beginning to distribute a film yourself and are raising money from investors, you must tell them. Either they or someone else will have to put up the print and ad money. If you make the film first without the distribution funds, you may not find other investors for the additional money. The other problem is forecasting the revenues, as all of your comps for profitable films are going to be ones that have been distributed by professionals.

FILMMAKER STRATEGIES

David Versus Goliath

Many filmmakers let fate determine which way they will go in terms of distribution: studio or independent. This decision has no right or wrong answers, only options. The studio brings with it deep pockets, backup advice from experienced producers, strong marketing, and the ability to retain screens. Independent distributors bring an intimate knowledge of the low-budget market, the ability to disseminate films carefully over time, and a willingness to take a chance. Weigh your options carefully before making a decision.

There is wisdom to the thought, "Just get the film made." Over the years, though, I have come to believe that raising money and making the film may actually be the easy part. Getting a good distribution deal for the film and financial deal for yourself and your investors is where the real work begins.

One filmmaker's meat is another's poison. Before going into any negotiations, be clear on your goals. The distribution decision is the major reason that you went through the exercise of listing

TABLE 6.1

Pros and Cons of Studio Versus Independent

ELEMENT	STUDIO	INDEPENDENT
Greenmail	Often	Seldom
Backup	A lot	A little
Upfront Money	Generous	Practical
Types of Films	Blockbuster	Small to moderate
Overrun Financing	Yes	Forbidden
Distributor Cutoff	Quick	Moderate
Bureaucracy	Heavy	Filmmakers
Net Profits	Seldom	Often
Producer's Capital	None	Some

your wants and desires in Chapter 2, "The Company." You may seek advice and counsel from others, but in the end, you must make your own decisions. Table 6.1 helps you identify the pros and cons of studio and independent distribution.

The studio's backup system is a safety net for the new film-maker. There are experienced producers on the lot, and executives are often dispatched to location to solve problems. This might be an advantage or a disadvantage. The independent filmmaker, on the other hand, usually completes the film before finding a distributor and thus has far more freedom during the filmmaking process. Distributors generally do not have extra people to hang around the set and tell you how to direct or produce.

The nature of independent distribution supports smaller-budget films. In the studios, it is hard to make a film with a smaller budget. They've got union salaries, overhead, and extra costs galore. Independent distributors have to run a tighter ship. Certainly, when looking for financing, their goal is a small budget. The size of the budgets for studio films usually leads to less imaginative and less chancy films being made. The independent system, meanwhile, embraces new and eclectic films. Studios maintain large bureaucracies, which make reaching a decision very difficult and time consuming. The less cumbersome independent process enables quicker decisions because there are fewer chefs in the kitchen.

The studio's financial resources generally favor generous salaries for producers, directors, and cast. With independent films, above-the-line money is often cut to lower the budget to make it doable. Most studios assume a certain level of budget overrun with pictures and have the resources to support it. Conversely, private equity investors expect the budget you give them to be the final number. Underestimating can be dangerous because investors may not make up the shortfall. (More on this subject in Chapter 9.)

Studio distribution, as we have seen, is generally "get 'em out fast and wide." Historically, the studios have had neither the time nor the inclination to pamper a film through its release. It goes out everywhere with a lot of publicity. In addition, the studios have a short attention span. Films that fail to find their audiences quickly enough are pulled to make room for other titles that might have broader appeal. Independent distributors, on the other hand, often have the knowledge and patience to give special care to eclectic films. Many are geared to let a film find its audience slowly and methodically. Of course, there are some independent distributors whose forte is the mass-appeal genres. Most independents, though, have an expertise for releasing films with smaller budgets and lesser-known names.

Historically, the studios' desire to share in the small-film market used to last for only a brief time. Studios have gone through cycles of acquiring smaller films, then forgetting about them. By buying indie companies, the studios manage to keep a hand in the niche market. Many of these specialty divisions have become labels, however. For independent companies, the niche markets are their business.

Earlier, we noted that your chances of a net profit on a studio film are low. There is a greater chance of having a real net profit at the end of the day with an independent film, although it is not guaranteed. The best policy in the movie business usually is to get what you can in the beginning—just in case.

The Control Factor

Filmmakers are well aware of the fact that studios retain the right to change anything they please—title, director's cut, and so on—and sometimes they assume that independent distributors will not want control over these things. Wrong! All distributors want to control the title and the cut. The only way to have total control over your film is to finance and distribute it yourself.

With the studios, the filmmaker's lack of control over projects is the stuff of which legends are made. Once your project goes into the system, it may be the last time you recognize it. If you are the writer, the finished picture may bear little resemblance to your original. Normally, there is far more control in independent filmmaking, but absolute control is a myth. An independent distributor will not allow you to have your way with everything. Novice filmmakers often are surprised at their lack of control. If only to protect themselves, distributors feel that they need these rights. Their biggest concern is to have a salable product, and, especially with neophyte producers and directors, they have no idea what they may be getting. A film that is too long, that drags in various places, or that includes scenes that were not approved in the original script will be a problem. Most independent distributors would rather deal with a finished film. That way, they know what they are getting before making an agreement, and they can request certain changes before obtaining the film. The latter is why turning over a finished film is no guarantee for the filmmaker of retaining the elusive "final cut."

Be Aware

When going into a distribution negotiation meeting, know what items are important to you. Talk to your attorney and get a feel for your deal-breakers—that is, the points on which you will not negotiate. No matter what someone says to you verbally, written agreements are what count. For example, if having a hand in the marketing is important to you, try to have it included in the contract. Be advised that many distributors will not concede this item. They may listen to what you have to say, but they want the final decision.

Learn from the experiences of others. One novice filmmaker sent his distributor 40 minutes of finished film and 45 minutes of dailies. Although the distributor had said that they wouldn't change a frame, they used the dailies to change the film to meet their standards. In addition, they took a frame from a scene that was not in the finished film to use for the poster. This allowed the distributor to promote the film as belonging to a different genre than it actually did. Will the average distributor do this? Probably not, but it is your responsibility to check out the people you will be dealing with to see how they have handled other filmmakers' projects.

In the final analysis, you must enter into the distribution agreement with care. Make sure your rights are spelled out. If you see the term *standard agreement*, ask for a definition. Finally—and I cannot say this often—get the advice of an attorney who specializes in independent film distribution before signing anything.

Deliverables

While there isn't room in this book to go into all the aspects of distribution, I want to mention the delivery items. When you see the initial distribution contract and a small advance, remain calm. You have additional expenses. The filmmaker is responsible for delivering certain items to the distributor—another reason for having that detail-oriented attorney. Your lawyer will know whether or not those items are normally the expense of the filmmaker. They will include such things as type of print, M&E (music and effects) tracks, music cue sheets, continuity script, MPAA rating certificate, E&O (errors and omissions) insurance policy copyright certificate, still photographs, and copies of all contracts and agreements. This is not a complete list but gives you an example. Refer to Robert Seigel's "Distribution Deal Points" download on the book's companion website.

WHAT DO YOU TELL INVESTORS?

The salient facts are here, but you must decide how much explanation to include in your plan. Always keep your description short and to the point. The Distribution section of your business plan should run two or three pages at most.

On the other hand, do say something useful. Unless they are professional movie investors, your investors know even less than you do about distribution; as with other subjects, you have to dispel any wrong impressions they might have. Many investors think that their production financing gives them control of the distributor, too. In addition, some have been known to assume that the distributor will repay them all the production costs upfront before the film is released. These notions may prevent you from finding a distributor; in that case, no one will ever see your film.

Before you propose to take charge of all the marketing and promotional strategies yourself or decide to self-distribute your films, ask yourself a question: Who is going to make decisions? The idea may sound great—it will give you control—but there may well be pitfalls. Remember: If you do not know how to drive a car, you're either not going to get far or crash.

Getting a distribution deal is never a given. I make a point of saying that the specifics of the distribution deal and the timing of all money disbursements depend on the agreement that is finally negotiated. In addition, the timing of the revenue and the percentage amount of the distributor's fees differ depending on the revenue source. You must always remind investors that you are making estimates based on general industry formulas.

If you leave investors with the impression that distribution automatically comes with making the film, you may end up with a bigger problem than you ever imagined. I have seen many business plans that have a single statement—"We will get a distributor"—as the entire Distribution section. As you should realize by now, this approach is not the best. Never leave your investors in the dark, but don't attempt to talk about something you haven't looked into yourself. Do your research before writing your plan and explain the essentials.

By the way, attorneys will warn you that a phrase like "We expect to negotiate with a distributor" can create some difficulties for you down the road. Instead of "expect to" (or, worst of all, "will"), say that you "aim" or "intend" to get distribution. Then you will be in good shape to give investors confidence while shielding yourself from later legal problems.

7

Distribution: Nontheatrical and the Wild West

It's still the Wild West

—LOGAN MULVEY, CEO, GODIGITAL

In every seminar, online class, and by email, I am asked about writing business plans for feature films to go direct to smart phones, home video, cable, VOD (and all its version, such as TVOD, SVOD, etc.), Amazon, iTunes, Netflix, Hulu, Xbox, and any other nontheatrical platforms currently in operation. All of these changes are exciting and becoming increasing important to the entertainment business. The problem with all this is: where is the money?

That question shines a bright light on a challenge. I have to assume that you bought this book with the intention of writing a business plan to raise money from other people. You can write about the industry, markets, and budget your costs for all the nontheatrical platforms, but you don't have the information on revenues, distribution costs, and fees for individual films to make a forecast. When distributors and financial consultants call it the "wild west," you know that segment of the industry is still in its infancy.

A BIT OF HISTORY

In earlier editions of the book, this chapter included discussions of documentaries, large-format (IMAX) films, and direct-to-various ancillaries. There wasn't enough data to create financials for those formats. In 2004, I felt there was enough worldwide information for docs to move them to move them to Chapter 5. In 2009, I began to formulate a method for doing business plan for large format films. For this edition, I have given those two formats their own chapter (12) along with animated films, so that I could give you a fuller explanation of how their financials differ from the standard formula in Chapter 11.

In the rest of this chapter, we are going to look at the history of the new media segments and where those markets are now. The same applies to the older ancillaries when films are sent directly to them skipping the traditional theatrical. Once you have the facts, you can decide how to proceed. At some point in time, the information you need will exist; however, I doubt that it will be in the next five years.

NEW MEDIA

Right now everyone's still just trying it out to see what works. The world will really change when things like Apple TV come online and you have more penetration into homes. Hal Sadoff, financial consultant and former Head of International and Independent film for ICM, was talking about digital distribution and streaming.

New Media has always been with us. As discussed earlier, we are now focusing on the "newer" digital media and their rights. More and more companies have become involved with digital distribution. In 1999, CinemaNow was the first company offering secure digital distribution of a studio movie, 1997's *Heaven's Burning* with Russell Crowe. In 2006, Movielink and rival CinemaNow announced that they would offer permanent downloads of movies from several major studios day-and-date (on the same day as) with their DVD release. Movielink, which started in 2002, was a partnership of MGM, Paramount, Sony, Twentieth Century Fox, Universal Studios, and Warner Bros. Meanwhile, Lionsgate, MGM, and Sony made their movies available for download-to-own through CinemaNow. Other companies began making films available on a nonexclusive basis to both systems. Finding that Movielink wasn't the cash cow it had been expected to be, the original partners finally sold the service to Blockbuster in August 2007. Blockbuster shut down the Movielink site in December 2008, in favor of downloading directly from the

Blockbuster website itself. In 2011, the Dish Network purchased Blockbuster and created blockbusterhome.com.

Other players kept coming into the Internet market. Amazon, Best Buy (which purchased CinemaNow), Hulu, WalMart's Vudu, and iTunes selling films and other entertainment programming for download on the Internet, and websites such as Netflix and Hulu (through Hulu Plus) stream filmed entertainment to home viewers as rentals. Diverse devices for personal viewing of films (including Xbox, Wii, video iPod, iPhone, and iPad) are continuing to gain ground in the marketplace, expanding the potential revenues from home video and other forms of selling programming for viewing. As usual, the impact of these new technologies is expected to keep growing significantly over the next 5 to 10 years.

There are both services through which you can download your films directly and distributors who will make Internet deals. The argument is that distributing through theaters is very expensive compared to the vast audiences you can reach on a single day through the computer without making multiple prints. To get to a theater screen, you have gatekeepers. You usually have to go through distributors and convince bookers/exhibitors that they should both put your film on the screen.

Streaming of films by distributors like Netflix has started to be included in the home video numbers that DEG publishes. It reportedly costs Netflix 80 cents to send a DVD out and get it back. The company has a 12,000-title catalog available for unlimited streaming at $9 a month.

With the Internet, theoretically anyone can download their film with a choice of several software systems. The technology not only is empowering, but allows you to send any film anywhere without a rating or, technically, censors to worry about. (There are ways to shut off technology as recent political events have demonstrated, but that isn't part of this discussion.)

So what's the problem? Why I am including this information here, rather than in Chapter 6? First of all, the movies being watched are primarily ones that have gone out theatrically. Second we only know macro numbers for those. Information on individual films for how many people are downloading, what are the revenues, and so on doesn't exist.

Then, there is the question of not only what people will pay, but also how much will come back to the filmmakers. We know what different sites charge for a customer to download, but we aren't sure what the share is for the filmmaker. Many download sites are ad-supported. There is no common split the way that we can track with brick-and-mortar stores or Netflix.

YouTube

YouTube, which made its debut in 2005, was founded by three former PayPal employees, it allows users to upload and share videos. Google bought it in November 2006 for $1.65 billion. While much of their site is dedicated to shorter videos, in November 2008, YouTube reached an agreement with MGM, Lionsgate Entertainment, and CBS that will allow the companies to post full-length films and television shows on the site, accompanied by advertisements. This created competition for other sites, especially Hulu. However, the films being released to the site by companies are mostly older and theatrically distributed films for which any additional income is welcome. As for the amount of that additional income, your guess is as good as mine.

In May 2010, YouTube reported that the site was serving more than two billion videos a day, but described the downloads as "mostly the television audience." In January 2012, YouTube stated that the figure had increased to four billion videos streamed per day. Still it is reported that most of the four billion videos that YouTube now streams worldwide every day do not make money. In addition, in 2012, studios and other distributors made deal with the service to provide feature films for download as they come into the rest of the home video market.

Short Films

In the previous editions of this book, there was a chapter on the distribution of short films. YouTube and its Google parent are the main reason that chapter is no longer included. As the 2009 edition was being printed, David Russell, the President of Big Film Shorts and major source of information, closed his company. With the number of free videos being downloaded daily from the new 800-pound gorillas in the short-film business, the marginal revenues that had existed for the films disappeared.

Second Screens

Television was the original second screen. Now it refers to electronic devices with even smaller screens—smart phones, iPads, game consoles. The big step forward that Google took in 2005 allowing download to cell phones, which I like to refer to as "short attention span theater, seems like ancient history. There appears to be no limit to how many of these devices. Still, most of the data has to do with what people download from television. According to a study published in January by Yahoo's advertising division, 86 percent of people who use the mobile Internet use their mobile device while watching television. Of those using their mobile device, 25 percent say they are browsing content related to the program they are watching. Netflix users were less interested in streaming movie title in 2012 than a year earlier, according to data released by Nielsen based on a study in April that year.

Business Models

A distributor whom I know and respect very much told me in 2009 that the thing I had left out of the previous edition is that the digital wave was heading for the shore like a tsunami and that it is going to change the fundamentals of distribution. That still hasn't happened. Many in the business are bullish about the future. We keep hearing that once the market is "fully developed," it will be a boon for independent filmmakers. We have to ask, though, how long a time before the prophesied boon will be more than another aftermarket for films that have been released theatrically first.

Distributors specializing in "digital only" keep appearing in the market. Companies like GoDigital, Gravitas, and SnagFilms will take your film direct, while still contracting at times for theatrical releases. The major independent companies, like The Weinstein Company, IFC, and Magnolia, have separate labels devoted to digital. Unfortunately, there is no industry standard for how all this works. According to reports, digital distributors look for 20 to 30 percent of receipts, minus any fees or sub-distributor fees. That compares to the 50 percent that theatrical exhibitors keep. How the contract details read of any of those deals varies. The range of digital deal structures is wide, as no one has a firm idea of the best way to go. The biggest problem that you will have in investigating the thought of "direct-to" is recognizing hype when you read it. In addition, what relates to a large company that can afford to take a flyer sending films directly to online may not be useful for the average filmmaker. I look at all as full employment for attorneys.

How is someone going to know that your film is available for download? You have to tell them. With social networks and email marketing, self-marketing keeps growing. Nevertheless, you still need some advertising push to alert people that your film is available. And how many of them are going to download? We don't know that.

Direct-to-DVD

Sales of direct-to-DVD films have continued going down since 2009. Premier releasing into this market remains mainly a market for studios, releasing new version so franchise films or a sequel to a theatrically released film with a genre market. It has been particularly lucrative for The Walt Disney Company that capitalizes on its family-film themes.

Independents have had less success. "Starting in 2007, independent distributors sold more foreign direct-to-video films than the studios, and this trend continued until 2011 when the studios eclipsed the indies once again," David Paiko, VP of home entertainment at research provider Rentrak, told *Variety*. According to reports, titles now typically generate only hundreds or tens of thousands of dollars instead of amounts in the millions. With less upside potential, the distributors that previously worked this market tend to prefer a digital model now with VOD. In addition, a film that does well on VOD first will be send to DVD if it performs well.

Another interesting wrinkle in the direct-to business is the life expectancy of any company with which you might be negotiating. This year, two clients were negotiating with two different companies for direct-to domestic ancillary and foreign sales. Before they could return the signed contracts, each company was bought by someone else. Both had to go through new negotiations. One did, and the other decided to walk away. It is too early to know how much, if anything, the filmmaker will make.

Occasionally, someone tells me that they have written a business plan for direct-to-DVD. When I ask what they used for data, the answer is, "You don't want to know." I advise readers not to go down that road. With the lower upfront expenses, however, you might be best off with a direct-to-VOD business.

WHAT CAN YOU TELL INVESTORS?

The short answer is, "Not much." Clearly, things are changing. It is the timing that is the problem. If you are planning to distribute your own films directly through the Internet or any other new media technology, there currently is not enough money from Internet downloads for indie films. For forecasters, five years always seems like a long time away. It can be in terms of new devices but not necessarily for changes in how a filmmaker can monetize them.

With the lack of data available about individual films, we are left with only anecdotal stories about how much money individuals have made selling their own films from their websites. Clients have told me about money that has been made. In most cases, it was for short films (before the wide world of freebies) and for "no-budget" films under $50,000. Filmmakers appear on panels who say that they have made $3 to $5 million by selling their films only over the Internet. It sounds impressive. However, these reports are subjective and very few. In addition, when you push them to the length of time it took, the answer may be eight years. They also have spent a great deal of time getting the information out to the audience, similar to our discussion of marketing methods for films on crowdfunding sites in Chapter 9.

If you have the resources yourself to make anything—short-, medium-, or feature-length and want to put it on the Internet, go ahead. If someone wants to put up money without any need for getting it back, make them your best friend. But you can't honestly imply that they will make money. As discussed earlier, there are no deal standards and only sketch financial information relating mostly to studios.

Nevertheless, keep tracking what is happening. Put your own Internet browser to good use and follow all the companies and sites mentioned earlier. I will end with the same sentences that I wrote in 2009. All the above information is presented for your use. You should proceed as you think best. I agree with Director Michael Apted and President of the Director's Guild of America at that time, who said, "All the talk is the Internet and all the deals we did for the future. In a sense, that's sort of fog. The real money and the real deal are in traditional media."

8

Risk Factors: Truth in Advertising

A little uncertainty is good for everything.
—HENRY KISSINGER

Every business plan requires a statement of risk, in which you tell investors what a high-risk investment this is. Make it clear that nothing is guaranteed. No entrepreneur likes a risk statement, but it is a protection for you. In a limited liability company (LLC) or limited partnership, your attorney will insert one whether you like it or not. You are well advised to do this in any proposal for funds. With a risk statement included in your business plan, investors cannot later claim that they did not know that the investment was unpredictable. Even though it seems obvious to you, and probably to them, assume nothing and state the facts anyway. If things should go awry and people lose money, they tend to sue.

A risk statement can be a very short statement or a long explanation. Sometimes, I see risk statements as long as 14 pages in business plans that I haven't written. This is excessive for a business plan, but appropriate for the legal document.

SHORT STATEMENT

I always put a short statement like the following in the Executive Summary.

Investment in the film industry is highly speculative and inherently risky. There can be no assurance of the economic success of any motion picture, since the revenues derived from the production and distribution of a motion picture depend primarily upon its acceptance by the public, which cannot be predicted. See the "Risk Factors" section of the Investor Offering Memorandum for further particulars.

Long Version

I also put the following long statement before the Financial section. Some attorneys will feel that the short statement is enough. If you have an attorney putting together the Investor Agreement, ask her. If you are handing out the business plan separately from the legal document, include the following statement. You don't need to copy this page, as it is downloadable from both the book's companion website and http://www.moviemoney.com.

RISK FACTORS

Investment in the film industry is highly speculative and inherently risky. There can be no assurance of the economic success of any motion picture since the revenues derived from the production and distribution of a motion picture depend primarily upon its acceptance by the public, which cannot be predicted. The commercial success of a motion picture also depends upon the quality and acceptance of other competing films released into the marketplace at or near the same time, general economic factors, and other tangible and intangible factors, all of which can change and cannot be predicted with certainty.

The entertainment industry in general, and the motion picture industry in particular, are continuing to undergo significant changes, primarily due to technological developments. Although these developments have resulted in the availability of alternative and competing forms of leisure time entertainment, such technological developments have also resulted in the creation of additional revenue sources through licensing of rights to such new media, and potentially could lead to future reductions in the costs of producing and distributing motion pictures. In addition, the theatrical success of a motion picture remains a crucial factor in generating revenues in other media such as videocassettes and television. Due to the rapid growth of technology, shifting consumer tastes, and the popularity and availability of other forms of entertainment, it is impossible to predict the overall effect these factors will have on the potential revenue from and profitability of feature-length motion pictures.

The Company itself is in the organizational stage and is subject to all the risks incident to the creation and development of a new business, including the absence of a history of operations and minimal net worth. In order to prosper, the success of [the name of your film here] will depend partly upon the ability of management to produce a film of exceptional quality at a lower cost which can compete in appeal with higher-budgeted films of the same genre. In order to minimize this risk, management plans to participate as much as possible throughout the process and will aim to mitigate financial risks where possible. Fulfilling this goal depends on the timing of investor financing, the ability to obtain distribution contracts with satisfactory terms and the continued participation of the current management.

9

The Financial Plan: How It Works

It's very important that every movie I do makes money, because I want the people that had the faith in me to get their money back.

—DIRECTOR QUENTIN TARANTINO

Shuffle a pack of playing cards. Now spread them out face down and pick one card. If it is the ace of spades, you win; if it is not, you lose. Your chances of getting the right card are 1 out of 52. These odds are better than the odds of finding independent money for your film. Do not be discouraged, though. Many filmmakers face these odds each year—and win.

Film is probably the worst investment anyone could ever make. It is considered risky and capricious. If risks were measured on a scale of 1 to 10, movies would rate a 15. One might as well go to Las Vegas and throw the dice—in fact, those odds are probably better. Why would anyone invest in films, then? From a purely financial standpoint, it is a gamble for which there is a big payoff. In addition, there are many subjective reasons for investing in films, such as personal ideals, creative participation, and being part of the glitter and glamour. The specific people and firms those are likely to fund films change, but the modus operandi remains the same. Some of the different sources of financing will be relevant for your situation, others will not. Some are dynamic; some are static. As studio executives and production companies go through cycles, so do forms of financing.

By this point, you are well on your way to a finished proposal. You have explained the basic information—your company, your film(s), the industry, the market, and the distribution process. You have your goals and objectives well in hand. Now here is the kicker. Popular agent lore (spread by agents) is that if a script is not interesting after the first 10 pages, it gets thrown onto the "forget it" pile. Something similar can be said of investors and business plans. Investors typically read the Executive Summary first and the Financing section second. If they are still interested, they read all the delicious text between the two. This does not mean that all the in-between material is irrelevant, just that the primary emphasis is on the ins and outs of financing and how the numbers look.

When thinking about investors, most people picture a singularly rich person who swoops in and says, "Here's an extra $10 million I found in my drawer. Go make a film—no strings attached." Or they imagine a country suddenly passing a law guaranteeing you 100 percent of your film costs just for showing up. This is the stuff of which movie plots are made. Not impossible scenarios, but improbable ones. You may get lucky early on, but it is more likely that there will be false starts, dashed hopes, and months or years of frustration.

As the saying goes, "If it were easy, everyone would be doing it." The truth is that finding financing is hard work. If you think otherwise, forget it. There are almost as many ways to finance a movie as there are people reading this book. We will look at specific methods, but note that the full financing of your movie may be a combination of several methods.

With a business plan for a new filmmaker or company, there is an additional struggle. Whether you are asking a money source to invest in one film or several, creating a feeling of confidence is not easy. Any anxiety on the part of the investor about funding one of your films is magnified when committing to finance an entire company. Besides making successful films, you have to be able to run that company. The investor will be looking with great care, therefore, at the production team.

In your Financial Plan section, you will discuss how your films will find financing, but you should do this without restating this entire chapter. Only certain financial strategies will be appropriate for your particular projects or for the type of investor you are going after. Too much irrelevant information will only confuse your reader.

This chapter examines some of the specific sources of money: single investors (rich people), presales, coproduction and below-the-line deals, negative pickups, limited partnerships, and limited liability companies. In addition, it takes a brief look at bank loans. This chapter is meant to give you general knowledge of how film financing works; the intention is to make a complex subject easy to understand and to give you material for your business plan. It is not meant to be the complete and final word on the subject. For your own knowledge, do additional research on the specific financing techniques that you plan to use.

BEFORE YOU START

Before writing the financing section of your business plan, there are several guidelines to think about and follow. These concern the following:

- Seeking reality.
- Finding the best fit.
- Being careful what you promise.
- Being careful what they promise.
- Being able to explain it.

Seeking Reality

The way that one person financed a film yesterday may not be relevant to you today. This statement may appear to contradict what was said earlier about learning from other filmmakers, but it does not. We said it was sometimes the same formula, not necessarily the same people. Do not assume that you will find money in the same place. Who you approach, where they are, and what they want to know differs from investor to investor. Learn from the other filmmakers' experiences in their interviews in Chapter 13, "Other People's Money." They may prove useful to you. Keep in mind, however, that you may have totally different results to share in the next edition.

Finding the Best Fit

Filmmakers often believe that all money is equal; it isn't. Each source sets different requirements or conditions for the delivery of funds. You will be able to live with some of these, but not with others. For example, there may be too many fingers in the pie. Three intermediaries later, you will be paying out large sums to finders. Or prospective investors may have requirements that make getting the money not worthwhile. There may be content, length of time, or rate of return demands you cannot meet.

Worse, at the 11th hour, Ms. Investor may inform you that her husband has to play the lead in the film. Don't be discouraged. The right source for you is out there somewhere; seek until you find it.

Being Careful What You Promise

Making statements of absolute fact about financial conditions may be dangerous. An investor will hold you to whatever you promise. You might say, for example, "We will seek presales in order to recover at least some of the production financing upfront." That is not a promise, only a statement of intent. On the other hand, saying to people, "We will obtain presale commitments" is a promise. Unless you have commitments already in hand, you may be making a promise that you cannot keep. And be careful of implied promises. If you want to tell potential investors that Sony Pictures Classics paid less than $1 million for *Beasts of the Southern Wild*, be sure to say: "It was reported at the Sundance Film Festival that Sony Pictures Classics paid less than $1 million for domestic rights to *Beasts of the Southern Wild*."

In the discussion, point out that we don't always know what the actual deal is in reference to the figures quoted. I have seen investors refuse to approve a distribution deal because they assumed that "normal" purchase prices were twice the negative cost of the film. The typical verbiage that I use is:

> Deals at festivals vary greatly. The prices announced in the press may depend on specific boxoffice results, be advances against future revenue streams, or be total buyout prices with no further remuneration to the filmmakers and their investors. For most of the publicized dollar amounts, the negotiated agreement is not made public.

Being Careful What They Promise

Always take the stance that you have to see it to believe it. People do not have to be con artists to lead you astray; many just like to hear themselves talk. Even investment bankers are seen bragging at cocktail parties about financing films they didn't. If a money source (finder or actual) is saying, "The check is in the mail," your mantra should be, "Do not spend any money until the cash is in the production account." This warning applies to family and friends as well as bank executives. Check the paperwork. If you are not knowledgeable about financial terms and clauses, find someone who is. Look carefully in the fine print for how much cash this source is keeping. Do they have the resources to meet your needs or are they making a promise on behalf of some other entity that has never heard of you and probably never will?

Recently, a client told me that she wanted to work with a producer who had a certain A-list director and star attached and $50 million in the bank. My first question was: why do they need you? I was not being rude. She had never made a film and no particularly interesting connections. This fellow had $50 million and could go ahead with his director and an actress who had could bring in the audience on her name. While my client was thinking it over, I did an Internet search on Yahoo! I finally found a website for the film. The only people attached were family and friends; however, it said "no director attached" and didn't mention cast. There also was a statement that they were looking for money for an unspecified budget. It is fair to assume that having that much money you have an assistant who could update the website. Such searches only take a few minutes of your time but can save grief later.

Being Able to Explain It

If you cannot explain a financing scheme, do not include it. To my constant amazement, I often receive business plans to critique that are based on a complicated financing structure, usually in a foreign country, that the producer does not understand; nor has he ever found someone who has successfully used it. Longtime professionals, not just inexperienced filmmakers, will base entire companies on such schemes. Frankly, not only do many of these require several investment bankers to work through their complexity but also the majority either don't work or were fictional to begin with.

Be especially wary if an intermediary wants a substantial amount of money in advance. A finder gets paid when you have the money in the bank, not before. Request to see all the documents first. If you have to find an investor to make a deal work, you can bet your bottom dollar that your investor will ask for details about the financing, with examples of films financed. They'll also want a meeting with a principal (person who actually controls the other funding).

WHO ARE THEY?

Investors are gamblers no matter what their reasons, and film is one of the biggest gambles you can find. Others have personal reasons for investing in film. Private investors are equity players.

They take a portion of the profits in exchange for their capital. Until you take in partners, you own the whole pie. As partners come in, you start to slice the pie into little pieces, and as the old saying goes, "Them that has the gold makes the rules." The nature of an entrepreneur is to be filled with passion to accomplish a certain end. The hardest job for you may be your own emotional involvement when attempting to see things dispassionately from the investor's point of view.

Family and Friends

The first string of the investment team for has often been family and friends. Raising development money and the negative cost of films under $1 million is very difficult. Professional investors do not see enough of a return on such small investments. Mom and Uncle Harry are more likely to be willing to give you a chance. Kevin Smith funded the $26,575 budget for *Clerks* with credit card advances, the sale of his comic book collection, and a loan from his parents. It is hard to find anyone with the much room on the credit cards since the financial meltdown started in 2008. Filmmakers Alex and Stephen Kendrick raised the $100,000 budget for *Facing the Giants* as donations from church members, including family and friends. Since the introduction of the original crowdfunding platforms, primarily Kickstarter (launched April 2009) and Indiegogo (launched January 2008), much of this money has been donated through those websites.

I have been at a lot of panels where company executives will tell you that family and friends are the *only* source of money for low-budget films. This statement is false. Many films have been made with all the money coming from total strangers. When it comes to investment from those close to you, it is wise to have the same written agreements that you would have with total strangers.

Entrepreneurs

Private money comes most often from people in businesses other than entertainment. Entrepreneurial types who have made a killing in almost any industry may feel the lure of film. It takes a high roller at heart to start a firm and prosper with it. You can try the annual Forbes 400 for a listing of billionaires; however, you may have to travel to Hong Kong or Taiwan to speak with them. You don't have to go that far for what you need.

Investors have all sorts of reasons for taking this risk. Some are after big bucks, some are personal fans, and some want to give back to the community. Despite their reasons, investors are seldom seeking to lose money. I have seen scores of creative people forget their dreams rather than face the reality that, whatever the content, these are business deals as well.

There have always been wealthy people attracted by Hollywood. Many of them invested with studios in the early years. One of the first investors in DreamWorks was Paul Allen, co-founder of Microsoft. Over the past 15 years, however, a growing number of communications, real estate, Internet, sports, finance, and other billionaires have made pacts with experienced producers to start independent production and distribution companies. Phillip Anschutz, chairman of Qwest Communications International, has started several production companies, now combined into Walden Media. He also bought United Artists, Regal Cinemas, and Edwards Cinemas, which currently controls over 6,000 theater screens. Jeff Skoll, a co-founder of eBay, founded Participant Media, which has invested in both studio and independent films. Mark Cuban and Todd Wagner, the founders of http://www.broadcast.com, formed 2,929 Productions and Magnolia Distribution and bought the Landmark Theaters. The partners in Google have co-financed a film; they are also early investors in various areas of high-definition entertainment. Gary Gilbert, co-owner of the NBA's Cleveland Cavaliers, along with Usher and the Chairman and Vice Chairman of Quicken Loans has financed several movies, among them *Garden State*. Sidney Kimmel, a founder of Jones Apparel Group, formed Sidney Kimmel Entertainment, which has produced several films and has more in development. The late Adam Yauch of the Beastie Boys formed Oscilloscope Laboratories, which became a film producer and distributor in 2008. Bill Pohlad, the son of self-made billionaire Carl Pohlad (owner of the Minnesota Twins baseball team), formed River Road Entertainment.

In more recent years, Texas businessman Mark Hulme set up Five Star Pictures, which plans to finance and produce one film a year. The company's first film *is Jobs*, a biopic of Apple co-founder Steve Jobs. Gigi Prtizker, heiress of the Chicago Pritzger fortune ($1.7B), set up Odd Lot Entertainment. Saul Hudson better known as Slash, the former lead guitarist of Guns N' Roses followed in the footsteps of fellow rocker Rob Zombie by establishing Slasher Films (horror genre, of course).

The sons and daughters of the rich and maybe famous have brought many of their trust funds to film. Teddy Schwarzman, the son of Blackstone chairman and CEO Stephen Schwarzman, founded Black Bear Pictures. Allison Ellison, daughter of Oracle billionaire Larry Ellison, founded Annapurna Pictures, and Sarah Siegel-Magness and Gary Magness (Sarah Seigel's parents founded Celestial Seasonings teas, and Magness' parents founded cable company Tele-Communications Inc.) formed Smokewood Entertainment. Their first film was *Precious*.

All the people mentioned in the preceding paragraphs came into the business with a commitment to film but had various reasons. Some of them have a commitment to films with a message, others want to develop new technology frontiers, and others just love films. However, none of them intend to be spending their money foolishly. There are many in other countries of the world; and presumably, there are more out there waiting for the right opportunity.

WHERE ARE THEY?

How do you find them? I wish I could tell you. One thing I do know is that these are people who recognize that film operates on a different risk level than the businesses that made them or their relatives rich. Before the current economic conditions, several finders working with real estate investor groups have approached me about film, thinking that they could sell the idea to their syndicates. They couldn't. As a group, real estate investors are putting their funds into projects with less risk than film. Even then individuals from those syndicates were investing in limited liability companies (LLCs) and limited partnerships on their own. Until the real estate market turns around, film appears to many to be a better bet than that industry. It does not mean that film is any less risky than it has always been; it is a sign of how risky real estate has become.

Your own backyard is the first place to look for financing. Few filmmakers are born in Los Angeles; they migrate there. Nor are all of the investors born in Los Angeles. They are born and live in Ohio, Michigan, Iowa, Oslo, Sydney, Hong Kong, and so on. At least those are areas where many of my clients have found investors. (Don't call me for a list; it is proprietary—nonpublic, company-owned—information.) You may find untapped markets of entrepreneurs with lots of money from very unglamorous businesses, to whom the lure of the film world may be irresistible. Your best chance is in an area where there is not a lot of competition from other filmmakers—if there still is such a place. The entire financing deal can be conducted without anyone living in Tinsel town.

Giving a party is another strategy that I have seen some producers use to find interested investors. Since I am not an attorney, check the details with yours before proceeding. I have paraphrased some of the rules set out by Morrie Warshawski in his book *The Fundraising Houseparty* (available at http://www.warshawski.com). Although Morrie is focusing on raising money for nonprofit events, the same principles can be used for film fund-raising:

- Potential investors receive an invitation to come to a private home.
- The invitation makes it clear that this is a meeting to launch a film.
- Participants arrive and are served some sort of refreshments.
- The host or hostess explains why they personally feel it is a worthwhile project.
- Participants sit through a brief presentation—appearances by actors in the films, script reading, and so on.

- A peer (we might say shill) in the audience—someone articulate, respected, and enthusiastic—stands up and explains why she wants to be part of the project.
- Once you have established an individual's interest, you can contact her later with your documents about investing.

WHAT YOU GET

Equity investors will want at least a 50 percent cut of the producer's share in the film; some may even want a higher percentage. In recent years, filmmakers have offered the incentive with a return of 110 to 120 percent of the original investment before any split of net profits. No matter how many years you spent writing the scripts or how many hours you spent talking deals, it is their money. Before you start complaining, be glad your investors don't want 80 percent. Venture capital companies and professional film investors often require that much equity to put in seed money.

Filmmakers have a habit of promising "points" and film credits to people for their work in finding investors, making introductions to potential actors, or other steps involved in getting the project made. Directors and stars who are too expensive for the film's budget often are given points as a deferment of part of their salary. These points all come out of the filmmaker's share, unless an agreement is reached with investors. Besides points, filmmakers like to give away credits. Be careful what you promise. If you have one investor for the entire budget, he may want the title of executive producer (and deserves it). Some may want to remain anonymous, so all the other filmmakers wanting money don't contact them. In addition, be careful about the producer title. When your film is nominated for the Best Picture Oscar (I never said you couldn't indulge yourself with some fantasy), only three people can be listed according to the 2007 Academy of Motion Picture rules.

Reasonable Risk

Entrepreneurs often want money from investors with no strings attached as a reward for their creative genius. They do not want to be responsible for how the money is spent or for whether investors realize a gain. No doubt, you are a genius. But do not expect to get financing without showing the investor what kind of risk she is taking.

Early in this business, I tried to get financing for an entrepreneur who had a new idea for making films that would have a nontheatrical distribution in malls. One investor thought the idea was "sexy" and that the films could be taken national but that the business plan was so-so. The investor proposed to invest $5 million and then raise additional money from other investors; however, he wanted a revised business plan. My client would have none of this. "After all," he said, "investors are supposed to take a risk. If these people are not willing to take one, who needs them? I'm not going to waste all this time. Big guys in New York are interested." You can probably guess what happened. The client never heard from the "big guys," never got the first film made, and went back to his old job, never to be heard from again.

The moral here is not that people in New York are unreliable. Serious investors, whether they are in New York or Des Moines, will seldom make a final decision based on flash and dash. They want to see substance and detail. Even if someone likes your project, chances are you will hear, "Come back when you have a business plan."

The Big Payoff

The low-budget, big-return films are the hooks that lure many high rollers into the film business.

Films like *Once, Fireproof,* and *Napoleon Dynamite* can be irresistible. Very few other ventures, outside of Las Vegas, offer the potential of a 500 to 1,000 percent return on investment. At a lower percentage rate but nevertheless as alluring are *Black Swan, Slumdog Millionaire,* and *Courageous.* As a filmmaker, you must be ready to show prospective investors that the chance of making a killing may outweigh the risk of losing their money. Remember, though, that you can never promise a risk-free investment. And you do not want to tell them, "Ten million dollars is typical of advances and/or buyouts for $1-million films."

When all is said and done, it is the projected bottom line that builds the investor's confidence. You need to find similar films and track their dollar returns. Whether you are looking at a single film or a company, you must project your revenues and expenses, box office grosses and rentals, and cash flows over the next three to five years. (You will learn how to do that in the next chapter and through doing the exercises provided in the Financial files on Focal's companion website for this book.)

TYPES OF FINANCING

Crowdfunding for Donations

The original crowdfunding (sometimes called crowd sourcing) is a method of raising limited amounts of money without being governed by SEC (Securities and Exchange Commission) regulations. People donate to your film in return for a reward that a nonmentary reward, such as a DVD, T-shirts, or other memorabilia. The donors do not have any ownership in your film. It doesn't require a PPM or excessive paperwork and should not be confused with the updated traditional investment version of crowdfunding described under the Jump Start Act of 2012, described later in this chapter.

In this method of fund-raising, you create a website on an established platform. The most popular to date have been Kickstarter (kickstarter.com) and Indiegogo (indegogo.com). They are best used for development money, post-production money, or to finance a micro-budget film. You have to research the sites and pick the one that is best for you.

The basic differences between the two mentioned here are that Kickstarter has you set a funding goal and time-frame (usually up to 60 days) that must be met or all monies are returned to the donors. If the funding goal is raised, Kickstarter applies a 5 percent fee to the total amount but only if it is free. Indiegogo also has you set a funding goal, but you don't have to get to your goal. They charge 4 percent if you meet your funding goal or 9 percent on the money you raise if you do not reach your goal. Both have third party processors that charge at least a 3 percent fee.

The big question is: how do all those potential donors know about you and your project? You have to work the social websites, friends, family, and any forms of communication that you can think of to let them know. There are terrific stories on the Internet from people who have raised money. They have another thing in common, though. It is a lot of work!

Veteran documentary filmmaker Jennifer Fox raised over $150,000 for her latest project *My Reincarnation*, a portrait of a High Tibetan Buddhist teacher and his Western-born son. She had 518 backers, donating an average of $290 per person. Jennifer Fox told *The Hollywood Reporter* that it wasn't easy. You need to have a carefully orchestrated campaign with compelling marketing hooks. Irish filmmaker Alexandra Guinness told screendaily.com that she raised initial money for her film *Lotus Easters* that premiered at the Tribeca Film Festival in 2011 through a crowdfunding model. "The website and the crowdfunding model got us a small investment at the beginning to keep going, and it raised the profile and let people know we were there."

Presales

There are two main activities at markets like AFM and Cannes: seeking presales for as-yet-unmade films in order to finance production, and selling finished films. We are concerned here with the former. The seller (you or your U.S. distributor) has a booth or room and entices the buyers from each territory and medium (theatrical, DVD/Blu-ray, VOD, satellite, broadcast, and so on) to buy the ancillary rights (domestic or foreign) to your film in advance. (This is also called a *prebuy*.) In return, you receive a commitment and guarantee from the prebuyers. The guarantee includes a promise from that company to pay a specific amount upon delivery of the completed film. If deemed credible by one of several specialized entertainment banks that accept such "paper," the contract can be banked. Then the bank will advance you a sum, minus their discount amount.

In exchange for the presale contract, the United States or foreign buyer obtains the right to keep the revenue (rentals) from that territory and might also seek equity participation. The agreement can be for a certain length of time, a revenue cap, or both. The time period can be anywhere from 5 to 15 years, with 7 being customary. The biggest issue on a presale is to try to have name talent attached. At least talent that has marketability in the territory that the presale is coming from. The presale will not be in the form of a check, but a loan guarantee to take to a bank. Since a presale will not generally cover the entire budget, you may have to have equity for the balance of the budget.

Many filmmakers are under the impression that "in perpetuity" (forever) enters into this negotiation. These terms are not unheard of, but they are more likely to surface if you are transferring the copyright, or ownership, of the film. There is nothing to keep people with money in their hands from demanding as much as they can get. The buyer tries to make the length of time as long as possible, and the seller tries to make it as short as possible. Be careful of the stance you take. Some foreign companies have told me that if the filmmaker balks at 7 years, they will change the term to 10.

The "revenue cap" is a certain amount of money in sales, up to which the buyer gets to keep all the money. When negotiating these terms, buyers try to estimate the highest amount that the movie will make and then try to make that amount the cap. After the revenue cap is reached, the seller may start receiving a percent of the revenue or may renegotiate the deal.

Being the sole source of financing gives people much more power than if they are one of a group of funders. Yet any of these negotiations still depend on the "eye of the beholder." Any leverage depends on the desire of the buyer for the film.

Advances

In the past, cable, home video, and television syndication companies were major sources of production financing. Through advances, they funded all or part of a film's production in exchange for an equity participation and the rights to distribute the film in their particular medium. Although advances do not occur as frequently as they did in the early 1990s, particularly in video, they are still a potential form of production financing. As noted earlier, most domestic distributors prefer not to see fractionalized rights.

Always weigh this fact against the benefits of having an ancillary company as your main investor. The advance for a finished film is another matter. It may be a total buyout, have a revenue cap, or combine any number of characteristics common to presales.

Advantages and Disadvantages

The primary advantage of presales is that they offer you the chance to make your film. This source of money continues to be a workable one for new filmmakers. In addition, if you manage to reach your production goal over several territories, it lessens the impact that someone else can have on your film. Presumably, the fewer territories in which you presell or from which you receive advances, the more money you will be able to keep on the back end after distribution.

There are two disadvantages to this source of funding. First, you sacrifice future profits in order to make the film. Selling your film in advance puts you at a negotiating disadvantage. Companies that use presale strategies often give away much of the upside cash flow and profit potential from hit movies. Second, not all paper is bankable. You have to do a lot of research before accepting this kind of contract. Things change quickly, particularly in difficult economic times.

U.S. Film Incentives

Federal Film Incentive

In 2004, Congress passed the American Jobs Creation Act. Section 181 of that act provides for an incentive for film and television productions. Attorney Hal "Corky" Kessler of Deutsch, Levy & Engel has contributed the following explanation of the incentive (and the Jump Start Act). Under Section 181 of The American Jobs Creation Act, 2004, any taxpayer, company, or individual who invests in a qualifying film or television project under the act can deduct 100 percent of the investment as a loss in the year or years the money is spent. Regardless of budget, filmmakers can take advantage of the first $15 million (or $20 million in specific depressed areas). For television, it is either $15 or $20 million per episode for the maximum of 44 episodes. The triggering effect is when the money is spent.

On February 9, 2007, under the IRS temporary rules and regulations, the IRS answered many of the outstanding questions and concerns. It stated that Section 181 deductions may be taken only by the owner of a production, including pass through entities, who received investments from investors. The investors, who had no active participation in the production or were not a part of the production company, could only take their loss under Section 181 as a passive loss and not against ordinary income. The IRS temporary rules and regulations also stated, for the first time, that all contingent compensation, (residual or otherwise), when paid became part of the production budget.

Section 181 said that each qualified film or television project can expense out to the taxpayer investors an amount up to a maximum of $15,000,000 per film or $20,000,000 per film if a significant amount is filmed or paid in a low-income state. In television, the amount allowed to be expensed out to the taxpaying investors is up to a maximum of $15,000,000 or $20,000,000 per episode for up to 44 episodes. The original act was extended twice with the last extension ending in December 2011. The incentive still applies for any films that were qualified through appropriate methods before the Act expired. Any buyer of a certified 181 film project, wherein the copyright and all intellectual property is transferred to the buyer, can now receive new 181 benefits for the amount paid for and any finishing funds.

In May 2012, Congressman David Drier introduced a bill into the House of Representatives (H.R. 5793) "to amend the Internal Revenue Code of 1986 to extend the election to treat the cost of qualified film and television productions as an expense which is not chargeable to capital account. H.R. 5793 would amend the Internal Revenue Code of 1986 to extend the election to treat the cost of qualified film and television productions as an expense which is not chargeable to capital account." The bill would extend 181 until December 31, 2013. It was referred to the House Ways and Means Committee. With the house bill number, you can track the bill on the Internet. I will post any updates on the book's companion website.

Section 199

In addition to the tax reduction incentives under Section 181, the income received also has some tax reduction opportunities under Code Section 199 which was also added by the Act. Under the manufacturing sections of the Act, film production businesses are considered "manufacturing businesses." From 2010, manufacturing businesses can deduct from their qualified production activities income an amount equal to 9 percent of such income. This deduction may also apply to television productions. For example, if $100 is received after 2010, then the taxable income would be $91. A film could qualify under both sections. However, even if a film does not qualify for income tax benefits under Section 181, the film may be a "qualified film production" pursuant to Section 199 if (a) direct labor and overhead costs incurred within the United States account for 20 percent or more of the total costs of the film, and (b) 50 percent or more of the total cost of the film is spent on services performed in the United States. In addition, expenses incurred in Puerto Rico are allowed to take advantage of Section 199.

State Film Incentives

Currently, 37 states and Puerto Rico have incentives for certain qualified films. The incentives vary from rebates, tax credits for the film company, transferable tax credits (for local individuals/ companies enabling them to deduct all or a portion of their investment in the film), and other refunds of expenses. What line items are covered (salaries, below-the-line production spending) and the amount of the incentives (normally expressed as a percentage of the costs covered) differ from states to state. As states have been very competitive in trying to draw films to their communities, similar legislation is being drawn up in many of the remaining states. In addition, some states have assigned all their money for the next two to three years. If you know in which state(s) you want to film, go to their website to check all the details of the incentives. Print off the files and go over them with your line producer/unit production manager (UPM) and your attorney to see if the fit is good for you. If you aren't familiar with which states have incentives, consult the website of the Association of Film Commissioners International (http://www.afci.org).

A checklist of items to consider:

1. When will the incentive be paid? Most states do an accounting at the end of production before agreeing to a specific dollar amount; therefore, you need to raise your entire budget before you start filming.
2. If bringing crew from another part of the country is necessary, how does that cost mesh with the amount of incentive you hope to receive?
3. What has been the experience of other filmmakers dealing with the state's incentive regulations?

Jump Start Act of 2012

Crowdfunding

On April 5, 2012, the Jump Start Act, 2012, was signed into law. It consists of two distinct sections. The first is the Crowd funding portion. This is Crowd funding as an equity investment. Under the new laws, any new security created like an LLC is considered a new business; and, as such, if you have a Private Placement Memorandum and Limited Liability Documents and you are trying to raise $1 million or less ($2 million is some cases), you can now for the first time in the history of the SEC publicly solicit, market, and advertise your investment documents and investment opportunities. You can have unaccredited investors and accredited investors. For unaccredited investors, the limit is 35 and no investor can give more than the greater of $10,000 or 10 percent of their annual income, whichever is less. However, the investments must go through as SEC approved portal. The SEC is setting up the rules for same and portals must be first authorized by the SEC. When those rules are available, they will be posted on the book's companion website.

New Business

Under another section of the act, there is no dollar limit of the capital raise amount if you offer an investment only to accredited investors. You can publicly solicit, market, and advertise your investment documents and investment opportunities if you have Private Placement Memorandum, Limited Liability Documents and only offer the investment opportunities to accredited investors. The SEC will publish guidelines as to the level of due diligence to confirm the accuracy of any such claimed accreditation.

Negative Pickup

In the days when film companies had more cash, there were many negative pickups. The premise is that a studio or independent production company promises to pay the cost of the film negative (production costs) upon delivery of the completed picture. This agreement is taken to the bank, which then provides cash for production at a discount to the total value of the agreement. A discount is a reduction in the stated value of the note.

The Catch-22 here is that the bank has to believe that the studio or distributor will be able to pay off the loan upon delivery of the film (often a year from the date of the agreement). In the past, this was not as difficult to do as it is now. In the late 1980s, banks could count on the Majors, a few of the mini-Majors, and a very small number of distributors to make good on negative pickups. The entire situation has changed in the past several years. The financial problems of many of the large production companies are well known. In addition, the troubles and, in some cases, complete collapse of many financial institutions have created an even more dismal picture. Nothing can be taken for granted. Although there are still companies that will give you negative pickups, this is not a financing strategy that I would count on. As with distribution deals, show the documents for your negative pickup to a bank to see if the deal is acceptable.

Advantages and Disadvantages

One advantage of negative pickups is that the film is made without giving away a share of the company to someone else. In addition, a negative pickup with a major studio or distributor removes the angst of searching for a distributor.

On the other hand, the standard negative pickup agreement contains two loopholes that favor the distributor. First, the agreement has a built-in escape clause that says, in effect, "You must deliver the film we were promised." Any change in the script, even if it seems minor to you, can cause cancellation of the contract. Second, the contract also states that the finished film has to meet the distributor's standards of quality. Even if the movie is, shot-for-shot, the same as the script, the distributor can always say that the film's quality is not up to standards.

Limited Partnerships

Until the mid-1980s, limited partnerships were all the rage. Subscribers could deduct losses calculated at many times the amount of their original investment; taxwise, therefore, the losses sometimes were more beneficial than making profits. In 1986, the Tax Reform Act removed most of these benefits, however, and now the investors have to pray for successful films.

A limited partnership has two kinds of partners. The general partner has unlimited liability with respect to the obligations of the partnership and is active in management. The general partner chooses the investments and does not have to ask for the advice or agreement of the other partners. The limited partners, who provide all of the capital, share any profits or losses and are not actively involved in management. In addition, their liability is limited to the amount of their investment. Gains and losses flow through directly to the limited partners.

A public limited partnership must be registered with the SEC, and in the case of a public or private limited partnership, there must be a properly prepared prospectus that includes all the facts about the partnership. The overall package should include a business plan (be still, my heart!) and offering with subscription documents.

DO NOT WRITE YOUR OWN LIMITED PARTNERSHIP. In order not to pay attorneys, film producers are fond of cutting and pasting someone else's partnership agreement. I think I just emphasized that this is a bad idea. When it comes to fraud, working with unofficial documents is only one aspect. Any misrepresentation about the company's plans also constitutes fraud. The SEC and the Internal Revenue Service are not known for their sense of humor, and ignorance is not an acceptable defense.

Advantages and Disadvantages

On the plus side, the limited partners have no right to interfere with the creative process. Private placements provide a means to raise funds from multiple investors without having to negotiate different deals with each one. The subscription documents contain all the deal information.

There are disadvantages as well. Because of the complicated nature of all SEC regulations and the differences between public and private offerings, participating in one of these formats requires research and expert advice from an attorney. The law is complex, and ignoring any filing regulation (each state has its own requirements) may bring an order for you to cease and desist in your sale of the offering. Another disadvantage is that the producer or the purchase representative must have a previous relationship with the investor before approaching her with a specific offering.

Limited Liability Companies

In the past few years, a new financial structure, the LLC has become widely used. LLCs are a hybrid combination of the partnership and corporate structures. They are an attractive alternative to partnerships and corporations because the LLC provides limited personal liability to the investors, who are referred to as "members." They have a share in the profits as outlined in the offering document.

The LLC also provides a single level of tax. In the standard limited partnership, general partners (read "filmmakers" here) have personal liability for partnership debts, whereas limited partners in an LLC have no personal liability. Theoretically, the worst thing that happens is that they lose their investment. In addition, the limited partners cannot participate in management without jeopardizing their limited liability status.

In addition, an LLC member can participate in the entity's management without risking loss of limited liability. For federal tax purposes, the LLC generally is classified as a partnership. The same is true in most states—the operative word here being "most." I have clients who have formed an LLC in Michigan, for example, but not in Florida, where the LLC is taxed as a corporation. As there is no uniformity in the LLC statutes across states, creating an LLC with members in more than one state may be complicated.

The same rule that I stated for limited partnerships exists here: DO NOT WRITE YOUR OWN. Can I say that too often? From what I have seen, the answer is a resounding "No!" When you hire an attorney, however, be sure that he is someone with experience with both film and the particular form of Investor Offering that you are using. You do not want to pay for an attorney's learning experience.

When pass-through of revenue is of primary concern, strict conformance to IRS and state revenue accounting criteria should be considered before the LLC is chosen over other organizational structures. With new tax credit schemes (both state and federal) appearing on a regular basis, you also may need to consult with a CPA familiar with IRS statements.

Austin- and Los Angeles-based attorney Michael Norman Saleman prefers the limited partnership structure to limited liability companies (see later in this chapter). As he explains:

> *The reasons that I prefer the limited partnership to the LLC have to do with the fact that the law does not adequately protect the LLC Member investors by limiting them to their investment as the total amount of their potential losses, as it does for the limited partner investors in a limited partnership. For example, California law creates personal liability for LLC members if the LLC "veil" of protection is pierced, in the same manner as a corporation. That cannot happen to a limited partner. Also, there is nothing in the law that separates the control of the business from the managers and the members in the LLC as it does between the general partner and the limited partners in a limited partnership. In a limited partnership, should the limited partners attempt to involve themselves in the day-to-day operations of the*

partnership (i.e., production of the film), they would, by law, run the risk of assuming unlimited liability. With this safeguard in place, the producer may make the picture without having to worry about investor interference or attempts to wrest the production from the producers.

The LLC has become one of the most favored business structures for independent film investment. Producers frequently set up their own production companies separately as closely held corporations in which investors do not participate. LLCs are a hybrid combination of the partnership and corporate structures. The LLC is an attractive alternative to partnerships and corporations because the LLC provides limited personal liability to the investors who are referred to as "members." The LLC owns all distribution rights to the film, and investors have a share in the profits as outlined in the offering document. The LLC also provides a single level of tax like a partnership, however, unlike a formal partnership the filmmakers as managers of the LLC have no personal liability for business debts. The worst case for investors is the loss of their investment but there is no liability for any business debts. Limited partner investors cannot participate in management without jeopardizing their limited liability status, but if an investor becomes a manager, the member can participate in the entity's management without loss of limited liability. For federal tax purposes, the LLC may elect at the time of its formation to be treated as either a corporation or a partnership. Most states afford the same tax treatment to an LLC as its federal status. The operative word here is "most." As there is no uniformity in LLC statutes across states, creating an LLC with members in more than one state may be complicated.

The same rule that I stated for limited partnerships is applicable to the formation of an LLC. DO NOT CREATE YOUR OWN. The Operating Agreement for an LLC, which governs its business operations, is a complex document far more complicated than simply filing basic Articles of Organization and must be drafted with the assistance of legal counsel and often accounting advice.

Being Fair to Your Investors

When people invest in an LLC or a limited partnership, there is a payback schedule that is agreed to by both the filmmaker and investors. The investment agreements that are included in the financing package include the budget that you have prepared. Production Attorney and Producer William L. Whitacre of Orlando, whose clients include Haxan Films (*The Blair Witch Project*) Company, says:

> In a limited liability company investors are passive; however, once the investment structure is determined and funds have been accepted, there can be no change in that structure, since doing so would dilute the interests of the initial investors. Accordingly, it is extremely important to budget accurately in the beginning, and to establish an investment structure that will get you to the finish line (including postproduction and completion of an answer print or master) before accepting investment funds into a limited liability company, since your only alternative to raise additional capital would be to sell your own Producer's shares.

BANK LOANS

Bank loans are not associated with business plans per se. However, this discussion focuses on what you will tell potential investors, and bank financing may be relevant to your situation.

Banks are in the business of renting money for a fee. They have no interest in the brilliance of your potential films; they do not care that you are a nice person and have a sparkling reputation. By law, commercial banks (the ones that give you checking accounts) can only lend money based on measurable risk, and the only credit they can take is the collateral, or the assets being offered to secure the loan. The contracts that have already been discussed—negative pickups, distribution agreements, and presales—are such collateral (assets offered to offset the bank's risk). The bank does not have to worry about when you deliver the film or how the box office performs; it is the distributor who has that worry.

The cost of the loan is tied to the prime rate, which is the rate of interest that banks pay to borrow from the Federal Reserve. It is a floating number that may fluctuate significantly. Home lending rates, also based on the prime rate, are a good example. When the prime rate falls, everyone rushes to refinance their mortgages. In most commercial lending, loans to "low-risk" firms (e.g., major studios) can be 0.5 to 1 percent above the prime rate. On the other hand, a small production company, which represents a higher risk, would pay up to 3 percent above prime. Let's say that the bank is going to charge 2 percent points above prime and that prime is 9 percent. The total would be 11 percent. On a $1-million loan, therefore, the bank removes $110,000 ($1 million multiplied by 0.11). To hedge their risk, the bank also retains another 1 or 2 percent in case the prime rate goes up. If the bank charges 1 percent, another $10,000 is added to their retained amount. Now you are down to $880,000 for the film. The bank is not through with you yet, however. It also charges you for its attorneys' fees, which can range from $15,000 for a simple contract to six figures if several companies are involved. Of course, you will still have to pay your own legal fees.

Once again we come back to the subject of attorneys. The one who represents you must know the ins and outs of all these contracts, so you should hire an experienced entertainment attorney. Costs go up drastically if your attorney is charging you an hourly rate to learn how the entertainment industry works. General corporate attorneys may mean well, but they can be an expensive choice.

Advantages and Disadvantages

The first advantage of bank loans is that the producer is not personally liable for the loan; the bank can't take your house. A company is established for the production of the film, which is its only asset. In addition, many producers prefer to pay back a loan rather than give up equity. On the down side, the process to obtain a loan is expensive, and several parties and miles of paperwork are involved. Also, if the distributor defaults on the loan, the bank takes possession of the film.

COMPLETION GUARANTORS

Misunderstood by neophyte filmmakers is the role of the completion guarantor. This is not the person you go to for the rest of your production money; the guarantor's role is to provide an assurance that the film will be completed and delivered to the distributor. The contract with the producer or distributor allows the guarantor to take over the film to complete it, if need be. For the bond itself, the guarantor charges a fee based on the film's budget. The charges have been flexible over the past few years, depending on the state of the completion business. The bond is not issued until after funding is in place, however, and this fact is often difficult to explain to investors. To make matters worse, small films have trouble getting bonded anyway. The risk is too great for most guarantors to bond low-budget films. In the past few years, several of the biggest bond companies lost their financing from insurance companies when high-budget films failed. The active companies had their hands full with major productions, leaving them little time or inclination to consider your $1-million film. New companies have come into the market, making the completion bond more accessible for some smaller films. However, their staying power depends on the insurance companies that back them.

In many business plans for low-budget films, I no longer mention a bond, as I know they have no chance of getting one. Bonders seem to be constantly going in and out of the market and changing their requirements. Check the market before deciding what to say in your business plan. One suggestion is that you say you will "seek" a bond. If you say that you "intend" to get a bond, it implies a promise to the investor. Never promise what you don't already have, whether it is a financial document, an actor, or a director.

A completion bond is always desirable to protect both you and your investors financially. Accidents and bad weather can happen, but investors have the right to decide what exposure they want to have. As always, honesty is the best policy with your investors and yourself.

INTERNATIONAL INVESTORS

We hear a lot about European and Japanese investments in the American film community. In the early to mid-1990s, most of the foreign money went to studios or the formation of large production companies with experienced studio executives; $100 million was a favorite start-up amount. From the late 1990s to 2002, German investment funds grew like crazy. Investors looking for prestige, profits, and extraordinary tax breaks began funding as much big-budget output as they could. Some funds existed to fund studio films; others financed independent companies, such as the UK firm Intermedia (*Iris, K-19: The Widowmaker, The Quiet American*). As some high-budget films failed and the economy started to collapse worldwide, many of these funds closed. However, new ones came along to take their place. Any detail presented here would be out of date before you bought the book.

Generally, this money doesn't go to novice filmmakers. In tracking foreign money, you often run into finders who claim to have a special relationship with foreign money. Some do, many do not. Remember to check these people out. A finder should be paid a percentage of the money you receive from the investor, and only after the cash is in your bank account, as in any interaction with an intermediary. And, at the beginning of this journey, ask how many people there are between the finder and the money. If that person is going through two other people to obtain the money, have them agree to split one fee. For example, if your finder's fee is 5 percent, then all three split that money; otherwise, you are paying 15 percent in finders' fees. Naturally, this is always your choice. But don't get backed into a corner to pay out three times what you intended simply because you didn't get the facts straight upfront. And I can't stress enough, *do not* give them any money in advance.

International Coproductions

International coproduction deals are the result of treaty agreements between countries. Qualifying films are permitted to benefit from various government incentives provided by the country in which production will take place. However, coproduction agreements are not a charity event. A number of requirements may be imposed on the film by government treaty, including the following:

- The producer must be a resident of the host country.
- A certain percentage of above-the-line talent must come from the host country.
- A certain percentage of the technical crew must be residents of that country.
- Distribution must be done by a company located in the host country.
- A percentage of the revenues from the film must remain in that country.

Advantages and Disadvantages

The first advantage of coproduction is that the total budget may be smaller because of the advantages of filming in a cheaper locale. Second, because of the readjusted budget, you will have to find a smaller amount of hard cash. The right deal will cover most, if not all, of your below-the-line costs. Many films would still be only a gleam in the producer's eye if part of the actual cash burden had not been removed by a coproduction deal. In terms of disadvantages, you will still need to have hard cash for the above-the-line payroll—that is, the cast, director, writer, and production office staff. No film is made without these people, and they will not take IOUs, although some take deferred salaries. Another disadvantage is that finding enough skilled personnel in a host country could be a problem. If you end up having to fly key technical people from the United States to another country, you may end up with a budget burden that offsets the advantages of the coproduction deal.

EUROPEAN FINANCING

This separate section is courtesy of Thierry Baujard, Peacefulfish, a consultancy for financing the content industry in Berlin, Germany.

In Europe, coproduction is the most used option to finance projects within a country or with other countries. The term can be misleading as coproduction can simply be a collaboration between two companies or a collaboration that follows very strict rules that are indicated in an official contract between two or more countries.

This chapter is trying to give some background information and issues on how to develop coproduction financing in Europe for independent producers. Peacefulfish, a consultancy based in Berlin, Germany, can help you better understand the process, identify the right partners to raise the money, and develop the right business and finance plans that will make the most of the coproduction opportunities in Europe.

Coproductions

One way to finance your film is to look for a coproducer. Coproduction means sharing production costs, rights, and profits with another production company either from the same country or from a foreign country. In the case of a foreign country, there are two possible reasons: either the coproducer can access additional funding in the form of public subsidies such as grants, interest-free loans, or tax incentives, or the coproducer offers very low production costs.

If the main goal is to access public funding in the foreign territory, then there needs to be a coproduction agreement or a treaty between your country and the foreign one. Regarding Europe, there are two types of agreements to keep in mind: the European convention and bilateral treaties.

European Convention on Cinematographic Production

Note that the Council of Europe (COE) is *not* the European Union (EU)/European Commission; these are two completely different organizational entities.)

The European Convention aims to support European coproduction by enabling a film production to benefit from all national supports available through the participating producers. There have to be at least three established producers from different countries. Only these countries are relevant, which have ratified the Convention. If a producer from a nonmember country is involved, her contribution must not be more than 30 percent of the total budget.

Public Subsidies

In Europe, subsidies are playing a key role in film production. There are state-funded grants on three levels: the European level (provided by the EU and the COE), national level, and regional level. Subsidies have to be applied for and are granted if a project is approved by a board or commission depending on business and creative criteria.

European Level

At the European level, there are two relevant schemes: the MEDIA 2007 program (EU, duration 2007 to 2013) and EURIMAGES (Council of Europe). The EU is a community of currently European member states that collaborate to a level where some national sovereignty is handed over to EU bodies in order to make democratic decisions on specific matters of joint interest. The COE is an organization of currently European states that aims at increasing the awareness of a European identity and providing control and monitoring for human rights and democratic processes. The COE has no legislative powers.

The MEDIA 2007 program supports the audiovisual industry in Europe in the areas of training, development, distribution, promotion, and cinematographic festivals. For aspiring filmmakers, the areas of interest are mainly support for development. To be eligible for support, the applying company has to be registered in a country that participates in the MEDIA program. Currently, the MEDIA 2007 program has 32 members. The scheme could therefore also work for non-European companies in case they enter into coproduction with an eligible company. Apart from geographical eligibility, there are also requirements regarding the existence of the applying company (registered for at least 12 months) and proof of previous experience. However, there are no specific requirements of a company's turnover or profit. The amount of support granted can be up to 50 percent or even 60 percent of a part of the budget, depending on the kind of support and the respective threshold. For application forms as well as more information and deadlines, visit the EU's MEDIA website at http://ec.europa.eu/.

EURIMAGES is a funding program initiated by the Council of Europe aiming to support coproduction, distribution, and exhibition of European cinematographic works. Support is divided between coproduction, distribution, and exhibition for feature films, documentaries, and animation projects of at least 70 minutes in length. To be eligible for coproduction support, the project needs at least two producers from different EURIMAGES member states and has to have a European origin. Financially that means that at least 51 percent of the funding has to derive from EURIMAGES member states and no more than 30 percent of the funding can originate from non-European sources or one non-EURIMAGES country. For filmmakers outside EURIMAGES member countries, this means that the program becomes only of interest in the case of minority a coproduction. For more information, visit http://www.coe.int/Eurimages.

National Level and Regional Levels

Throughout Europe, most countries and many regions within the countries provide state support for the audiovisual industry. Foreign filmmakers can benefit from these support schemes through being part of a coproduction with one or more of these countries. If the participating countries have agreements with one another, national subsidies are accessible for international coproductions as well. In the following, different schemes are outlined based on their support budget, eligibility and selection criteria, funding aspects, and recoupment strategies. As with the U.S. state incentives, these change too frequently to detail in the book. You can use the Internet for up-to-date information. However, I would suggest working with a consultant like Peacefulfish to understand the complexities in each deal.

Banking

Only the five big European countries have developed film banking markets: France, Germany, United Kingdom, Spain, and Italy. The main film banking services that are provided are Interim Finance, Tax-Incentive Financing, Gap Financing, Working Capital/ Corporate Finance, and Bank Guarantee. On a European level, there is a development, which sees the European Investment Bank getting involved in film financing. So far, it is active in France, but support for specialized banks in other European countries is possible.

WHAT YOU NEED TO KNOW

Before looking at an example with some numbers, here is a list of questions you may like to consider when looking at coproductions:

1. Where is the main production company located? If you are located in the United States, consider coproducing with Canada, since Canada has a range of agreements with European countries.
2. Is your country part of a bilateral agreement of a European country or member of the European Convention on Cinematographic Production?
3. Is your country part of the EU?
4. Has your country signed the EURIMAGES agreement?
5. Are there national subsidies in your country?
6. Are there regional subsidies in your country?
7. Are there tax incentives in your country?

8. Are there broadcasters involved in presales or coproduction in your country?
9. Are there banks specialized in film financing in your country?
10. Which countries are most promising in entering into a coproduction with (choose your candidates and go through the previous questions for each of them)?

CASE STUDY OF A FICTIONAL FILM

Our fictional film project involves four production companies from France, Germany, Canada, and the United States. The budget is EUR 4 million. As in every coproduction, be it national or international, involved companies have to decide on their individual share of rights, territories, profits, recoupment positions, revenue corridors, etc. In a traditional coproduction, the coproducer from a certain country normally received the rights for that particular country and neighbor countries using the same language. The coproducer can also look for distribution (theatrical and TV) in the country.

France and Germany both have a bilateral agreement with Canada and are members of the European Convention on Cinematographic Production. The bilateral agreements and the convention secure the same option: to benefit from the coproducing countries' national supports. But if the convention is applied, the share of the total budget (and thus shares of rights, profits, etc.) for the United States and Canada can only be up to 30 percent (EUR 1.2 million). Through the coproduction treaty, you will be able to access funding from the other country.

That might not be enough considering the efforts such a multi-international production causes. However, even under the bilateral agreements with European countries, the obligation is that the majority needs to be held by European producers.

France and Germany are both part of the EU as well as members of EURIMAGES and are thus eligible for European subsidies. Both have national and regional subsidies. France has a tax shelter and two tax credits. Germany has the German Federal Film Fund. Both countries have cultural tests linked with their subsidies. The German-French broadcaster "arte" could be involved in presales or coproductions. France and to a lesser degree Germany have banks involved in film financing.

This is only a very rough idea of the complexity of international coproductions. There are extensive rules and obligations for each country referring to each financing tool. Due to local spend, majority requirements and cultural relevance finance might not be as easy to get as it seems at first glance. Many funds on a national level are selective aids; however, this can also be an advantage for producing in Europe since funding is not primarily aimed at commercial projects.

In addition, there are excellent production facilities and professional staff capacities available in Central Europe for a fraction of the price of the ones in established countries. If you are going to produce in or with Europe, it will be wise to get some professional help in dealing with the business plan, the financing strategy, and the legal aspects involved, as well as to benefit from an already established network of contacts in the European film industry.

For more information, please log on to http://www.pecefulfish.com or contact thierry@peacefulfish.com.

WHAT DO YOU TELL INVESTORS?

A section on financing assumptions is required as part of your business plan package. Give investors only relevant information, not everything in this chapter. Based on the assumption that your readers are not film sophisticates, you should explain what constitutes a presale agreement, a negative pickup, or whatever form of financing you will pursue. Be prepared to answer investors' questions.

They may ask you about the forms of financing that you have not included. You should be conversant enough with the pros and cons of various strategies to explain your choices intelligently. As mentioned earlier, it is unproductive to include financing methods that you do not plan to use. If you plan to use a limited partnership, for example, the business plan will be part of the offering; otherwise, there is no reason to discuss this form of financing. To do so would be to create a red herring for investors, confusing them with a nonexistent choice.

Along the same lines, you should be careful about considering options that may no longer exist. What Canada or Australia is doing in 2006 may not be relevant in 2008 or later. Financing patterns, like everything else in our culture, can be in or out of vogue from year to year. It is important to keep current with the business climate through the trades and other sources while writing your plan.

In Chapter 13, we discuss more about investors, who they are and what they want. As stated above, filmmakers share their investor experiences with you; however, let me share with you the words of one of them, Jay Spain, now. *Do your homework!*

10

The Financials: Forecasting While Keeping One Foot on Earth

It is a capital mistake to theorize before one has data.
—SHERLOCK HOLMES TO DR. WATSON

BEING IN THE PREDICTION BUSINESS

Nostradamus has become well known due to his dire predictions about December 21, 2012. If you are reading this book, we probably neither haven't been hit by a comet (or other fireball) nor has there been anarchy and World War III. As with predictions by other seers, there have been predictions by Nostradamus that have turned out to be completely wrong or totally misinterpreted. When I first started in the film business, several accountants insisted that I couldn't predict the future. I said, "Yes, but it is a lot of fun trying."

Then why do we do it? No one can afford to run a country, school, or film business without looking ahead. Whether you are planning one film or a slate, only when you have a clear picture of future results can you proceed with a feeling of confidence. In the past 150-plus years since moving images were shown with zoetropes, little has changed except the technology and net profits. In the beginning, there was no sound. Now actors talk, and we have 3D.

For filmmakers, predicting the revenue and costs associated with films to be made is a necessity. As long as you have a good rationale, you can't let fear stand in the way. Will you be right?

Chances are that audiences, critics, and other forces out of your control will interfere. Yet you need to have a rational basis for going ahead with the project and asking other people for money. This chapter reviews how to find data, what to do with it after you find it, and how to create your own financial forecasts.

Students often object to even looking up box office grosses for a class assignment. Their idea of a business plan is a synopsis of their film and, possibly, an idea of who wants to see it. Although important, these items are the given quantities on one side of the equation for estimating revenues and costs. Remember the investors? They are going to read the Executive Summary first and then go quickly to the financials. Money is the glue that holds these building blocks together.

A filmmaker recently asked me whether all my business plans showed films making a profit. The short answer is "Yes." Before investors hand over hard cash, they want to believe that your project will be profitable. A Mark Twain quote that I used to use at the beginning of this chapter is, "Get your facts: then distort them as you please." In rethinking the quote, I became concerned about the phrase "as you please." Partially, this is true. However, keep in mind that whatever the forecast, it has to look reasonable to "the person who has the gold."

Forecasting is an art, albeit not a precise one. Sophisticated business writers like to say that the one sure thing about a prediction is that it will be wrong; they are probably right. The value of a forecast is as a guide for making decisions; the better informed the forecaster, the closer to actual events the forecast will be. By researching history, obtaining the best data possible, looking for relationships among the data you find, and making assumptions about the future based on those relationships, you hopefully have a rational basis for your forecasts.

When writing your business plan, you have to decide which group of numbers tells your story best. The most recent data may be a year or two behind because of the flow of revenues. Rather than putting whatever spin on these statistics appeals to you, a few more years of historical information is needed. Remember our discussions about investors in the previous chapter? They value two things most of all: facts and common sense. Your goal is to show that the independent film market is robust and that profits can be made.

Anyone Can Do It

There is no mystery to forecasting revenues and expenses. You do not have to be an accountant or hold an MBA. You do not need previous knowledge of trend and regression analysis or internal rate of return. This jargon is used by financial whiz kids to speak to one another; life can go on without it. You can take numbers from the most credible sources and create projections that look feasible. You will take the elements that seem to influence the outcome of a film—genre, stars, director, distribution, revenues, and costs—and analyze how much you think each will influence the resulting revenue. The only math skills you will need are adding, subtracting, multiplying, and dividing, as well as an elementary understanding of ratios. Mix these skills with some good judgment and you have a forecast. If you can balance your checkbook, you can create a forecast.

FINDING THE DATA

What Are Comparative Films?

Forecasting requires that you use films that reasonably can be compared by theme, budget, and release date. Due to inflation, audience tastes, numbers of screens, and other film business trends, the industry standard has been five to seven years including the current one. I have always used the five most previous years plus the current year.

What makes a comparative (comp) film is a combination of factors. First of all, making an independently financed film does not mean that you can only use independent films. For low budgets, most of the films within a reasonable budget range are likely to be the only ones available. If you were making a film like *Knowing*, for example, with a budget of $37 million, it is likely that a majority of your comparative films will have been made by studios.

Secondly, what is a reasonable budget range? With a $2-million budget, I would like all comp films to be at $8 million or below on the high side. To find enough films, however, you may have to move the upper limit of budgets that you are using. In recent years, I have had to go to $10 million depending on the genre of the film. Nevertheless, as talented as you may be, don't use a $15 million film in this comparison. Production quality and cast become more important the higher you go.

With the advent of digital film, the concept of having a budget that includes a transfer to 35 mm is important. I have found it is often difficult for filmmakers to comprehend. At this point, of course, there aren't enough films to compare. As discussed earlier in the book, despite the number of digital screens, all the profitable low-budget films that I have found were released theatrically in both digital and 35 mm. What if you are shooting on 16 mm film? What will your film look like when it is transferred to other formats and shown on the big screen? When comparing your film to other movies, remember that the audience doesn't care what technical format you used to make the film, they care about what the film looks like and who is in it.

On a statistical basis, I feel that at least four to five films per year are required over the three years for which worldwide data are available. (Different assumptions that apply to documentaries, animated films, and large format are discussed in Chapter 12, "Breaking the Rules." In 2012, for example, those years are from 2008 to 2010.) Now that you have decided your time span and budgets, you can then start looking for films that fit.

Matching Your Film

Do they all have to be just like your film? Films can be similar in genre and subthemes; however, it is unlikely that at any budget you will find 15 films "just like yours." After all, your film is going to be unique. Therefore, start with your overall genre. You may have a crime drama. The film also could have action, romance, gay themes, coming-of-age, or a host of other themes.

The goal is to use films that relate to at least one of these. To fill out your list, budget also is a consideration. Since you are likely to be asked by an investor why you used certain films, have a reason for each film that you use. All you can do is your best to have a rationale for each film. There isn't a rule as to what will seem reasonable to a given investor.

The data that you gather about previously released films will serve two purposes: (1) show the profits of films recently released and (2) supply a basis for estimating the revenues *and* total costs for your films. The first part of your numerical story consists of showing what has happened with films that have already been produced and released. You use these examples to build a case for the ultimate success of your film. Select recent films that have a relation to your planned production in terms of genre, budget, or other common factors.

Genre is a common way to group films; however, use whatever characteristic you feel links these films together. But whatever your rationale for grouping films, use budget clusters that make sense. The films you include in your business plan depend on what is available. It is your choice whether to include films that have lost money. There is no database that includes all the films ever made, so you can't have a "fair" sampling no matter what you do. However, if you use only three films with extraordinary results—for example, *Paranormal Activity, Saw V*, and *The Devil Inside*—any projection you are being unrealistic. Your predictions will be recognized as such by most investors. Of course, with those films, you can't use *Avatar*, either. What is that? You think it not only doesn't relate in budget but in genre, also. You would be surprised at the comparatives I see in the business plans that filmmakers ask me to critique.

Recently, I did a business plan for a $3 million-thriller film. I went to http://www.proimdb.com and used the "power search" feature to look for thriller films released between January 2008 and December 2010. A list of 2,952 films came up. Of the films that were less than $10 million in budget, many had either no U.S. box office or one that was too minimal to use. There were two films that I felt I could use for forecasting in this particular business plan. I could use the higher budgeted films in the Markets section, where you can use a film of the same genre regardless of budget. For the comps, though, there still were crime and romantic drama films that were reasonable (notice how often that word pops up) to use, as the story lines and budget ranges fit this particular movie.

Where Do You Find Information?

The first step is to see what films you will want to use. I always use proimdb. The site is the best way to search for likely films by genre and keywords. For example, Crime is a genre and murder is a keyword. At the moment, the sites annual cost of $124.95 is small compared to the information you can find. It is the best way to know what films might be available.

Once you have picked the films you want, including budgets can be another question. Hopefully, most of the films you will know the budgets from the same source. Often you have to go to other sites. Since I recommend checking the total box office grosses at boxofficemojo.com, I would look there first. Otherwise, check for interviews with filmmakers and reviews in the public press. For current films, check television and radio shows for the appearance of a filmmaker. They often appear on the daytime and evening news and talk shows to promote their films. The film festivals are another place where you can gather extensive financial information. Many producers and directors of independent films attend and they will usually answer questions about not only the cost of their films, but also the source of their financing. People often feel more comfortable about revealing proprietary data when face-to-face.

Much has changed since the last edition of this book. Both *Variety* and *The Hollywood Reporter* websites used to be free to search. *THR* was sold, and you need a subscription to do extensive searching. *Daily Variety* data were subscription only, free and then behind a pay wall again. Currently, *Variety* is up for sale. However, the newer free sites, such as deadline.com and the wrap.com, are full of good information.

For the total domestic box office data, I double check oxofficemojo.com. Since the box office dollars include Canada and Puerto Rico, I refer to the grosses as domestic or North American rather than United States.

Revenues for ancillary dollars, both domestic and foreign and foreign box office, as well as the amount of the prints and ads (P&A) costs are harder to find. If you see this information on the Internet for free, the chances are that it is wrong. You need to have *credible* source for the data to withstand any challenge from an investor. To find all the data you will need for your three years of worldwide numbers, you will need to buy the information. I recommend Baseline (http://www.baselineresearch.com) as the current best source. Go directly to http://www.baselineintel.com. First, you can search to find out which films you want to use are in their database. Then, you can talk to the customer reps there to learn if they have any package deals for buying a group of films. The amount you have to pay is small compared to the amount you want to raise from investors.

In previous editions, I had a separate section for *average foreign revenues*. The section included a table of typical revenues from individual foreign territories for a $1.5-million film. With presales in flux and foreign territories giving more and more screens over to their locally made films, I don't feel it is appropriate to put together such a table at this time. Distributors either are giving very low numbers or saying that there aren't any foreign sales at all for low-budget independent films. As always, the foreign value of any film depends on the story, cash, etc. In addition, the trade papers have been reluctant to estimate such sales since. The trade papers used to have charts of foreign revenue with titles like "The Going Rate" and "Global Revenues." The last of those charts appeared in 2007. Note their names in case they reappear when the world economy gets on a better footing. When I feel there are real numbers, I will include the information on the book's companion website.

If you do use the tables from the trades, the range of likely prices is based on the distributors' experience in selling low-budget films. When forecasting, you always want to be conservative, so you would use the average return of dollars. For example, in Japan, you see that the high is $70,000 and the low is $20,000. This does not mean that all distributors will pay you $70,000; generally, the most they will pay is 10 percent of the budget. Use the average figure, which is $45,000.

You have to go with the best information you can get. Whatever tact you take, heed this warning: **DO NOT INVENT NUMBERS**. If lying does not bother you, getting caught in a lie will. Then the game will be over. If telling the truth isn't reason enough, you may have investors check some of your sources, which will be listed at the bottom of your tables. Or, as I have seen many times, some friend of theirs will claim he saw "something somewhere that was another number." Worse yet, your potential investor may have a relative or friend in the film business who can check the data. All sources will not necessarily have the same information; however, you want to be able to point to your sources as the most credible you could find.

ANALYZING THOSE PESKY NUMBERS

Did I say without fear earlier? You must analyze the data before putting them into your proposal. Be strong. You can do it. When collecting and analyzing, keep in mind another favorite quote from Mark Twain: "There are three kinds of lies: lies, damned lies, and statistics."

The discussion of financing and your presentation of comparative films, projections, and cash flows is the single most important section of your business plan. The filmmaker's job is to be honest and use common sense.

I have said it before, but filmmakers have convinced me that I cannot say it too often. This analysis is your job, not the investor's. Do not expect the investor to accidentally happen upon useful information while browsing through the 15 or 20 pages that you have photocopied or downloaded from a website. It is your duty to find useful information and present it in an easily understandable way.

Tables 11.3 through 11.6 included with the sample business plan (see Chapter 11, "Sample Business Plan") are examples of methods for presenting comparative films. The films listed in these tables are fictional but are based on the results of real films. These sample tables include the following items:

1. *Domestic theatrical rentals:* Domestic rentals are the portion of the North American theatrical box office that reverts back to the distributor (or producer). (The tables in the trades include Canadian box office figures in this total.) There has been confusion in recent years, as we also refer to DVD rentals. The term *domestic theatrical rentals* is the industry standard and should be used. As mentioned earlier, when working with numbers, you should avoid factoring in exceptional movies that would make all your averages too high. If you want to include *Fireproof,* list it and indicate in a footnote that it is in your chart for reference only. Just as on any given day any team can win, it is theoretically possible for any film to be a breakout hit.

2. *Domestic ancillary revenue:* The ancillary revenue includes all nontheatrical sources, such as DVD/Blu-ray, streaming, cable, free television, syndicated television, and pay-per-view. Distributors have been trying various formulations of revenue sharing as opposed to paying per unit. In addition, there are ongoing changes in the newer ancillary forms. However, new standards have not been set, and it is too early to know their effect on independent film. Pay-per-view is growing, although not as quickly as analysts have expected.

Specific numbers do not exist for individual films, so some analysts use a general estimate. Those estimates are derived mostly from studio films, so they are more appropriate for budgets over $15 million than for other films. Although release times (windows) into home video have become shorter for studio films, the windows for indies have remained the same on average. Cable and the premium channels are getting movies sooner than they used to, also. Be aware that although a few of the indie films financed by cable networks have had a U.S. theatrical release, most do not. In the past, PBS has also financed documentaries that have had a theatrical release prior to being shown on television.

3. *Foreign theatrical revenue:* The distributor is responsible for collecting money from other countries. In the United States, the industry assumes that the North American box office drives all the other windows. If a picture does not perform well in U.S. theaters, therefore, all other theatrical and ancillary venues may be worth less money. On the other hand, some films that have only moderate results in the United States do much better overseas. In addition, it is more frequent than earlier for an independent film to be released in either multiple countries at the same time or overseas before the United States.

To make the picture even murkier, there are films that do very well at the domestic box office and in domestic ancillary revenues, but have virtually no foreign revenues that are recorded. Depending on the gross profit of those films, they can still be used. The type of film and the stars often have a lot to do with these results. For example, Tyler Perry's *Madea* films have historically made big profits; however, the databases show little or no foreign revenue for them. On the other hand, certain U.S. television stars whose shows are marketed worldwide are important to filmmakers for the foreign markets. Before making any assumptions about the value of actors, however, it always is good to check with distributors.

4. *Foreign ancillary revenue:* Foreign ancillary presents a great opportunity. Television companies often buy exclusive product. The potential revenues for English-language

films, even small ones, in other countries remain much stronger than for foreign-language films in the United States. Markets have opened up in eastern Europe and Asia. China began to expand the number and types of U.S. films they would accept in 2011. Independent film companies established alliances with Chinese companies. For example, Relativity Media announced a strategic partnership with Huaxia Film Distribution Co. and Sky Land (Beijing) Film-Television Culture Development and, separately, is teaming with SAIF Partners and IDG China Media to launch the first Chinese-American distribution company, Sky Land Entertainment. While its U.S. entity always has made films with studios, Legendary Pictures created the independent Legendary East to work with Huayi Brothers, a Chinese film conglomerate, to make its coproductions. Then in 2012, China's Dalian Wanda Group (DWG) bought the second largest U.S. theater chain AMC Entertainment for $2.6 billion making DWG the world's biggest cinema owner.

5. *Total revenue:* This is rentals plus domestic ancillary plus foreign equal total revenue. The foreign dollars are assumed to have the exhibitor portion removed and, therefore, can be added to the domestic dollars to find total revenue. Always be sure that you are comparing apples to apples.

6. *Negative cost, P&A, and total costs:* We have already discussed finding the production, or negative costs, of the film. These are not the total costs, however. P&A are an important expense. It is necessary to include these costs to get a total profit picture. As films stay in distribution, the P&A costs grow. Therefore, if you are forecasting the initial release cost, indicate it. The most credible source for this type of information is still Baseline.

7. *Gross profit (loss):* Gross profit (loss) equals the revenue minus the direct expenses before the company's operating expenses. In this case, direct expenses are the negative and P&A costs. They relate directly to your film, as compared to the company overhead costs, which exist whether a film is in production or not. Notice the parentheses around the word *loss*. When preparing financial statements, use parentheses rather than minus signs to indicate negative

numbers. Both words can be written on the profit line. However, if there isn't a projected profit, you may want to rethink the whole idea.

FORECASTING WITHOUT FEAR

Now we come to your film. Here are two guidelines for projecting your revenues. First, be conservative. A generally accepted business principle is to forecast your income on the low end and your expenses on the high end. Probably, all filmmakers who have ever done a budget have padded it to be sure that they did not run out of money. You want to take the opposite path for revenues. If you are making a $1-million Indian-themed film, you would be fooling yourself to assume that the film will gross $141 million, as Oscar-winner *Slumdog Millionaire* did. It is nice to aspire to be an Oscar winner, but you can't plan on it.

Second, be honest. As long as the data of your historical films are as accurate as possible and the films you choose are comparable to those you plan to make, you should be all right. The type of comment I've heard most often from filmmakers with an inspirational film is, "Include *The Passion of the Christ* as an average film." Yes, here we are in 2012, and filmmakers with inspirational dramas want to include an extraordinarily successful movie from 2004 in the comparatives. Feel free to discuss it in your analysis as an example of an exceptional result to hold out the brass ring as a hook for the investor.

Assumptions

Before opening a new Excel table, you should write down your assumptions. Unless you have concrete reasons for the forecasted revenues in your tables, people may assume that you invented them. There has to be a thought process leading to these numbers. Since you have just written 15 or 20 pages for the preceding sections, you have already gone through the thought process. In most cases, the crucial elements have already been mentioned, and the list is a recap for your benefit and for the investor's. Do not expect readers to remember the specifics from the body of the business plan; you are not playing a game of hide and seek with the investor.

Explain your assumptions at the end of your Financing section, directly before the tables, to be sure that the reader knows how you came to your conclusions. If you do not do this, it may look like you have no rationale. Review the assumptions in the sample business plan both in the book and the files you have downloaded from the companion website before continuing.

Revenue and Expenses (Income Statement)

The *Projected Income Statements* (Tables 11.7 through 11.9), also known as the Statement of Revenues and Expenses, is the profit statement for each film. Likewise, the *Summary Projected Income Statement* (Table 11.1) indicates the bottom line for the company. In a one-film plan, you will have two tables of comparative films and Table 11.3 will show your net profit.

As I say in a preamble to the sample business plan, whether you are doing a business plan for one film or a company, the methodology is the same. In a one-film plan, you won't have summary tables. In the downloaded files, you will find a complete Financing section for one film using *Len's Big Thrill* from Chapter 11, as well as a sample business plan for one film.

The sample shows a straightforward production company in which all the income is from films. If you are planning to produce other products or have additional divisions, such as direct-to-DVD or distribution, you will need other methodologies and types of tables for those items. You will have to provide separate assumptions and cash flows for those products because they function differently from film. Then make a combined statement that includes all the products. Unless you are a very experienced filmmaker who already has owned a film company, however, I suggest don't diversify yet. Add other divisions after the initial film company is profitable.

Looking at our numbers, you can take the average or the median (the point above and below which half the films fall) of all the films, or you can give more weight to the more recent films. (Do not panic. The "how-to" is contained in the downloaded files.) It depends on whether you feel that the genre is gaining more audience approval or has been drawing the same amount of box office dollars for the past few years. You have to look at the available data and use good judgment.

Note that these tables show worldwide results. As you will not have these for the two most recent years, you want to include a table for each film (Tables 11.4 and 11.6) that shows the box office and budgets only for those years.

The net profit (loss) line is the sum of the company's revenues and expenses. Commonly, the phrase "before taxes" is added to indicate that this is a preliminary income forecast. Do not let these phrases throw you. An accountant can easily prepare these statements for you.

Cash Flow Statement

A cash flow statement shows the timing of incoming revenue and outgoing cash. The dollars will not come in all in one week or one month. Table 11.10 shows the cash flows for the individual films, and the summary is given in Table 11.2. Notice that in the columns for the tables, I have used generic terms—Year 1, Year 2, Year 3, and so on. If you are looking for the production money, your year starts when that money is in the bank. To specify the first year—for example, 2013—could create a problem. What if you are still wandering around two years later looking for money? Finding money and getting the cash in your bank account is hard; no need to announce it to your current prospect.

In addition, each year is further divided into quarters. This seems to make the most sense for showing cash flow. I would shy away from individual months. There is no way to actually track each month. Unless you have the distributor's monthly accounts for various films in front of you, there is no way to track such data accurately. You have to give your investor a readable document, even if you aren't crazy about the idea. Use my formula. I retest it with each new edition.

In the sample cash flow statements, all of the production money is outgoing in Year 1. I have assumed one year from the beginning of production to the end of post-production. (The exceptions in this cash flow scenario are animated and large format films, which are discussed in Chapter 12.) I use six months (two quarters) before I indicate the release of the film.

An independent filmmaker won't know the actual timing in advance, unless she is doing her own distribution. There is no average length of time between end of post-production and the release date for an independent film. Even if you already have a distribution agreement in place, you won't know. (I am making an assumption that vertically integrated companies like Lionsgate and Relativity Media aren't buying this book to find out how to calculate cash flows.) In order to make the table readable, I skip the two quarters before distribution starts and make it clear that the plan is not promising a specific interval. Note there is the following comment at the bottom of the table: "For reference only. How and when monies are actually distributed depends on the contract with the distributor."

The first rentals are shown during the quarter in which distribution begins. Throughout the year, we track domestic grosses week to week to find trends in the number of theaters and the amount of grosses. Going through that exercise will reveal a pattern that you can use. Average release "windows" give you an idea of the money flow from other sources. Most films don't stay in the theaters longer than six months; however, due to some long stays in the theater, I have a small amount of revenue still coming in a third quarter. The median stay for independent films is about four and a half weeks.

We can track when films go into home video but not necessarily how long they are there. In addition, there may be a different method on how the dollars flow back to your distributor, the head of your revenue food chain. Therefore, I have chosen to include them, as the distributor normally does the accounting for money that is owed to the filmmakers and their investors—once a year.

For foreign revenues, all sources are grouped into one number. Not all films are released the same way. Some countries actually legislate the time period; in other cases, the distributor negotiates it. Some films go directly to home video, which is a more popular distribution method in Europe and Asia. Trying to figure this out country by country would be excessive. The timing has been very fluid lately, so it is a good idea to research the topic to keep current. The films go into foreign release in the third quarter of Year 2, approximately seven months after the domestic release date.

The total line is the sum of the incoming cash minus the outgoing cash. Do not panic over minus totals. While your film is being made, there is no revenue. The amount of eventual profit is the deciding factor. In companies, the minus total may last longer than in a one-film plan. As in Table 11.2, depending on how often you plan to start pre-production on the next film, the costs for the next film coming in, as well as the P&A money spent by the distributor may keep a negative number in the cumulative total for several years. In a multipicture company, the cash flow statement allows you to see whether you will have enough money coming in to keep production going.

Overhead (Administrative) Expenses

This table is used only for a business plan with multiple films. In the overhead table (Table 11.11), I have not included specific numbers. It is meant to show you what line items you may have to use. These differ from film to film, city to city, and country to country. While the films are clearly fake, I don't want to take the chance that the reader someone will copy the dollars in my overhead sample. You must research what those costs are in your community. In addition, add anything that is specific for you and leave out line items that don't relate to your film. The total for your overhead expenses is then adjusted by the net profits for each of your films.

An ongoing company has its past history to report, along with a statement of its present position. Your accountant will do the serious reports for you, such as Sources and Uses of Funds, Balance Sheet, and so on. These go into your Financing section along with the other tables. As new companies have less to report, don't worry. Just report what there is. There may or may not be a bank account worth mentioning. Present information that must be included in the business plan, even for a very small company.

If you are setting up a company, you will have ongoing expenses, far less than those of the studios, of course. These general administrative costs include salaries that are not attributable to a specific film budget as well as all of the company's tools of the trade—office equipment, telephone charges, entertainment costs, and so on. Your company may have fewer people or no salaried employees at all. Before Year 1, there are generally start-up expenses. You may rent an office, option a script, buy a computer, or scout locations in the Dardanelles. Any expenses that are necessary to get your company going are shown in this table. Even if you wait for investment funds before doing any start-up, list these costs separately. Some of them—like the computer—are one-time costs.

Like everything else, administrative costs are projected over the time period of the business plan. Look ahead to the number of films that you plan to make three or four years down the road. You may need additional office staff, more office space, or increased development money. Everyone knows that these numbers are guesstimates; however, as a general rule, you should include all the expenses you can think of. On the other hand, do not give yourself a salary of $1 million. I see this item in a lot of companies that never get funded. Because you are partners with the investor, your salary should be moderate.

What If I Have Only One Film?

No matter how often I mention it in the book, filmmakers often don't understand that the biggest difference between doing a one-film plan and a slate of films is more films and tables. A one-film plan has the same text sections with perhaps less text in each one. As a filmmaker (producer, director), you are the manager of a small company. The other big difference is that any expenses need to be in the budget of the film rather than a separate overhead. Don't overburden this poor film with your car and house payments. Include only those things that belong in a film budget. You will be splitting those massive (let's be positive) profits with your investors.

The layout is the same for one film as for multiple films, but fortunately you have less number crunching. Your first table will be comparative films for the past three years (or four if you need them) for which you have worldwide numbers. Your second table will be the two years for which you only have U.S. box office and budgets. Then you have an income statement (without the overhead) and a cash flow statement, which will be similar to any of the individual films in the sample business plan.

THE NEXT STEP

Review Chapter 1, "The Executive Summary," and then study the sample business plan in Chapter 11. Work through the sample in the downloaded files from the companion website. Feel free to use this format as a guide in writing your own plan.

Have fun, and good luck!

Sample Business Plan for a Fictional Company

The sample business plan in this chapter shows the forecasts and cash flows for a company planning to produce three films. Due to space considerations, it is not practical to include separate business plans for both a single film and a company plan. They both follow the same format, but with some modifications. All of the costs for a one-film plan should be included in the budget, and summary tables are not necessary. Of course, the reader also has to modify the text that is shown in the book to relate to one film. For more information and detail on how to create the forecasts and cash flow, please refer to the "Financial Worksheet Instructions" on the companion website for this book.

Table 11.11 has the format for an overhead table. It is only meant to show some of the line items that you need to consider and has no data to match the Company Overhead numbers in Table 11.1. Not all companies will need all the line items, and some may have more. In addition, the place that the filmmaker lives and/or is filming will make a difference in the specifics for each expense. For example, rent in New York will not be the same as rent in Missoula or Berlin. One-film plans do not have an overhead table, as all your expenses are in the budget.

If you plan on accessing a state or country film incentive, include it after the section on Strategy but *before* Financial Assumptions. Tax incentives for films are not included in the sample business plan. Whether in the United States or other countries, incentives change on a regular basis. In some cases, they may be discontinued altogether or simply run out of funds to apply for after a period of time. Be sure to tell investors to check with their own tax advisors to see how a specific incentive would affect them. In addition, do not subtract potential incentives from your total budget. In the case of most U.S. state incentives and many of those in other countries, there is an accounting done by the governing body at the end of production before the actual dollars are awarded. The statement that you qualify for an incentive is not a guarantee on the amount of money you will receive.

CRAZED CONSULTANT PRODUCTIONS

THE BUSINESS PLAN

CONTROLLED COPY

Issued to: _____

Issue Date: _____

Copy No.: _____

For Information Contact:

Louise Levison

Crazed Consultant Productions

c/o Business Strategies

4454 Ventura Canyon Ave. #305

Phone: 818-990-7774

TABLE OF CONTENTS

1 / THE EXECUTIVE SUMMARY

Strategic Opportunity

- North American box office revenues in 2011 were $10.2 billion
- Revenues for independent films in 2011 were $3.4 billion, or 34 percent of the total North American box office
- Worldwide revenues from all sources for North American independent films were over $9 billion in 2011
- Worldwide box office revenues for 2011 were $32.6 billion
- The overall filmed entertainment market is projected to reach $45.1 billion in the United States in 2013 and $102.2 billion worldwide

The Company

Crazed Consultant Productions (CCP) is a startup enterprise engaged in the development and production of motion picture films for theatrical release. The first three films will be based on the *Leonard the Wonder Cat* books by Jane Lovable. CCP owns options on all three with two books already in print and a third currently being written. The books have sold 25 million copies in 12 countries. The movies based on Lovable's series will star Leonard, a half-Siamese, half-American shorthair cat, whose adventures make for entertaining stories, and each of which includes a learning experience. The movies are designed to capture the interest of the entire family, building significantly on an already established base. CCP expects each film to stand on its own as a story.

The Company plans to produce three films over the next five years, with budgets ranging from $500,000 to $10.0 million. At the core of CCP are the founders, who bring to the Company successful entrepreneurial experience and in-depth expertise in motion picture production. The management team includes President and Executive Producer Ms. Lotta Mogul, Vice President/CFO Mr. Gimme Bucks, and Producer Ms. Ladder Climber.

The Films

Leonard's Love: Natasha and her cat Leonard leave the big city to live in a small town, where they discover the true meaning of life.

Len's Big Thrill: Leonard charms the director during Natasha's audition for a movie and becomes a bigger star than Uggie the dog.

Cat Follies: His movie career gone, Leonard takes up professional ice skating. Discovered by a movie mogul, he is once again on top as a movie star.

The Industry

The future for low-budget independent films continues to look impressive, as their commercial viability has increased steadily over the past decade. Recent films, such as *My Big Fat Siamese*, *Cat Surfers*, and *My Week with Phoebe*, are evidence of the strength of this market segment. The independent market as a whole has expanded dramatically in the past 15 years, while the total domestic box office has increased 80 percent. At the 2005 through 2009 Academy Awards, four of the five films nominated for the Best Picture Oscar were independently financed. Technology has dramatically changed the way films are made, allowing independently financed films to look and sound as good as those made by the Hollywood studios, while remaining free of the creative restraints placed upon an industry that is notorious for fearing risks. Widely recognized as a "recession-proof" business, the entertainment industry has historically prospered even during periods of decreased discretionary income.

The Markets

Family films appeal to the widest possible market. Films such as the *Tweetie Bird* films, *Me and My Doberman*, and *My Big Fat Siamese* have proved that the whole family will go to a movie that they can see together. For preschoolers, there are adorable animals, while tweens and teens get real-life situations and expertly choreographed action, and parents enjoy the insider humor. The independent market continues to prosper. As an independent company catering to the family market, CCP can distinguish itself by following a strategy of making films for this well-established and growing genre.

Distribution

The motion picture industry is highly competitive, with much of a film's success depending on the skill of its distribution strategy. As an

independent producer, CCP aims to negotiate with major distributors for release of their films. The production team is committed to
making the films attractive products in theatrical and other markets.

Investment Opportunity and Financial Highlights

CCP is seeking an equity investment of approximately $13.5 mil-
lion for development and production of three films and an additional $1.0 million for overhead expenditures. Using a moderate
revenue projection and an assumption of general industry distribution costs, we project (but do not guarantee) gross worldwide revenues of $109.4 million, with pretax producer/investor net profit of
$22.3 million.

2 / THE COMPANY

CCP is a privately owned California corporation that was established in September 2011. Our principal purpose and business are to create theatrical motion pictures. The Company plans to develop and produce quality family-themed films portraying positive images of the household cat.

The public is ready for films with feline themes. Big-budget animal-themed films have opened in the market over the past five years. In addition, the changing balance of cat to dog owners in favor of the former is an allegory for changes in society overall. The objectives of CCP are as follows:

- To produce quality films that provide positive family entertainment with moral tales designed for both enjoyment and education.
- To make films that will celebrate the importance of the household cat and that will be exploitable to a mass audience.
- To produce three feature films in the first five years, with budgets ranging from $500,000 to $10 million.
- To develop scripts with outside writers.

There is a need and a hunger for more family films. We believe that we can make exciting films starting as low as $500,000 without sacrificing quality. Until recently, there was a dearth of cat films. We plan to change the emphasis of movies from penguins, pigs, and dogs to cats, while providing meaningful and wholesome entertainment that will attract the entire family. In view of the growth of the family market in the past few years, the cat theme is one that has been undervalued and, consequently, underexploited.

Production Team

The primary strength of any company is in its management team. CCP's principals Lotta Mogul and Gimme Bucks have extensive experience in business and in the entertainment industry. In addition, the Company has relationships with key consultants and advisers who will be available to fill important roles on an as-needed basis. The following individuals make up the current management team and key managers.

Lotta Mogul, Executive Producer

As Executive Producer, Lotta Mogul will oversee the strategic planning and financial affairs of the Company. She previously ran Jeffcarl Studios, where she oversaw the production and distribution of over 15 films. Among her many credits are *Lord of the Litter Box*, *The Dog Who Came for Dinner*, *Fluffy Goes to College*, and the Feline Avengers franchise, which earned more than $600 million. Before moving into film, Mogul was Vice President of Marketing at Lendaq, an American multinational corporation that provides Internet-related products and services.

Gimme Bucks, Producer

With 10 years experience in the entertainment industry, Gimme Bucks most recently produced the comic-action-thriller *Swarm of Locusts* for Forthright Entertainment. He made his directorial debut on *Cosmic Forces*, which Wondergate is releasing in 2013. Bucks also has been a consultant to small, independent film companies.

Better Focus, Cinematographer

Better Focus is a member of the American Society of Cinematographers. He was Alpha Numerical's director of photography for several years. He won an Emmy Award for his work on *Unusual Birds of Ottumwa*, and he has been nominated twice for Academy Awards.

Ladder Climber, Co-Producer

Ladder Climber will assist in the production of our films. She began her career as an assistant to the producer of the cult film *Dogs That Bark* and has worked her way up to production manager and line producer on several films. Most recently, she served as a line producer on *The Paw* and *Thirty Miles to Azusa*.

Consultants

Samuel Torts, Attorney-at-Law, Los Angeles, CA
Winners and Losers, Certified Public Accountants, Los Angeles, CA

3 / THE FILMS

Currently, CCP controls the rights to the first three *Leonard the Wonder Cat* books by Jane Lovable. The books will be the basis for its film projects over the next five years. In March 2011, the Company paid $10,000 for three-year options on the first three books and first refusal on the next three. The author will receive additional payments over the next four years as production begins. The *Leonard* series has been obtained at very inexpensive option prices due to the author's respect for Lotta Mogul's devotion to charitable cat causes. Three film projects are scheduled.

Leonard's Love

The first film will be based on the novel *Leonard's Love*, which has sold 10 million copies. The story revolves around the friendship between a girl, Natasha, and her cat, Leonard. The two leave the big city to live in a small town, where they discover the true meaning of life. Furry Catman has written the screenplay. The projected budget for *Leonard's Love* is $500,000, with CCP producing and Ultra Virtuoso directing. Virtuoso's previous credits include a low-budget feature, *My Life as a Ferret*, and two rock videos, *Feral Love* and *Hot Fluffy Rag*. We are currently in the development stage with this project. The initial script has been written, but we have no commitments from actors. Casting will commence once financing is in place. As a marketing plus, the upcoming movie will be advertised on the cover of the new paperback edition of the book.

Len's Big Thrill

Natasha is an actress in her late thirties still trying to get her big break in Hollywood. She lives in a small one bedroom in Marina del Rey. On a good day, she can see the ocean if she stands on the furthest corner of her narrow balcony. Her closest companion is her cat, Leonard. He has been through many auditions with Natasha, quietly sitting on the sidelines while she tries for that big break. To make matters worse, Natasha has just gotten a final notice to pay her rent or be evicted.

One day in September, Len accompanies Natasha while she auditions for yet another movie role. Getting the lead in this movie would solve her current financial problems. Restless with the wait at the audition, Leonard struts across the room. Seeing the cameraman, he looks directly into the camera and appears to smile. The director, Simon Sez, is captivated by Len's natural ease in front of a camera. He thinks the cat actually is posing. Then he gives the cat some stage directions—run across the room, jump on the chair, and pretend to sleep—that Leonard appears to follow. The cameraman, Wayne, doesn't believe it. He points out to Simon that household cats are hard to train and seldom follow verbal directions from a stranger.

When Natasha reads for her role, Simon is equally captivated by her. He wants to make a deal for both Natasha and Leonard to be in the film, but she is hesitant. Simon explains that he wants to rewrite the script to feature Leonard as the cat who saves his mistress from a burning building. After years of waiting for her big break, Natasha feels that he wants to hire her only to get Leonard into the film. In addition, she thinks that Simon may be one of those directors who are more interested in a one-night stand with actresses. Natasha declines the part for both of them and leaves the studio with her cat.

Simon refuses to give up. He sends flowers and calls every day. When serious attempts don't work, he tries humor. One day a fellow dressed as a Siamese cat shows up at the door with a singing telegram. The song, written by Simon, is from another cat begging her to let him play with Leonard on the set. On another day, UPS delivers a box of movie posters showing both Natasha and Leonard posing in front of a burning building. The posters are accompanied by fake online reviews about the "new" actress, Natasha, who is sure to win an Academy Award for Best Actress. Then, he has former girlfriends call her to extol his virtues and guarantee that he is one of the good guys. Finally, he calls and invites her for coffee to discuss the project.

The coffee business meeting turns into lunch that turns into dinner. Natasha realizes that she is attracted to this man; however, she worries that having a relationship with him may just be her own desire for the movie part and the paycheck. Simon assures her that his intentions are honorable. He suggests that they put any personal relationship on the back burner, so that she will feel comfortable. He says that she was the best actress to test for the part. Leonard's antics would add that much more to the film. He is willing to go with the original script, if Natasha wants. After thinking about it for a week, Natasha decides to go ahead with the film including the cat's part.

Despite Wayne's misgivings, Len is a natural in front of the camera. Although they hire a trainer for him, he prefers to follow Natasha's requests. As a true Siamese, he doesn't like commands. The film is a smash with audiences. Walking the red carpet turns out to be one of Len's favorite activities. Finally realizing they are in love, Natasha and Simon marry, giving Len the biggest thrill of all.

Cat Follies

The third book in the series is currently being written by Lovable and will be published in late 2013. The story features a dejected Leonard, whose films aren't drawing the audiences they used to. No matter what Natasha and Simon, his human parents, do, they can't cheer up our cat. Desperate to find something to encourage Len, they take him for ice skating lessons. Amazed at Leonard's agility on skates, his teacher contacts the Wonderland Follies, who sign Leonard to a contract. He is an immediate hit with the audience, especially the young people. As luck would have it, one night film mogul Harvey Hoffenbrauer is in the audience. Seeing the reaction of both kids and adults to Leonard, he decides to make a film of the follies. Soon Leonard is back on top.

4 / THE INDUSTRY

The future for independent films continues to look impressive, as their commercial viability has increased steadily over the last decade. Recent films, such as *My Big Fat Siamese*, *Cat Surfers*, and *My Week with Phoebe* are evidence of the strength of this market segment. In addition, every year since 2006, an independent film has won the Academy Award for Best Picture: *Crash* (2006), *The Departed* (2007), *No Country for Old Men* (2008), *Slumdog Millionaire* (2009), *The Hurt Locker* (2010), *The King's Speech* (2011), and *The Artist* (2012). As studios cut back, equity investors have been moving into the independent film arena. Lately, falling salaries, rising subsidies, and a thinning of competition have weighted the financial equation even more in favor of the investor. In addition, revolutionary changes in the manner in which motion pictures are produced and distributed are now sweeping the industry, especially for independent films.

The total North American box office in 2011 was $10.2 billion. The share for independent films was $3.4 billion, or 34 percent of the 2011 total. Revenues for North American independent films from all worldwide revenue sources for 2011 are estimated at more than $9 billion. Worldwide box office revenues totaled $32.6 billion in 2011. Projections for 2013 are for the overall filmed entertainment market to reach $45.1 billion in the United States and $102.2 billion worldwide. Once dominated by the studio system, movie production has shifted to reflect the increasingly viable economic models for independent film. The success of independent films has been helped by the number of new production companies and smaller distributors emerging into the marketplace every day, as well as the growing interest of major U.S. studios in providing distribution in this market. Also, there has been a rise in the number of screens available for independent films.

Investment in film becomes an even more attractive prospect as financial uncertainty mounts in the wake of Wall Street bailouts and international stock market slides. Widely recognized as a "recession-proof" business, the entertainment industry has historically prospered even during periods of decreased discretionary income. While the North American box office was down 4 percent in 2011, it is up 14 percent year-to-date. "In mature markets such as the United States, the business can be more cyclical in the short term, driven by product supply and distribution patterns," National Association of Theatre Owners President John Fithian stated. "In the long term, however, domestic revenues continue to grow … 2012 looks to be another growth year." Senator Thomas Dodd, Chairman and CEO of the Motion Picture Association of America (MPAA), declared at the December 2011 Asia Pacific Screen Awards, "I am proud to report that the film industry remains a key driver of economic growth around the globe."

Motion Picture Production

The structure of the U.S. motion picture business has been changing over the past few years at a faster pace, as studios and independent companies have created varied methods of financing. Although studios historically funded production totally out of their own arrangements with banks, they now look to partner with other companies, both in the United States and abroad, which can assist in the overall financing of projects. The deals often take the form of the studio retaining the rights for distribution in all U.S. media, including theatrical, home video, television, cable, and other ancillary markets.

The studios, the largest companies in this business, are generally called the "Majors" and include NBC Universal (owned by Comcast Corp.), Warner Bros. (owned by Time Warner), Twentieth Century Fox Film Corporation (owned by Rupert Murdoch's News Corp.), Paramount Pictures (owned by Viacom), Sony Pictures Entertainment, and The Walt Disney Company. MGM, one of the original Majors, has been taken private by investors and is being run as an independent company by Spyglass Entertainment Co-Chairmen Roger Birnbaum and Gary Barber. In most cases, the Majors own their own production facilities and have a worldwide distribution organization. With a large corporate hierarchy making production decisions and a large amount of corporate debt to service, the studios aim most of their films at mass audiences.

Producers who can finance independent films by any source other than a major U.S. studio have more flexibility in their creative decisions, with the ability to hire production personnel and secure other elements required for pre-production, principal photography, and post-production on a project-by-project basis. With substantially less overhead than the studios, independents are able to be more cost-effective in the filmmaking process. Their films can be directed at both mass and niche audience, with the target markets for each film dictating the size of its budget. Typically, an independent producer's goal is to acquire funds from equity partners, completing all financing of a film before commencement of principal photography.

How It Works

There are four typical steps in the production of a motion picture: development, pre-production, production, and post-production. During development and pre-production, a writer may be engaged to write a screenplay or a screenplay may be acquired and rewritten. Certain creative personnel, including a director and various technical personnel, are hired; shooting schedules and locations are planned; and other steps necessary to prepare the motion picture for principal photography are completed. Production commences when principal photography begins and generally continues for a period of not more than three months. In post-production, the film is edited, which involves transferring the original filmed material to digital media in order to work easily with the images. In addition, a score is mixed with dialogue, and sound effects are synchronized into the final picture, and, in some cases, special effects are added. The expenses associated with this four-step process for creating and finishing a film are referred to as its "negative costs." A master is then manufactured for duplication of release prints for theatrical distribution and exhibition, but expenses for further prints and advertising for the film are categorized as "P&A" and are not part of the negative costs of the production.

Theatrical Exhibition

There were 42,390 theater screens (including drive-ins) in the United States out of approximately 150,000 theater screens worldwide in 2011, per the most recent report of the MPAA. Film revenues from all other sources are often driven by the U.S. domestic theatrical performance. The costs incurred with the distribution of a motion picture can vary significantly depending on the number of screens on which the film is exhibited. Although studios often open a film on 3,000 to 4,000 screens on opening weekends (depending on the budget of both the film and the marketing campaign), independent distributors usually tend to open their films on fewer screens. Theatrical revenues, or "box office," are often considered an engine to drive sales in all other categories. Not only has entertainment product been recession-resistant domestically but also the much stronger than expected domestic theatrical box office has continued to stimulate ancillary sales, such as home video and digital, as well as raising the value of films in foreign markets.

Television

Television exhibition includes over-the-air reception for viewers through either a fee system (cable) or a "free television" (national and independent broadcast stations). The proliferation of new cable networks since the early 1990s has made cable (both basic and premium stations) one of the most important outlets for feature films. Although network and independent television stations were a substantial part of the revenue picture in the 1970s and early 1980s, cable has become a far more important ancillary outlet. The pay-per-view business has continued to grow thanks to continued direct broadcast satellite (DBS) growth. Pay-per-view and pay television allow cable television subscribers to purchase individual films or special events or subscribe to premium cable channels for a fee. Both acquire their film programming by purchasing the distribution rights from motion picture distributors.

Home Video

In 2011, overall consumer spending on home video totalled $18.0 billion, according to the Digital Entertainment Group, consisting of $14.6 billion from DVD/Blu-ray sales and rentals and $3.4 billion from digital download (including electronic sell-through, video on demand [VOD], and subscription streaming). Annual spending on Blu-ray discs jumped 20 percent, hitting $2 billion for the first time. At the same time, total penetration of Blu-ray disc playback devices—including set-top box and game consoles—reached 40 million households in 2011, an increase of 38 percent. Consumers also purchased more than 27 million HDTVs during 2011, raising HDTV penetration to 74.5 million households.

The VOD market for paid rentals is currently ruled by pay TV services, but the Internet-on-demand (iVOD) market is growing in strength, according to the NPD Group. Pay TV VOD services hit $1.3 billion in revenue for 2011, according to NPD, while the iVOD market reached $204 million. Including the services of iTunes, Amazon, Vudu, and others, iVOD reached 7 million users, compared to 40 million for pay TV VOD. Internet VOD also poses a possible challenge for pay TV's nonmovie services. "IVOD users reduced their time spent watching TV shows, news and sports via pay TV companies by 12 percent between August

2010 and August 2011," said Russ Crupnick, Senior Vice President of Industry Analysis for the NPD Group. "Pay TV operators now must not only defend their movie VOD revenues but also counter an emerging threat to basic programming." Note that all findings are based on NPD's VideoWatch tracking service, which does not consider free or paid viewings of TV shows, subscription services, such as Netflix streaming, or free movies included in pay TV subscriptions.

International Theatrical Exhibition

Much of the projected growth in the worldwide film business comes from foreign markets, as distributors and exhibitors keep finding new ways to increase the box office revenue pool. More screens in Asia, Latin America, and Africa have followed the increase in multiplexes in Europe, but this growth has slowed. The world screen count is predicted to remain stable over the next nine years. Other factors include the privatization of television stations overseas, the introduction of DBS services, and increased cable penetration. The synergy between international and local product in European and Asian markets is expected to lead to future growth in screens and box office.

Future Trends

Revolutionary changes in the manner in which motion pictures are produced and distributed are now sweeping the industry, especially for independent films. Web-based companies like Movielink (owned by Blockbuster), Amazon's Video on Demand, CinemaNow, and Apple's iTunes Store are selling films and other entertainment programming for download on the Internet, and websites such as Netflix and Hulu (through Hulu Plus) stream filmed entertainment to home viewers as rentals. New devices for personal viewing of films (including Xbox, Wii, video iPod, iPhone, and iPad) are gaining ground in the marketplace, expanding the potential revenues from home video and other forms of selling programming for viewing. Although there may not be a notable impact of the new technologies at present, their influence is expected to grow significantly over the next five years.

5 / THE MARKET

The independent market continues to prosper. The strategy of making films in well-established genres has been shown time and time again to be an effective one. Although there is no boilerplate for making a successful film, the film's probability of success is increased with a strong story, and then the right elements—the right director and cast and other creative people involved. Being able to greenlight our own product, with the support of investors, allows the filmmakers to attract the appropriate talent to make the film a success and distinguish it in the marketplace.

CCP feels that its first film will create a new type of moviegoer for these theaters and a new type of commercial film for the mainstream theaters. Although we expect *Leonard's Love* to have enough universal appeal to play in the mainstream houses, at its projected budget it may begin in the specialty theaters as the blockbuster *Sylvester Barks at Midnight* did. Because of the low budget, exhibitors may wait for our first film to prove itself before providing access to screens in the larger movie houses. In addition, smaller houses will give us a chance to expand the film on a slow basis and build awareness with the public.

Target Markets

Family-Friendly Films

Family-friendly films appeal to the widest possible market, with *Leonard's Love* and its sequels having a multigenerational audience from tweens to grandparents. *Variety* and industry websites have said that family films boost the box office. John Fithian, President of the National Association of Theater Owners, said, "Year after year, the box office tells an important story for our friends in the creative community. Family-friendly films sell." Previously thought of only as kids' films, family-friendly movies now offer a new paradigm of family entertainment. Production and distribution companies know that wholesome entertainment can be profitable. "Movies that have a good message for [young people] that adults enjoy are universally embraced," says Tom Rothman of Twentieth Century Fox.

Cat Owners

The two most popular pets in most Western countries have been cats and dogs, with cats outnumbering dogs in 2011, according to a study by the American Pet Products Manufacturers. In the United States, there are 86.4 million pet cats compared to 78.2 million pet dogs. The statistics reveal that 39 percent (44.3 million) of households own at least one pet dog compared to 33 percent (38.4 million) that own cats. This seeming contradiction is due to the fact that the average household with a cat owns at least two. Overall, pet ownership is currently at its highest level since the first study, with 115.5 households owning a pet in 2011 compared to 71.1 million households in 1988.

The time has finally come for the cat genre film. Felines have been with us for 12 million years, but they have been underappreciated and underexploited, especially by Hollywood. Recent studies have shown that the cat has become the pet of choice. We plan to present domestic cats in their true light, as regular, everyday heroes with all the lightness and gaiety of other current animal cinema favorites, including dogs, horses, pigs, and bears. As the pet that is owned by more individuals than any other animal in the United States, a cat starring in a film will draw audience from far and wide. In following the tradition of the dog film genre, we are also looking down the road to cable outlets. There is even talk of a cat television channel.

CCP plans to begin with a $500,000 film that would benefit from exposure through the film festival circuit. The exposure of our films at festivals and limited runs in specialty theaters in target areas will create awareness for them with the general public. In addition, we plan to tie-in sales of the Leonard books with the films. Although a major studio would be a natural place to go with these films, we want to remain independent.

Demographics

Moviegoers of All Ages

The *Leonard* films are designed to appeal to everyone from children to their grandparents. It plays to younger ages better than many animated films, while still bringing in the whole family demographic. The MPAA counts all moviegoers from ages 12 to 90 in specific groups in their annual "Theatrical Market Statistics" analysis. Young adolescents, teenagers, and young adults comprised 46 percent of the movie audience in 2011, according to the most recent MPAA report. Those over 40 comprised another 39 percent.

The moviegoers dubbed "tweens" (ages 8-12) has emerged as a force at the box office during the past several years. According to recent market research figures, this group numbers about 30 million and accounts for more than $50 billion in spending. Since the MPAA's audience data groups ages 2 to 11 together, we can't present a separate audience percentage for children and tweens. According to the numbers, youngsters would be 15 percent of the audience.

Social Media and Self-Marketing

An important marketing component for any film, especially during its opening weekend, is word of mouth. Without incurring additional costs, it is possible for the filmmakers and their many colleagues to supplement the marketing strategy of a distribution company by working through niche channels to spread word of mouth about the film. Typically, film companies use the Internet to great effect with "viral" marketing. It is a strategy that encourages individuals to pass on an email or video marketing message to others, creating the potential for exponential growth in the message's exposure and influence. The recipients of those emails then forward them to their friends. As with any mainstream marketing, the strategy starts with the people at the top, the opinion makers or "influencers," and their channel partners, and it extends through the ranks to the people who see films the first weekend. They then spread the word to everyone else.

Complementing this approach are the more purely social networks. It is a $1.0-billion industry projected to grow to $2.4 billion by the end of 2012. Facebook, Twitter, LinkedIn, and other social networking sites have more than doubled since 2007, according to Forrester Research. Facebook (one billion users in August 2012, according to The Associated Press) and Twitter (140 million users in March 2012, according to the company itself) in particular have clearly become one of the focus sectors in media and entertainment. With their large communities, finding "friends" of similar film tastes in a social network is fairly easy. Twitter has become a force in the success of many films. Fans blog reviews on their own web pages or even make a video recording of their reactions and post these to YouTube, their own sites, or a social networking page and then "tweet" the link to their followers, thus informing friends and Web surfers about a film and influencing their opinions. In addition, some celebrities gather huge followings on Twitter, using the website to address their fans directly and plug their projects not only at time of release but also throughout filming to create anticipation.

There are also websites that are Web-based marketplaces where filmmakers and fans connect to make independent films happen through small individual contributions to funding and other forms of support. Fans get the opportunity to discover and impact the films of tomorrow, while getting insider access and VIP perks for their contributions.

6 / DISTRIBUTION

The motion picture industry is highly competitive, with much of a film's success often depending on the skill of its distribution strategy. The filmmakers' goal is to negotiate with experienced distribution companies in order to seek to maximize their bargaining strength for potentially significant releases. There is an active market for completed motion pictures, with virtually all the studios and independent distributors seeking to acquire films. The management team feels that the Company's films will be attractive products in the marketplace.

Distribution terms between producers and distributors vary greatly. A distributor looks at several factors when evaluating a potential acquisition, such as the uniqueness of the story, theme, and the target market for the film. Since distribution terms are determined in part by the perceived potential of a motion picture and the relative bargaining strength of the parties, it is not possible to predict with certainty the nature of distribution arrangements. However, there are certain standard arrangements that form the basis for most distribution agreements. The distributor will generally license the film to theatrical exhibitors (i.e., theater owners) for domestic release and to specific, if not all, foreign territories for a percentage of the gross box office dollars. The initial release for most feature films is U.S. theatrical (i.e., in movie theaters). For a picture in initial release, the exhibitor, depending on the demand for the movie, will split the revenue derived from ticket purchases ("gross box office") with the distributor; revenue derived from the various theater concessions remains with the exhibitor. The percentage of box office receipts remitted to the distributor is known as "film rentals" and customarily diminishes during the course of a picture's theatrical run. Although different formulas may be used to determine the splits from week to week, on average a distributor will be able to retain about 50 percent of total box office, again depending on the performance and demand for a particular movie. In turn, the distributor will pay to the motion picture producer a negotiated percentage of the film rentals less its costs for film prints and advertising.

Film rentals become part of the "distributor's gross," from which all other deals are computed. As the distributor often re-licenses the picture to domestic ancillaries (i.e., cable, television, home video) and foreign theatrical and ancillaries, these monies all become part of the distributor's gross and add to the total revenue for the film in the same way as the rentals. The distribution deal with the producer includes a negotiated percentage for each revenue source; for example, the producer's share of foreign rentals may vary from the percentage of domestic theatrical rentals. The basic elements of a film distribution deal include the distributor's commitment to advance funds for distribution expenses (including multiple prints of the film and advertising) and the percentage of the film's income the distributor will receive for its services. Theoretically, the distributor recoups his expenses for the cost of its print and advertising expenses first from the initial revenue of the film. Then the distributor will split the rest of the revenue monies with the producer/investor group. The first monies coming back to the producer/investor group generally repay the investor for the total production cost, after which the producers and investors split the money according to their agreement. However, the specifics of the distribution deal and the timing of all money disbursements depend on the agreement that is finally negotiated. In addition, the timing of the revenue and the percentage amount of the distributor's fees differ depending on the revenue source.

Release Strategies

The typical method of releasing films is with domestic theatrical, which gives value to the various film "windows" (the period that has to pass after a domestic theatrical release before a film can be released in other markets). Historically, the sequencing pattern has been to license to pay-cable program distributors, foreign theatrical, home video, television networks, foreign ancillary, and U.S. television syndication. As the rate of return varies from different windows, shifts in these sequencing strategies will occur.

The business is going through a changeover between screens that play 35-mm films and those that accept digital, which makes a difference in the cost of what we usually call "prints." Traditional 35-mm prints typically cost $1,200 to $1,500 each. Using film prints, a high-profile studio film opening on as many as 3,000 to 4,000 screens in multiple markets (a "wide" release) can have an initial marketing expense of $3.5 to $6 million, accompanied by a very high-priced advertising program. The number of screens diminishes after opening weekend as the film's popularity fades.

By contrast, independent films typically have a "platform" release. In this case, the film is given a build up by opening initially in a few regional or limited local theaters to build positive movie patron awareness throughout the country. The time between a limited opening and its release in the balance of the country may be several weeks. This keeps the cost of striking 35-mm prints to a minimum, in the range of over $1 million, and allows for commensurately lower advertising costs. Using this strategy, smaller budgeted films can be successful at the box office with as few as two or three prints initially and more being made as the demand increases. In the new digital system, the distributor pays $800 to $900 fee per theatrical screen on which the film is exhibited. For independent films that are in theaters for at least two months on an escalating number of screens, adhering to the platform release pattern, the overall distribution cost can still run between $1 and $2 million.

Distributors plan their release schedules not only with certain target audiences in mind but also with awareness of which theaters—specialty or multiplex—will draw that audience. Many specialty theaters remain print oriented, while multiplexes are rapidly converting to all digital. How much is spent by the distributor in total will depend on which system, and which release pattern, best serves each film.

7 / RISK FACTORS

Investment in the film industry is highly speculative and inherently risky. There can be no assurance of the economic success of any motion picture since the revenues derived from the production and distribution of a motion picture primarily depend on its acceptance by the public, which cannot be predicted. The commercial success of a motion picture also depends on the quality and acceptance of other competing films released into the marketplace at or near the same time, general economic factors, and other tangible and intangible factors, all of which can change and cannot be predicted with certainty.

The entertainment industry in general, and the motion picture industry in particular, are continuing to undergo significant changes, primarily due to technological developments. Although these developments have resulted in the availability of alternative and competing forms of leisure time entertainment, such technological developments have also resulted in the creation of additional revenue sources through licensing of rights to such new media and potentially could lead to future reductions in the costs of producing and distributing motion pictures. In addition, the theatrical success of a motion picture remains a crucial factor in generating revenues in other media such as videocassettes and television. Due to the rapid growth of technology, shifting consumer tastes, and the popularity and availability of other forms of entertainment, it is impossible to predict the overall effect these factors will have on the potential revenue from and profitability of feature-length motion pictures.

The Company itself is in the organizational stage and is subject to all the risks incident to the creation and development of a new business, including the absence of a history of operations and minimal net worth. In order to prosper, the success of the Company's films will depend partly upon the ability of management to produce a film of exceptional quality at a lower cost that can compete in appeal with high-budgeted films of the same genre. In order to minimize this risk, management plans to participate as much as possible throughout the process and will aim to mitigate financial risks where possible. Fulfilling this goal depends on the timing of investor financing, the ability to obtain distribution contracts with satisfactory terms, and the continued participation of the current management.

8 / FINANCIAL PLAN

Strategy

The Company proposes to secure development and production film financing for the feature films in this business plan from equity investors, allowing it to maintain consistent control of the quality and production costs. As an independent, CCP can strike the best financial arrangements with various channels of distribution. This strategy allows for maximum flexibility in a rapidly changing marketplace, in which the availability of filmed entertainment is in constant flux.

Financial Assumptions

For the purposes of this business plan, several assumptions have been included in the financial scenarios and are noted accordingly. This discussion contains forward-looking statements that involve risks and uncertainties as detailed in the Risk Factors section.

1. Table 11.1, Summary Projected Income Statement, summarizes the income for the films to be produced. *Domestic Rentals* reflect the distributor's share of the box office split with the exhibitor in the United States and Canada, assuming the film has the same distributor in both countries. *Domestic Other* includes home video, pay TV, basic cable, network television, and television syndication. *Foreign Revenue* includes all monies returned to distributors from all venues outside the United States and Canada.
2. The film's *Budget*, often known as the "production costs," covers both "above-the-line" (producers, actors, and directors) and "below-the-line" (the rest of the crew) costs of producing a film. Marketing costs are included under Print and Advertising (P&A), often referred to as "releasing costs" or "distribution expenses." These expenses also include the costs of making copies of the release print from the master and advertising and vary depending on the distribution plan for each title.
3. *Gross Income* represents the projected pretax profit after distributor's expenses have been deducted but before distributor's fees and overhead expenses are deducted.

4. *Distributor's Fees* (the distributor's share of the revenues as compared to his expenses, which represent out-of-pocket costs) are based on 35 percent of all distributor gross revenue, both domestic and foreign.
5. *Net Producer/Investor Income* represents the projected pretax profit prior to negotiated distributions to investors.
6. Table 11.2 shows the *Summary Projected Cash Flow Based on Moderate Profit Cases*, which have been brought forward from Table 11.10.
7. The films in Tables 11.3 and 11.4 are the basis for the projections shown in Tables 11.7 and 11.8. Likewise, the films in Tables 11.5 and 11.6 are the basis for the projections in Table 11.9. The rationale for the projections is explained in (8) below. The films chosen relate in theme, style, feeling, or budget to the films we propose to produce. It should be noted that these groups do not include films of which the results are known but that have lost money. In addition, there are neither databases that collect all films ever made nor budgets available for all films released. There is, therefore, a built-in bias in the data. Also, the fact that these films have garnered revenue does not constitute a guarantee of the success of this film.
8. The three revenue scenarios shown in Tables 11.7 and 11.8—low (breakeven), moderate, and high—are based on the data shown in Tables 11.3 and 11.4. Likewise, Table 11.9 is based on the comparative films in Tables 11.5 and 11.6. We have chosen films that relate in genre, theme, and/or budget to the films we propose to produce. The low scenario indicates a case in which some production costs are covered but there is no profit. The moderate scenario represents the most likely result for each film and is used for the cash flows. The high scenarios are based on the results of extraordinarily successful films and presented for investor information only. Due to the wide variance in the results of individual films, simple averages of actual data are not realistic. Therefore, to create the moderate forecast for Tables 11.7 through 11.9, the North American box office for each film in the respective comparative tables was divided by its budget to create a ratio that was used as a guide. The North American box office was used because it is a widely accepted film

industry assumption that, in most cases, this result drives all the other revenue sources of a film. In order to avoid skewing the data, the films with the highest and lowest ratios in each year were deleted. The remaining revenues were added and then divided by the sum of the remaining budgets. This gave an average (or, more specifically, the mean variance) of the box office with the budgets. The ratios over the five years represented in the comparative tables showed whether the box office was trending up or down or remaining constant. The result was a number used to multiply times the budget of the proposed film in order to obtain a reasonable projection of the moderate box office result. In order to determine the expense value for the P&A, the P&A for each film in the comparative tables was divided by the budget. The ratios were determined in a similar fashion, taking out the high and low and arriving at a mean number. For the high forecast, the Company determined a likely extraordinary result for each film and its budget. The remaining revenues and P&A for the high forecasts were calculated using ratios similar to those applied to the moderate columns. In all the scenarios, and throughout these financials, "ancillary" revenues from product placement, merchandising, soundtrack, and other revenue opportunities are not included in projections.

9. *Distributor's Fees* are based on all the revenue exclusive of the exhibitor's share of the box office (50 percent). These fees are calculated at 35 percent (general industry assumption) for the forecast, as the Company does not have a distribution contract at this time. Note that the fees are separate from distributor's expenses (see **P&A** in (2)), which are out-of-pocket costs and paid back in full.

10. The *Cash Flow* assumptions used for Table 11.10 are as follows:
    a. Film production should take approximately one year from development through post-production, ending with the creation of a master print. The actual release date depends on finalization of distribution arrangements, which may occur either before or after the film has been completed and is an unknown variable at this time. For purposes of the cash flow, we have assumed that distribution will start within six months after completion of the film.

b. The largest portion of print and advertising costs will be spent in the first quarter of the film's opening.

c. The majority of revenues generally will come back to the producers within two years after release of the film, although a smaller amount of ancillary revenues will take longer to occur and will be covered by the investor's agreement for a breakdown of the timing for industry windows.

d. Following is a chart indicating estimated entertainment industry distribution windows based on historical data showing specific revenue-producing segments of the marketplace:

WINDOW	MONTHS AFTER INITIAL THEATRICAL RELEASE	ESTIMATED LENGTH OF TIME
Domestic Theatrical	—	3–6 months
Video-on-Demand	3–6 months	3–6 months
Domestic Home Video (Initial)	3–5 months	6–12 months
Domestic Pay-Per-View	3–5 months	6 months
Digital Streaming	5 months	1–2 years
International Theatrical	Variable	6–12 months
International Video (Initial)	6–9 months	9–12 months
Domestic Pay Television	12–15 months	18 months
International Television (Pay or Free)	18–24 months	12–36 months
Domestic Free Television (Network, Barter, Syndication, and Cable)	3 or more years	14 years

11. Company *Overhead Expenses* are shown in Table 11.11.

TABLE 11.1

Crazed Consultants Productions Summary Projected Income Statement (Millions of Dollars)

FILMS	REVENUE					COSTS			DISTRIBUTOR'S GROSS PROFIT	EST. DIST. FEES	PRODUCER/ INVESTOR GROSS	COMPANY OVERHEAD	NET PROD./ INVESTOR INCOME
	DOMESTIC			FOREIGN	TOTAL	BUDGET	P&A	TOTAL					
	BOX OFFICE	RENTALS	ANCILLARY										
Leonard's Love	2.0	1.0	2.2	1.8	5.0	0.5	1.0	1.5	3.5	1.8	1.7	0.07	1.6
Len's Big Thrill	10.5	5.3	11.6	9.5	26.4	3.0	3.3	6.3	20.1	9.2	10.9	0.47	10.4
Cat Follies	26.0	13.0	31.2	33.8	78.0	10.0	30.0	40.0	38.0	27.3	10.7	0.45	10.3
TOTAL	38.5	19.3	45.0	45.1	109.4	13.5	34.3	47.8	61.6	38.3	23.3	1.0	22.3

TABLE 11.2

Crazed Consultants Productions Summary Projected Cash Flow* Based on Moderate Profit Cases (Millions of Dollars)

FILMS	YEAR 1				YEAR 2				YEAR 3				YEAR 4				YEAR 5				YEAR 6
	QTR. 1	QTR. 2	QTR. 3	QTR. 4	QTR. 1	QTR. 2	QTR. 3	QTR. 4	QTR. 1	QTR. 2	QTR. 3	QTR. 4	QTR. 1	QTR. 2	QTR. 3	QTR. 4	QTR. 1	QTR. 2	QTR. 3	QTR. 4	QTR. 1
Leonard's Love	(0.1)	(0.2)	(0.1)	(0.1)	0.0	0.0	0.2	0.1	0.5	0.3	0.3	0.4	0.4								
Len's Big Thrill					(0.7)	(0.9)	(0.9)	(0.5)	0.0	0.0	2.2	0.4	3.4	2.0	1.4	2.3	2.2				
Cat Follies									(2.5)	(3.0)	(3.0)	(1.5)	0.0	0.0	(6.2)	(1.9)	5.8	5.4	5.1	8.1	4.4
TOTAL CASH	(0.1)	(0.2)	(0.1)	(0.1)	(0.7)	(0.9)	(0.7)	(0.4)	(2.0)	(2.7)	(0.5)	(0.7)	3.8	2.0	(4.8)	0.4	8.0	5.4	5.1	8.1	4.4
CUMULATIVE CASH FLOW	(0.1)	(0.3)	(0.4)	(0.5)	(1.2)	(2.1)	(2.8)	(3.2)	(5.2)	(7.9)	(8.4)	(9.1)	(5.3)	(3.3)	(8.1)	(7.7)	0.3	5.7	10.8	18.9	23.3

*For reference only. How and when monies are actually distributed depends on contract with distributor. Print and advertising, which the distributor spends, are paid back first, then the production budget.

Source: Business Strategies

TABLE 11.3

Crazed Consultants Productions Gross Profits of Selected Comparative Films with Varied Genres for Two Films* with Budgets $500,000 to $7.5 Million Years 2008–2010 (Millions of Dollars)

FILMS	DOMESTIC REVENUE			FOREIGN REVENUE (c)	TOTAL REVENUE (d)	COSTS			DISTRIBUTOR'S GROSS PROFIT (e)
	BOX OFFICE	RENTALS (a)	OTHER (b)			BUDGET	P&A	TOTAL	
2008									
Cat Surfers	12.4	6.2	17.0	18.9	42.1	2.0	2.7	4.7	37.4
Eat, Pray, Groom	3.8	1.9	6.8	4.3	13.0	1.5	1.6	3.1	9.9
Evil Reptiles	4.0	2.0	9.0	2.0	13.0	0.7	5.0	5.7	7.3
I Hope They Have Fish in Heaven	7.0	3.5	9.0	3.0	15.5	3.0	4.0	7.0	8.5
Twilight Butterflies	9.0	4.5	12.0	10.0	26.5	3.3	4.6	7.9	18.6
2009									
Aardvark with the Bee Tattoo	8.0	4.0	9.8	4.6	18.4	3.4	4.5	7.9	10.5
Fireflies in the Woods	3.6	1.8	5.0	8.1	14.9	2.0	2.9	4.9	10.0
Goats of March, The	4.0	2.0	4.0	2.5	8.5	0.9	3.2	4.1	4.4
My Big Fat Siamese	9.0	4.5	12.0	21.9	38.4	3.0	8.0	11.0	27.4
Time Traveler's Turtle, The	12.0	6.0	15.0	6.0	27.0	7.0	5.0	12.0	15.0
2010									
Being Buffy: A Cat's History	15.0	7.5	25.0	16.0	48.5	7.5	7.0	14.5	34.0
Chinchillas in Paris	6.0	3.0	7.0	4.0	14.0	4.0	2.0	6.0	8.0
My Week with Murphy	7.0	3.5	7.5	5.0	16.0	2.0	5.0	7.0	9.0
Opossums Are Fine, The	8.0	4.0	10.0	7.0	21.0	3.0	3.5	6.5	14.5
Tinker, Tailor, Spider	3.0	1.5	2.2	5.0	8.7	0.5	2.0	2.5	6.2

(a) Rentals equal distributor's share of U.S. box office.
(b) Domestic Revenue Other includes television, cable, video, and all other nontheatrical sources of revenue.
(c) Foreign Revenue includes both theatrical and ancillary revenues.
(d) Total Revenue equals Domestic Rentals, Domestic Other, and Foreign.
(e) Gross Profit before distributor's fee is removed.

*The amounts obtained by these comparable films do not constitute a guarantee that *Leonard's Love* and *Len's Big Thrill* will do as well.

...iness Strategies

TABLE 11.4

Crazed Consultants Productions Selected Comparative Films with Varied Genres* for Two Films* with Budgets $500,000 to $8.0 Million U.S. Box Office and Budgets Only Years 2011–2012 (Millions Of Dollars)

FILMS	BOX OFFICE	BUDGET
Alien Horses	9.0	3.5
Crazy Chimps	16.0	8.0
Devil Mice	20.8	4.0
Ferret Flight	1.8	0.6
Iron Koala, The**	30.0	5.0
Mongoose Kingdom	7.5	3.0
Phoebe: Killer Cat	12.0	4.0
Spy Geese	5.0	0.5
War Sheep	6.0	1.0

*The amounts obtained by these comparable films do not constitute a guarantee that *Leonard's Love and Len's Big Thrill* will do as well.

**Still in North American distribution as of August 5, 2012.

Note: Domestic ancillary and all foreign data generally are not available until two years after a film's initial U.S. release; therefore, this table includes U.S. domestic box office only.

Source: Business Strategies

TABLE 11.5

Crazed Consultants Productions *Cat Follies* Gross Profits of Selected Films with Varied Genres* with Budgets of $8.0 to $30.0 Million Years 2008–2010 (Millions Of Dollars)

FILMS	DOMESTIC REVENUE			FOREIGN REVENUE (c)	TOTAL REVENUE (d)	COSTS			DISTRIBUTOR'S GROSS PROFIT (e)
	BOX OFFICE	RENTALS (a)	OTHER (b)			BUDGET	P&A	TOTAL	
2008									
Inglorious Pigs	18.0	9.0	38.0	36.0	83.0	10.0	5.0	15.0	68.0
Julia and Jasper	40.0	20.0	70.0	58.2	148.2	8.0	23.0	31.0	117.2
Maggie: Spirit of the Bones	66.0	33.0	98.0	78.0	209.0	15.0	47.0	62.0	147.0
Paranormal Wasps	38.0	20.0	53.7	54.6	128.3	11.0	46.0	57.0	71.3
Spider's Speech, The	74.3	37.1	69.4	106.3	212.8	30.0	34.0	64.0	148.8
2009									
Angel Goes Boating	40.0	20.0	84.8	106.3	211.1	13.0	68.4	81.4	129.7
Cat Who Played with Water, The	16.0	8.0	22.0	43.0	73.0	8.0	32.0	40.0	33.0
My Dove Tweetie	36.0	18.0	50.0	40.0	108.0	15.0	11.1	26.1	81.9
Strange Case Against Mosquitoes, The	70.0	35.0	110.0	120.0	265.0	25.0	10.5	35.5	229.5
Time Traveler's Turtle, The	54.0	27.0	64.0	46.0	137.0	20.0	18.3	38.3	98.7
2010									
Caterpillar in Black, The	19.1	9.5	25.1	58.5	93.1	16.0	18.0	34.0	59.1
In the Land of the Rhinoceros	45.7	22.8	37.9	45.0	105.7	20.0	30.0	50.0	55.7
Joyful Singing Parrots	16.0	8.0	30.2	20.0	58.2	8.0	10.0	18.0	40.2
Mission Pelicans	37.7	18.9	50.0	46.0	114.9	21.0	13.1	34.1	80.8
Zebras in Space	25.5	12.7	28.9	36.4	78.0	10.0	14.2	24.2	53.8

(a) Rentals equal distributor's share of U.S. box office.

(b) Domestic Other Revenue includes television, cable, video, and all other non theatrical sources of revenue.

(c) Foreign Revenue includes both theatrical and ancillary revenues.

(d) Total Revenue equals Domestic Rentals, Domestic Other, and Foreign.

(e) Gross Profit before distributor's fee is removed.

*The amounts obtained by these comparable films do not constitute a guarantee that *Cat Follies* will do as well.

☞ Business Strategies

TABLE 11.6

**Crazed Consultants Productions *Cat Follies*
selected Comparative Films with Varied Genres*
With Budgets $7.0 to $23.0 Million U.S. Box Office and
Budgets Only years 2011–2012** (Millions Of Dollars)

FILMS	BOX OFFICE	BUDGET
Cat Who Kicked the Litter Box, The**	15.0	9.0
Diary of a Brave Devilfish	55.9	20.0
Legend of the Praying Mantis	35.0	15.4
Lemur Lawyer, The	43.0	17.0
Mikie at Midnight	40.0	12.0
Parakeets Are All Right, The	23.4	7.0
Penguins with Benefits	87.0	23.0
Young Panther	36.0	8.5

*The amounts obtained by these comparable films do not constitute a guarantee that *Cat Follies* will do as well.

**Still in North American distribution as of August 6, 2012.

Note: Domestic ancillary and all foreign data generally are not available until two years after a film's initial U.S. release; therefore, this table includes U.S. domestic box office only.

Source: Business Strategies

TABLE 11.7

Crazed Consultants Productions *Leonard's Love*
Projected Income Low, Moderate, and
High Results (Millions of Dollars)

		LOW	MODERATE	HIGH
U.S. BOX OFFICE REVENUE		0.5	2.0	15.0
Domestic Rentals	(a)	0.3	1.0	7.5
Domestic Other	(b)	0.7	2.2	16.5
Foreign	(c)	0.9	1.8	13.5
TOTAL DISTRIBUTOR GROSS REVENUE		1.9	5.0	37.5
LESS:				
Budget Cost		0.5	0.5	0.5
Print and Advertising		0.7	1.0	6.0
TOTAL COSTS		1.2	1.5	6.5
DISTRIBUTOR'S GROSS INCOME		0.7	3.5	31.0
Distributor's Fees	(d)	0.7	1.8	13.1
NET INCOME BEFORE ALLOCATION TO PRODUCERS/ INVESTORS		0.0	1.7	17.9

Note: Box office revenues are for reference and not included in the totals. These projections do not constitute guarantees as how well this film will do.

(a) Box office revenues are for reference and not included in the totals. Fifty percent of the box office goes to the exhibitor and 50 percent goes to the distributor as Domestic Rentals.

(b) Domestic Other Revenue includes television, cable, video, and all other nontheatrical sources of revenue.

(c) Foreign Revenue includes both theatrical and ancillary revenues.

(d) Distributor's Fee equals 35 percent of Distributor's Gross Revenue.

Source: Business Strategies

TABLE 11.8

Crazed Consultants Productions *Len's Big Thrill*
Projected Income Low, Moderate, and
High Results (Millions of Dollars)

		LOW	MODERATE	HIGH
U.S. BOX OFFICE REVENUE		3.0	10.5	38.5
Domestic Rentals	(a)	1.5	5.3	19.3
Domestic Other	(b)	3.0	11.6	42.4
Foreign	(c)	1.2	9.5	34.7
TOTAL DISTRIBUTOR GROSS REVENUE		5.7	26.4	96.4
LESS				
Budget Cost		3.0	3.0	3.0
Print and Advertising		0.7	3.3	12.2
TOTAL COSTS		3.7	6.3	15.2
DISTRIBUTOR'S GROSS INCOME		2.0	20.1	81.2
Distributor's Fees	(d)	2.0	9.2	33.7
NET INCOME BEFORE ALLOCATION TO PRODUCERS/INVESTORS		0.0	10.9	47.5

Note: Box office revenues are for reference and not included in the totals.

These projections do not constitute guarantees as how well this film will do.

(a) Box office revenues are for reference and not included in the totals. Fifty percent of the box office goes to the exhibitor and 50 percent goes to the distributor as Domestic Rentals.

(b) Domestic Other Revenue includes television, cable, video, and all other nontheatrical sources of revenue.

(c) Foreign Revenue includes both theatrical and ancillary revenues.

(d) Distributor's Fee equals 35 percent of Distributor's Gross Revenue.

Source: Business Strategies

TABLE 11.9

Crazed Consultants Productions *Cat Follies* Projected Income Low, Moderate, and High Results (Millions of Dollars)

		LOW	MODERATE	HIGH
U.S. BOX OFFICE REVENUE		10.0	26.0	60.0
Domestic Rentals	(a)	5.0	13.0	30.0
Domestic Other	(b)	15.0	31.2	72.0
Foreign	(c)	20.0	33.8	78.0
TOTAL DISTRIBUTOR GROSS REVENUE		40.0	78.0	180.0
LESS:				
Budget Cost		10.0	10.0	10.0
Print and Advertising		16.0	30.0	50.0
TOTAL COSTS		26.0	40.0	60.0
DISTRIBUTOR'S GROSS INCOME		14.0	38.0	120.0
Distributor's Fees	(d)	14.0	27.3	63.0
NET INCOME BEFORE ALLOCATION TO PRODUCERS/ INVESTORS		0.0	10.7	57.0

Note: Box office revenues are for reference and not included in the totals.

These projections do not constitute guarantee that *Cat Follies* will do as well.

(a) Box office revenues are for reference and not included in the totals. Fifty percent of the box office goes to the exhibitor and 50 percent goes to the distributor as Domestic Rentals.

(b) Domestic Other Revenue includes television, cable, DVD, and all other nontheatrical sources of revenue.

(c) Foreign Revenue includes both theatrical and ancillary revenues.

(d) Distributor's Fee equals 35 percent of Distributor's Gross Revenue.

Source: Business Strategies

TABLE 11.10

Crazed Consultants Productions Combined Cash Flow for Three Films* Based on Moderate Profit Cases
(Millions of Dollars)

	YEAR 1				YEAR 2				YEAR 3				YEAR 4				YEAR 5				YEAR 6
	QTR. 1	QTR. 2	QTR. 3	QTR. 4	QTR. 1	QTR. 2	QTR. 3	QTR. 4	QTR. 1	QTR. 2	QTR. 3	QTR. 4	QTR. 1	QTR. 2	QTR. 3	QTR. 4	QTR. 1	QTR. 2	QTR. 3	QTR. 4	QTR. 1
Leonard's Love																					
Production Budget	(0.1)	(0.2)	(0.1)	(0.1)	0.0	0.0															
Print and Advertising					(0.5)		(0.1)		(0.3)			(0.1)									
Domestic Rentals					0.7		0.2		0.1												
Domestic Ancillary									1.1												
Foreign Revenue							0.5	0.4	0.4	0.3	0.4										
Distributor Fees							(0.9)		(0.9)												
Len's Big Thrill																					
Production Budget					(0.7)	(0.9)	(0.9)	(0.5)	0.0	0.0											
Print and Advertising									(1.8)	(0.4)	(0.8)		(0.3)								
Domestic Rentals									4.0	0.8			5.8								
Domestic Ancillary											0.5		0.8								
Foreign Revenue									2.7	2.3			2.7	1.4	2.3						
Distributor Fees									(4.8)				(4.4)								
Cat Follies																					
Production Budget									(2.5)	(3.0)	(3.0)	(1.5)	0.0	0.0							
Print and Advertising													(15.9)	(7.5)	(3.9)	(2.7)					
Domestic Rentals													9.7	1.3		2.0					15.6
Domestic Ancillary													15.6		15.6	9.8	8.1				2.7
Foreign Revenue													9.8			8.1	5.1	5.1	8.1	8.1	(13.9)
Distributor Fees													(13.4)			(13.4)	(2.7)				
TOTALS	**(0.1)**	**(0.2)**	**(0.1)**	**(0.1)**	**(0.7)**	**(0.9)**	**(0.7)**	**(0.4)**	**(2.0)**	**(2.7)**	**(0.5)**	**(0.7)**	**3.8**	**2.0**	**(4.8)**	**0.4**	**8.0**	**5.4**	**5.1**	**8.1**	**4.4**
CUMULATIVE TOTAL	**(0.1)**	**(0.3)**	**(0.4)**	**(0.5)**	**(1.2)**	**(2.1)**	**(2.8)**	**(3.2)**	**(5.2)**	**(7.9)**	**(8.4)**	**(9.1)**	**(5.3)**	**(3.3)**	**(8.1)**	**(7.7)**	**0.3**	**5.7**	**10.8**	**18.9**	**23.3**

*For reference only. How and when monies are actually distributed depends on contract with distributor. Print and Advertising are usually paid back first, then the production budget.

Source: Business Strategies

TABLE 11.11

Crazed Consultant Productions Sample Overhead Expenses
Format First Five Years

	YEAR 1	YEAR 2	YEAR 3	YEAR 4	YEAR 5
President					
Executive In Charge of Production					
Office Manager					
Payroll Taxes					
Salaries					
Travel and Entertainment					
Office Rent					
Office Supplies & Equipment					
Publicity/Promotion/ Advertising					
Dues and Subscriptions					
Legal Fees					
Accounting Fees					
Telephones					
Utilities					
Parking Spaces					
Security					
Insurance					
Repairs and Maintenance					
Freight/Air Couriers					
Other					
Total Non-payroll					
TOTAL OVERHEAD EXPENSES					

Note: This table includes examples of the line items only. You must choose the line items that are appropriate for your company and fill in the data. One-film plans do not have overhead.

12

Breaking the Rules: Documentary, Animation, and Large Format

The secret of breaking rules in a way that works is understanding what the rules are in the first place.

—MUSICIAN RICK WAKEMAN

WHY ARE THESE FILMS DIFFERENT?

I also could have said "All Roads Lead to Rome." A lot of people like to say variations of "rules are made to be broken." But I feel both convey the wrong message. The important message in this chapter is not that we should throw out all the rules but know when they need to be slightly bent to fit the situation. Not jut any road leads to Rome, but there is more than one.

The business plan outline does not change for documentary, animated, and large format (i.e., IMAX) films. You still have the same list: Executive Summary, The Company, The Film, The Industry, The Markets, Distribution, Risk Factors, and Financial Plan. However, the specifics within some of these sections vary. Each format treated in this chapter has specific areas that have to be treated differently than the "rules" laid down in the rest of the book. In addition, all the formats differ from each other in some aspects. This chapter takes you through how to treat each one and gives you examples for forecasting.

DOCUMENTARY FILMS

History

Documentary films became mainstream 10 to 12 years ago. Until 2002, I didn't write any business plans for theatrical documentaries. The reason is simple: There weren't enough of them that had earned significant revenues worth talking about. The majority of feature-length docs were made for television. The success of *Roger & Me* in 1989 began the re-emergence of the nonfiction film as a credible theatrical release. Then throughout the 1990s and continuing to present day, theatrical docs have continued to grow in prominence and popularity with audiences.

After a few successful films in the early 1990s, *Hoop Dreams* (1994) attracted a lot of attention by reaching U.S. box office receipts of $7.8 million on a budget of $800,000. The same year, *Crumb* reached a total of $3 million on a budget of $300,000. In 1997, a Best Documentary Oscar nominee, *Buena Vista Social Club*, made for $1.5 million and grossing $6.9 million, scored at the box office and with a best-selling soundtrack album.

Michael Moore's 2002 *Bowling for Columbine* raised the bar for documentaries by winning the Oscar for Best Feature Documentary and the Special 55th Anniversary Award at Cannes and by earning $114.5 million worldwide. The same year, *Dogtown and the Z-Boys, The Kid Stays in the Picture, I'm Trying to Break Your Heart,* and *Standing in the Shadows of Motown* all made a splash at the box office. The success of these releases was not anything like *Columbine*, which had a political and social message, but was noticeable nevertheless. In 2003, *Spellbound* seemed to confound the forecasters by drawing a significant audience, as did *Step into Liquid, The Fog of War,* and *My Architect*. The following year, 2004, Michael Moore surprisingly—and convincingly—bettered his own record with *Fahrenheit 9/11*, which was made for $6 million and earned more than $300 million worldwide. Distributors found more documentaries that they liked: *Riding Giants, The Corporation, Touching the Void,* and the little doc that could, *Super Size Me* (made for almost nothing and earning $35.2 million at the box office). In 2005, there were the popular *Mad Hot Ballroom, March of the Penguins, Enron: The Smartest Guys in Town,* and *Why We Fight*. In 2006, another breakout in terms of monetary success was *An Inconvenient Truth* (made for a reported $1.5 million and earning $75.3 million worldwide). Featuring a fledging actor, former Vice President Al Gore, undoubtedly added to the film's popularity.

In 2007, the critics said that documentaries were "dead," as Michael Moore's *Sicko* was the most significant entry in the genre. Made for $9 million, it earned a respectable $53 million worldwide. For you and me (and our investors) that would be considered a success. To paraphrase yet another Mark Twain quote, the reports of the box office death for theatrical docs was greatly exaggerated. In 2008, another genre broke through the barrier with Nathan Frankowski's *Expelled: No Intelligence Allowed* with perhaps the opposite end of that social discussion shored up by Larry Charles' *Religulous*. We also saw the biographical film about a tightrope walker *Man on Wire*. From 2009 to mid-2011, some of the significant docs are *Buck*, *Cave of Forgotten Dreams*, *Exit Through the Gift Shop*, *Inside Job*, *Page One: The New York Times*, and *Pina*. As this edition is going to press, the first half of 2012 has brought *Bully* and *Jiro Dreams of Sushi*. You can see the variety of subjects.

Synopses

In Chapter 3, "The Films," I make a big deal about telling the investors how the story ends. If you don't know the entire storyline and ending of the film, you probably should wait to raise money. Investors aren't looking for surprises with narrative films.

A favorite quote that I used in seminars is: "In feature films the director is God; in documentary films God is the director," Director Alfred Hitchcock.

With all documentaries you are making a film about a real subject. Nevertheless, there are still two general types of storylines: historical time and future time. Historical documentaries have an ending before you start making the film. The term *historical* is less a reference to time than that you and the investors know the ending of the story. With future time, or what I usually refer to as real-time documentaries, you are recording actual events as they happen. For example, you are curious how the latest miracle drug was discovered, tested, and won approval from the Federal Drug Administration. You are doing historical research. For your investors, there is a clear storyline outline plus an ending to the story. You still may discover facts along the way that weren't known before, but your synopsis will look a lot like that for a fiction film.

In a real-time documentary, you are raising money to look at health issues through a specific study. You may know what you wish the results to be; however, you won't know until after the study is over. While I insist on the "whole storyline including the ending" with fiction films, it is not possible to know in advance how this story will end. The synopsis will include a description of why you are making the film, what the study will include, and what you anticipate the results will be. An example for the last lines of the synopsis might be:

> *The entire process will be captured on film. This visual record of the transformations in the test subjects will prove _____. The results of this experiment in _____ may directly and indirectly affect the over 100 million people living with supposedly incurable _____.*

Interviews

Many documentaries are based on a large number of interviews. If you have already conducted some of the interviews, then list those people with their credentials. If you haven't already conducted the interviews, be careful how you mention people. I treat the contemplated list of interviews the same way as I treat listing stars in a film. You may want to talk to Queen Elizabeth in your film. If you already have an affirmative response from her (or her social secretary), include her in your list of interview. Otherwise, "people we would like to interview" is really the same as naming stars who never heard of you. The interviewees give credibility to your potential film for the investor. Whether equity or grant money, it is not a good idea to get funded by making promises you can't keep.

The bios for these interviews are listed attachments to the synopsis in the same way you would list actors. However, in the making of many documentaries, there are advisors who may help with structuring the film but not be part of it. These people I always list in the "Company" section under Advisors (different from consultants such as myself, the attorney, and the accountant) with one line stating their current or most recent special credential. An example of such a listing is: Buffy Celery, Head of Agricultural Production, Foods and Us.

Markets

The target markets for documentaries are the same as those for fiction films, save one group. Documentary audiences themselves are the first target audience to list. For example, the paragraph I used in a recent documentary reads:

> *Documentary films have entered the mainstream. Throughout the 1990s and into the 21st Century, documentary films have gained prominence and success on the theatrical screen. Part of the reason is the quality and diversity of the films. Documentaries ranging from the political and* Inside Job *to personal stories like* Buck *and the music-centered* Pearl Jam Twenty *are among nonfiction films that have earned substantial sums at the box office. Audiences eager to see intellectually stimulating, well-crafted fare are being drawn to theaters showing documentaries, resulting in attendance figures that have increased the value of these films in the home video, cable and foreign markets. In addition, a substantial portion of the television audience for documentaries—estimated by Nielsen Media Research at 85 percent of U.S. television households—appears unwilling to wait six to 12 months for a documentary to get to cable and longer for network television. Analysts also suggest that audiences' interest in reality television has helped documentary films build their growing theatrical audience. In addition, sales agents have said that documentaries that are more cinematic, with song scores and the evolution of characters, can be pitched more easily and sold in much the same way as dramatic features.*

The rest of the market section is the same as that for fiction films. Every documentary has a subject, be it political, economic, inspirational, historic, sports related, and so on. Fiction films with the same genres or themes can be used as examples in the market section as well as to show interest in the subject, although they can't be used as comparatives for forecasting.

The discussion of audience ages depends on the subject of the documentary. The main market for most will be an audience over 30, especially if the subject is economic or political. Musical, sports, and other docs depend on who or what is being featured. For example, a film about skateboarders might draw in a younger audience, and one featuring a baseball, football, or basketball star from the 1950s or 1960s would draw in baby boomers first.

Forecasting

In the previous two chapters, I made a big point that you need the worldwide numbers over the most recent three years available with 14 to 15 films to do my method of forecasting. Unfortunately, documentary, as well as animated and large format films, is not available in enough numbers every year to follow that rule. Due to the limited number of films and the lack of some information, you will probably have to go back more than five years to have at least 10 films to compare. There is more responsibility placed on you, the filmmaker, to be sensible and logical throughout the process. I know that many of you would rather never think about numbers. However, your investors do. Your forecast must look rational to them.

Which documentaries to use and which not to use is a choice you will have to make. There is more flexibility in terms of genres and themes for what films you can, but your decision-making process has to be reasonable. The first step is to look at everything in your story. If you are making a film involving political/economic/social subject, there are a lot of choices. These subjects tend to be what many filmmakers want to explore, especially in difficult times. They reach a broader audience, particularly with all the turmoil that has been going on around the world. I can't give you a hard-and-fast rule for which documentaries to use; it has to be your choice. One of my favorite docs for which to do the financials was Jonathan Holiff's *My Father and the Man in Black*. His father was Johnny Cash's personal manager. In addition to being about a father/son relationship, the themes in the story are varied. A short review read: "From hillbilly juke joints in the Deep South to the grandeur of London's Royal Albert Hall, from ditches and jail cells all the way to the White House." This gave me a lot of latitude in choices.

Budgets

There also were films that I wanted to used based on their box office results; they were not in the database due to lack of data. Often, I don't have any reference to a documentary budget until the database has worldwide numbers. Reason number one given by many documentary filmmakers is that they have made the film over a long period of time and didn't keep records of how much money was involved. It is true that many are made with a combination of cash from grantors and in-kind contributions, so a filmmaker has to keep careful financial records to know the real number. Or, reason number two, they choose not to tell us which happens far more often than with other feature films. Therein is the biggest problem with writing a business plan around a documentary film. It often is difficult to find the costs for the docs that are most applicable. However, it is far more doable now due to the number of films that have been released. If you are raising money from other people—whether individuals or grant organizations—you must know your budget. Even if you are using your own money, please figure out your budget ahead of time. When I first came into the business, filmmakers often raised money as they went along. Those times are gone. Documentary filmmakers are expected to be professional.

The range of applicable films to use normally is very narrow with theatrical documentaries. The majority of docs that appear profitable have budgets between $150,000 and $2 million. I always counsel clients to plan on making their film for $2 million or less. Even with a moderate box office, there are many sources for revenue. Specialized films often benefit from additional marketing that is not in the normal plan for film distribution companies. In addition to the traditional distribution channels of which Netflix and other commercial sites are now part, there tend to be more alternative and advocacy groups through, both nationally and internationally, though which documentarians can sell their film.

Table Layouts

As mentioned earlier, with items, such as budget and ancillary, harder to obtain, I may go back right to 10 years to have at least 10 films. Therefore, instead of breaking the films into three years to have a trend in the ratios, I keep them in a single list as in Table 12.1. For most documentary business plans, I have this one table with the current films listed here with only box office and budget. It depends on how many films are available with both numbers. If there are four or more, then I will have a second table similar to the one for narrative films. As with other films, the box office also has to give the impression that the film will be in the plus category in dollars. If the budget is $3 million and the final box office is $42,000, you don't need to include a film with a loss in your forecasting.

As when making a table of other feature films, list the extraordinary films when they are appropriate (i.e., *Hunting Snipe* in Table 12.1), but do not include them in your forecasting process. Even though it is tempting to use their high revenues, remember that your investor probably will know better. You want him to have confidence in you.

TABLE 12.1

Crazed Consultant Productions Documentary Sample: The Film Selected Comparative Documentary Films* Revenues and Costs Years 2003–2010 (Millions of Dollars)

FILM: WORLDWIDE RESULTS	DOMESTIC REVENUE			FOREIGN REVENUE (c)	TOTAL REVENUE (d)	COSTS				DISTRIBUTOR'S GROSS PROFIT (e)
	BOX OFFICE	RENTALS (a)	OTHER (b)			BUDGET	P&A	TOTAL		
Amazon Wonder Fish	2.0	1.0	4.0	2.0	7.0	0.5	3.5	4.0	6.7	3.0
Controlling the Wolpertinger	3.5	1.7	5.0	3.0	9.7	1.0	2.0	3.0	7.9	6.7
Finding Yamashita's Eagle	1.9	0.8	3.5	1.6	5.9	1.0	0.1	1.1	4.8	4.8
Hunting Snipe***	32.0	16.0	60.0	15.0	91.0	0.5	10.0	10.5	68.8	80.5
Jackalope of Sherman Oaks	1.5	0.7	1.8	0.6	3.1	1.2	0.3	1.5	1.5	1.6
Lobster Dreams	3.0	1.5	3.2	4.0	8.7	1.8	2.0	3.8	4.4	4.9
Magnificent Gambozino	1.2	0.6	3.6	3.2	7.4	1.0	1.2	2.2	5.1	5.2
Shetlands at Work	2.2	1.1	2.4	0.2	3.7	1.5	0.9	1.9	1.8	1.8

Wild Haggis of Scotland	8.0	4.0	10.0	4.8	18.8	2.0	5.8	7.8		11.0
Singing Bees, The	2.8	1.4	6.0	1.5	8.9	1.4	0.5	1.9	6.0	7.0
Touching Snapping Crabs	18.0	9.0	23.8	2.0	34.8	3.0	3.2	6.2	16.0	28.6
Wild Haggis of Scotland	8.0	4.0	10.0	4.8	18.8	2.0	5.8	7.8		11.0

U.S. BOX OFFICE ONLY AVAILABLE, YEARS 2011–2012

Dullahan, The	3.4				1.1	
Saving the Lox**	2.6				3.0	
U.S. vs Lizards, The	5.0				0.18	

*The revenues generated by these comparable films do not constitute a guarantee that *Documentary Sample: The Film* will do as well.

**Still in North American Distribution as of July 21, 2012.

***Due to its extraordiary results, *Hunting Snipe* is not included in the forecast.

(a) Rentals equal distributor's share of U.S. box office.

(b) Other includes television/cable, home video, and all other nontheatrical sources of revenue.

(c) Foreign Revenue includes both theatrical and ancillary revenues.

(d) Total Revenue equals Domestic Rentals, Domestic Other, and Foreign.

(e) Gross Profit before distributor's fee is removed.

Sources: Business Strategies, SNL Kagan Financial, Baseline Studio Systems, *Variety, screendaily.com, boxofficemojo.com*

Note that fiction films are not included into a forecast for a documentary. They have a wider audience appeal and usually wider distribution. All of the revenue windows for a fiction feature are going to show higher grosses. Using them would mean that you are fooling not only yourself with an unlikely net profit number but also your investor.

On the other hand, a successful documentary in the same budget range as your feature film and good results can be used in that plan. For example, *Inside Job* can fit in a low-budget film plan that deals with financial crisis, crime, and politics, themes that have become more prevalent in recent years. As we always are looking at a conservative revenue projection for our "Moderate" column, using a film that has done well with a lower net profit result is not a problem.

Finishing

Once you have set up your comparative table, you are ready to follow the forecasting method outlined in Chapter 10 and in the "Financial Worksheet Instructions" in the book's companion website. The only difference will be one average ratio to use for forecasting your revenue. Otherwise, forecast your revenues and expenses and create your cash flow with the same methodology used for narrative films.

ANIMATED FILMS

Independents

It is likely you have a budget that is far lower than that of the studios—probably between $5 million and $50 million. If you are trying to raise $150 or $200 million independently for your first animated film, I would suggest rethinking your plan. You can write the business plan, but be realistic about where you are going to find the money. As with documentaries, much of the business plan for an animated film is the same as other feature films. There are specific areas that differ, however.

Industry

The changes in technology affect the making of animated films to a greater extent than other movies. Although 2D still exists, 3D is involved in a majority of films. In addition, the techniques have changed. I usually put in a short animation section as either a part of the Industry Section or a separate section directly following it. In either case, it should have its own heading. Below is a sample of what might be in the business plan. You would want to expand on whatever format you are using. If your film is to be in 3D, for example, then follow the animation paragraph with an explanation of 3D and examples:

> *Traditional animation (also called cel animation or hand-drawn animation) was the process used for most animated films of the 20th century. Cel animation utilized the phenomenon of "persistence of vision," which can be created in several different ways. Some forms of animation can be traced to ancient times, but narrative animation did not really develop much until the advent of cinematography. One of the first people to use animation in film was the Frenchman George Melies, the silent film director featured in the live-action film Hugo. Many of the full-length animated films through the years have been made by studios, advances in technical methods and the ability to lower costs have brought independent companies into the animation business. DreamWorks Animation, The Weinstein Company, Lucasfilm and Aardman Animations are just a few of the independents making animated films today. By the beginning of the 21st century animators' drawings began to be either scanned into or drawn directly into a computer system.*

Markets

As with other genres of film, the audience is specific and knows what it likes. Techniques and storylines are discussed in other sections of the business plan. The demographics make a big difference with how you pitch animated films to investors.

Moviegoers of All Ages

Assuming that a good filmmaker "thinks market" before starting a film, there are two ways of designing an animated film. Either it is made for children who adults might accompany or it is designed for teens and older. The theory is that DreamWorks Animation's formula is to make films primarily for adults that may be entertaining for younger moviegoers as well; for example, the *Shrek* films play to everyone from 8 to 80. Certainly, older audiences still feel that these films play better on a big screen and want to see it in the theater initially.

Many of the films are designed to appeal to everyone from children to their grandparents. Due to the paucity of G-rated live-action films, animation is often not in competition for the same audience as live-action films that are released concurrently. They can play to younger ages better than many other films, while still bringing in the whole family demographic. Parents often go to check out a film before taking a very young child. Grandparents go to enjoy the activity with the rest of the family.

The Motion Picture Association of America (MPAA) reports the attendance levels of moviegoers from 12 to 90 in specific groups in their "Theatrical Market Statistics." There are no data for those under 12. Since the MPAA's audience data groups ages 2 to 11 together, we can't present a separate audience percentage for children and tweens. According to the data, "youngsters" would be 15 percent of that audience, but we don't know what ages are included in "youngsters." Here, we have a conundrum. There is a big difference between a film fit for a four-year-old and one for a pre-teen. For example, one animated film may be aimed primarily at children aged 12 and under. Another animated film, with a slightly more hip theme and a pop music soundtrack, may entertain children but also draw in teenagers and young adults. DreamWork's hits *Shrek* and *Shrek 2* were geared for the very young to the very old, while Tokuma's *Princess Mononoke* skewed to teenage viewers.

A part of the definition for a G-rating reads: "nothing in theme, language, nudity, sex, violence or other matters that, in the view of the Rating Board, would offend parents whose younger children view the motion picture." Despite the rating (which the MPAA makes clear is not a certificate but an opinion of a panel), some adults may feel that there may be activity in the film that is not appropriate for little Sally. Looking at 15 animated films released in the United States from January 2011 to July 2012, only one—*Gnomeo & Juliet*—was rated G, and it was a Disney film. All others were PG. If you feel that you want to make an independent film for young children and don't have any, talk to parents for their viewpoint.

Unlike the customers for other forms of films, the core market for animated films isn't really moving into other media. Kids who are watching these films generally aren't the ones downloading them from the Internet. That may change; but for now, the majority of parents are more than willing to take their little ones to the cinema. Besides being a valued family outing, they are teaching their children to appreciate movies. The good news about those very young children is that they are a boon to home video companies. Their parents tend to buy discs that they can play over and over again on child-level technology.

Financials

Budgets

As with documentaries, you will need to go back more than five years to have enough films for a proper forecast. How far back depends on what is available in terms of budget. The business plans for animated films that I am doing in 2012 generally have worldwide data from 2004 to 2010. While 12 films is a better statistical sample for making a forecast, I often have to settle for 10.

While there are a number of animated films every year, the majority are in the $120–$200 million-plus range. As much as you might think your $5-, $10-, or $20-million film compares, it doesn't. Nevertheless, the range of budgets for comparative films is much wider. In the early years of this decade, there were a number of successful animated films that were made for less than $10 million. Unfortunately, in the last few years, there have been very few. With a low-budget film, you may have to go as high as $40 million when seeking titles for comparison. Even for a film budgeted at $40 million, I don't go above $90 million in choosing comparatives. I also stay in this century. There have been too many technical improvements over the years have films from an earlier period.

Table Layouts

The Table 12.1 format should be used for animated films to show the worldwide revenues and expenses through the most current year available; however, there will be enough films from the most recent two years to create a second table similar to the layouts described in Chapter 10. The forecasting for an animated film also follows the methodology in Chapter 10. Animated films do differ in creating the cash flow table. Experienced filmmakers of animation with whom I have worked always have assumed two years for the production cost rather than one year. I recommend that you do the same. Otherwise, use the same percentages for calculating the spread for the prints and ads cost, domestic and foreign revenues, and distributor fees.

TABLE 12.2

Crazed Consultant Productions Sample Cash Flow for Animated Films Projected Cash Flow* Based on Moderate Projection (Millions of Dollars)

	YEAR 1				YEAR 2				YEAR 3				YEAR 4				YEAR 5
	QTR. 1	QTR. 2	QTR. 3	QTR. 4	QTR. 1	QTR. 2	QTR. 3	QTR. 4	QTR. 1	QTR. 2	QTR. 3	QTR. 4	QTR. 1	QTR. 2	QTR. 3	QTR. 4	QTR. 1
Budget	0.13	0.13	0.15	0.15	0.14	0.12	0.09	0.09									
Print and Advertising											0.53	0.13	0.25	0.09			
Domestic Rentals											0.75	0.15	0.10				
Domestic Ancillaries													0.50				0.50
Foreign Revenue													0.29	0.24	0.5	0.24	0.08
Distribution Fees													35% of Revenue to This Point				35% of Revenue From q2Y3 to Q5 Yr3

*For reference only. How and when monies are actually distributed depends on contract with distributor.
Prints and advertising are usually paid back first, then the production budget.
Note: Totals may not add due to rounding.
Prepared by Business Strategies

LARGE-FORMAT FILMS

History

Large-format films are made by several companies, among which are the IMAX Corporation, studios, and independent producers. They are commonly referred as IMAX films, since the industry started at EXPO '70 in Osaka, Japan, when IMAX Corporation of Canada introduced "the IMAX; Experience" at the Fuji Pavilion. These days, however, IMAX produces fewer of the films, but an overwhelming percentage of the "giant" screens. Warner Bros. is another studio producer, and there are independent producers discussed later in this chapter. Based on information from the IMAX Corp. and bigmoviezone.com, in July 2012, there were 672 giant screens worldwide with 643 of them IMAX screens (510 commercial multiplex, 20 commercial destination, and 113 institutional in 52 countries).

Until 1997, these theaters were located in museums, science centers, and other educational institutions, as well as a few zoos. In 1997, IMAX introduced a smaller, less-expensive projection system that was the catalyst for commercial 35-mm theater owners and operators to integrate their theaters into multiplexes. Currently, these films are 40 to 50 minutes long.

The first independent producers of these films were Greg MacGillivray and the late Jim Freeman. They began with surfing films in 1973. The cameras they used weighed 80 pounds, but they paid IMAX to make a camera with better specifications. Since that time, the MacGillivray Freeman Company has led the independent way with 20 productions. Among the other independent producers are nWave Pictures, 3D Entertainment, National Geographic Cinema Venture, and 3ality Technica.

Formats

In 2002, IMAX introduced a process to convert 35-mm film to 15/70 (15 perforations/70-mm process), which is their standard. Known as DMR, for digital remastering, the process started a new wave of converting longer feature films to be shown on the larger screens. There is ongoing controversy about whether fiction features belong to a giant screen. However, that is for you to decide. Suffice it to say that the economies of scale are different.

Another controversy erupted when IMAX introduced a new digital screen to multiplex theaters in 2009. Since 2004, the size of the IMAX screens has been 76 × 98 feet (23 × 30 m), while the new screens are 28 × 58 feet (8.5 × 18 m). The newer systems cost $1.5 million to get up and running compared to $5 million for an "original" IMAX. The company's multiplex agreements allow the removal of the lower portion of seating in stadium-seat venues, creating the perception of greater screen size and viewing immersion. Presumably, the remastering of 35-mm films boosts image resolution and brightness. Then there is the question if you can call them "giant screens." An IMAX representative insisted that "It's isn't a particular width and height of the screen. It's about the geometry." In the end, the audience will decide. They won't care about how much it cost to make the film, equip the theater, or remaster the film. They will care how it looks to them, and whether they should have been charged $5 more for a film that isn't on a six-story screen.

Synopses

Films produced as large-format films, as compared to the remastered films, have always been documentaries, and this rule still applies. Therefore, the synopsis for a film is essentially like those discussed in the "Documentary" analysis earlier. They are in both historical and future time. In putting together a business plan, list advisors in the company section and people appear in the film as attachments after the synopsis.

Markets

As with other documentaries, I use IMAX audience as the first target market to discuss. Then use other genres and themes in the films. The demographics are going to relate to the stories in the films.

Financials

That brings us to the bottom line for these films. Sources of data have been few. The *LF Examiner* discontinued box office information as of December 2005, Editor/publisher James Hyder said on the publication's website:

> *Readers are advised not to assume that the box office information on LF films provided here (or in other publications or Web sites) is complete or representative of the entire LF film market. In the conventional film industry, an independent agency collects and tabulates box office data directly from theaters for all films in release. Box office data for LF films are not reported the same way. Some LF distributors choose to provide data for their films to trade publications, but the practice is not universal, nor are the data independently audited or verified. In general, distributors that choose to report do so for the perceived marketing value. Therefore, films reporting their box office numbers are typically stronger than average. Films doing poorly generally cannot afford or prefer not to report. However, this does not mean that all films that do not report are poor performers. Some would undoubtedly place in the top half of these lists. But their distributors have chosen not to report because they believe weekly box office numbers are not a very useful measure of the LF industry's performance. We agree.*

That being said, *Variety* does print box office dollars. I have always used the *Variety* data, as it is the only reference to commercial box office revenue that we have. As the *Variety* data includes only the films released in commercial theaters, revenues from institutional venues are not known.

The previously mentioned independent companies tend to finance films from the profits of their own films. Independent filmmakers generally have been funding films as they would other documentaries—with grants, corporate donations, and funds from specific groups that may have a social or business interest in the subject of the film. Obtaining financing from equity investors appears to be rare for individual filmmakers; nevertheless, we need to have a format for approaching them.

Expenses

The problem comes on the cost side—not only the budgets but also how distributors of giant-screen films calculate their fees. Since we can use only films for forecasting for which the budgets are known, there always will be films that cannot be used as comparatives. Both the budgets and the prints and ad costs are included on the Baseline website.

There is a difference in the split, however. In addition, in over 12 years of covering this part of the film industry, I have never found a written analysis of the split between the distributor and the producer. This lack of financial knowledge also makes it difficult to approach equity investors with a business plan. Anecdotally, various filmmakers and distributors have told me that the split is the opposite of what we would assume for an independent film— 65 percent to the distributor and 35 percent to the producer. There is further difficulty concerning the search for accurate figures. After interviewing filmmakers and distributors at the annual conference of the Giant Screen Theater Association and, prior to that group, at the Large Format Cinema Association (in 2006, the LFCA merged with the Giant Screen Cinema Association to form GSTA), I have learned that the ongoing independent producers, MacGillivray Freeman, nWave, and others, have made profits from earlier films and, in some cases, distribute their own films. The best we can do at this time is to use this information, along with additional information that we get from Baseline to present a business plan.

Table Layouts

The tables for comparative films are set up similarly to the ones for animated films. Large-format films also are released in varying numbers over the years. To have 10 or 12 films to use as comparatives, you are likely to have to start with a year seven to nine before the current year. For example, in 2012, I might have a range of 2004 to 2012. The forecast is also set up the same way as the other tables. The difference is that the distributor's fee is 65 percent of the total revenue.

An individual large-format film can appear on screens off and for several years. *T-Rex*, was originally released in October 1998. makes irregular appearances on *Variety*'s box office list, including last few months in 2012. Table 12.3 shows the cash flow spread a large-format film. The production cost in this example is the e spread as an animated film. Whether live-action or animated , the time consumed is likely to be similar.

The domestic revenues are based on the study of independent released from 2003 to 2011. The data show an average of 94 nt of the domestic revenue coming in over six quarters in the

TABLE 12.3

Crazed Consultant Productions Sample Cash Flow for Large Format Films Projected Cash Flow* Based on Moderate Projection (Millions of Dollars)

	YEAR 1				YEAR 2				YEAR 3				YEAR 4				YEAR 5	
	QTR. 1	QTR. 2	QTR. 3	QTR. 4	QTR. 1	QTR. 2	QTR. 3	QTR. 4	QTR. 1	QTR. 2	QTR. 3	QTR. 4	QTR. 1	QTR. 2	QTR. 3	QTR. 4	QTR. 1	QTR. 2
Budget	0.13	0.13	0.14	0.14	0.14	0.12	0.09	0.09										
Print and Advertising									0.09	0.53	0.13	0.25	0.09					
Domestic Rentals											0.15	0.26	0.26	0.15	0.12	0.06		
Domestic Ancillaries															0.50		0.50	
Foreign Revenue														0.29	0.24	0.15	0.24	
Distribution Fees																65% of Total	0.08	65% of Total
TOTAL																		
CUMULATIVE TOTAL																		

*For reference only. How and when monies are actually distributed depends on contract with distributor. Print and advertising are usually paid back first, then the production budget.
Note: Totals may not add due to rounding.
Prepared by Business Strategies

time frame that we had. While with some studio films significant amounts of revenue can come in over a longer period of time, for many of the films later revenue is in small amounts.

The rest of the revenue is spread similarly to the other films. The distributor fee represents the 65 percent mentioned earlier.

13

Other People's Money: Them That Has the Gold Makes Some of the Rules

Raising money for a movie is like hitchhiking—It could be the first ride, it could the thousandth. But you have to stay out there with your thumb out and just wait. And you also have to know when not to get into the car.

—JOHN SAYLES DIRECTOR

There are almost as many answers to what investors expect as there are investors. Whether individuals, companies, or nonprofit organization and no matter where they are in the world, each has their own criteria and idiosyncrasies. Specific customs of relating to individuals and doing business may be different from country to country, but investors are similar in terms of their goals. Since the business plan is a sales (not a legal) document, it is your job to learn as much as you can about your potential "customers" and focus on their needs.

HOW DO YOU FIND AN INVESTOR?

The Sayles quote always has been one of my favorites, as it emphasizes that you may find your money immediately or it may take a very long time. If investors all were similar and lived in the same place, I wouldn't tell you where that place was. I'd be a very rich person funding films. Even *finders*—people who find money for films for a living—will tell you that it isn't easy. If a finder promises the money or insists on money upfront, you may want to move on to someone else.

While many filmmakers go to Los Angeles or New York to seek equity investors, they find that others are throwing business plans at people in those two centers of commerce every day. Any potential investors in those towns already have been approached by too many friends and neighbors. If you are from Fort Wayne (IN), Hibbing (MN), or Cincinnati (OH), my advice is to go back home. You have more connections there and, hopefully, less competition from other filmmakers.

WHAT DO THEY WANT?

Artistic Expression

Some investors are drawn to films that have more literary qualities than mainstream films. The definition of "literary" is in the eyes of the beholder. We used to call these art films, but specialty is a better term. Normally, the term is assigned to films that appear to be based on a higher level of expression and writing. Or they are experimental.

You should make an attempt to create realistic expectations for both you and your investor. If you are lucky, his desire to be associated with quality will outweigh the high return he wants for his investment. On the other hand, if he cannot afford more money and does not want to join with additional investors, move on. Put your energy into finding partners whose outlook and resources are a match for your project.

Filmmakers still tell me (and the investor) that their film is "just like" Merchant-Ivory's *A Room with a View*. It still is held as an example of an artistic film. After all, it is based on a novel by E. M. Forster. Unfortunately, they want to make it at 1986 prices ($850,000) and reap the box office of *The Help* ($213 million worldwide). The budget of *The Help* was $25 million. Your rationale may sound good to the investor, but it isn't a good portrayal of the real market for your film.

Special Interests

If you can find an investor whose sensibilities agree with the theme of your film, you may be able to create a workable collaboration. If your story takes place in Western Texas, then a good choice is to go to people in that area first. Other projects are funded by individuals, because it emphasizes a hobby or passion of theirs. As I mentioned in a previous chapter, many sports figures have become fascinated with film. Currently, I have several clients with football-, baseball-, or soccer-themed films. The first contacts they are making are with players and owners of teams.

The line between business and altruism can be a thin one. Still, few people will become involved in a feature film without considering its commercial possibilities. Jeff Skoll, for example, who was the first President of eBay and named the wealthiest Canadian by Forbes, formed Participant Media to make films on current social and political topics with the express purpose of inspiring social change. In many cases, the company even co-distributes with its focus on social media. The company still looks at the viability of the project beyond its societal interests.

Nonprofit organizations have funded all or part of for-profit films that fit with their particular mandate. The increase in the success of inspirational films with themes of good versus evil and redemption has brought more charity-based religious and nondenominational organizations into the market. Having been involved with writing several business plans for filmmakers who were seeking money from such organizations, I can assure you that most look at the project as a whole not only as their special interest.

Big Returns

People do invest in films with the primary purpose of making money. Independent films that are more mainstream in terms of story and demographic appeal are likely to appeal to investors to whom a big pay day is the biggest attraction about putting their money into film. Like a gambler in Vegas, this type of investor is playing the odds. As a matter of fact, several well-known poker players have become investors in films.

PITCHING YOUR PROJECT

The "Elevator" Pitch

In a seminar, a filmmaker asked me what kind of pitch you do if you are not in an elevator. The term *elevator pitch* is not meant to be taken literally. The idea is that you may be in a social or networking gathering, or indeed in an elevator going from the first to second floor," and have 30 to 45 seconds to attract interest. You are at AFM. You and Ryan Kavanaugh, founder of Relativity Media, are the only people in the elevator. Or you are waiting for the valet to bring your car around after a film seminar, and Mr. Local Mogul is standing next to you. What will you say?

Plan now. Don't wait until you are in the elevator or standing on the curb to think of something. Develop and rehearse it. Try it out on other people. You want to make a good impression, as well as create interest. In terms of the business plan, it is also the logline that you will put in the Executive Summary. This does not mean things like "It is *Avatar* meets *Juno*." You want a well-honed sentence or two that summarizes the idea of your film in a way that will make the investor want to speak or read further.

At the most basic level, an elevator pitch is a sales tool that helps you get the meeting you get the investor immediately interested in your film. Avoid the cookie cutter "insert your name here" templates that you'll find on the Internet. You want your pitch to stand out and be unique. On the other hand, the listener has to understand what you are talking about. Make it both sensational and simple at the same time. Make it concise, clear, and very short.

Below are two examples used by clients who raised money for their films in the last year. They show the difference between an elevator pitch and a synopsis.

> Elevator pitch: *The Kogi tribe of South America wants the world to know that if humanity doesn't stop digging into Earth and taking its minerals and resources, the planet will die.*
>
> Short synopsis: *Modern, scientific, rational people don't believe it, of course, but now the contemporary descendents of an advanced ancient civilization want to demonstrate that they really do have such knowledge. Members of the Kogi tribe, living in South America primarily in Colombia, are coming forward to prove their wisdom is sound, and to share their knowledge, because they sincerely believe it is the key for mankind's survival. They believe that man's ignorance about how to live in balance with nature is precipitating an environmental apocalypse that cannot be avoided unless humans learn to understand the natural world in a fundamentally new way.* [From the documentary feature *Aluna*, directed by Alan Ereira]

Elevator pitch: *Simon, a scientist who has come to Mexico to develop an important breakthrough, takes refuge in an orphanage under siege when local authorities and organized crime try to seize control of his mysterious invention.*

Short synopsis: *Simon Orwell is a brilliant student whose life has taken a series of wrong turns. At the point of giving up on his dreams, he gets a call from an old professor who has discovered a breakthrough in a device that would create unlimited energy, and he needs Simon's help. But the professor is killed and Simon assaulted by members of a powerful drug cartel. He takes refuge in a local orphanage where he meets Harold Finch, who walked away from a lucrative career with NASA and consulting Fortune 500 companies to serve a higher cause. With Harold's help, Simon sets out on a quest to uncover who killed the professor and why, but in the process discovers the secret to both the world-changing device and his own unlimited potential.* [From the feature *Unlimited*, directed by Nathan Frankowski]

Filmmakers Share Their Investor Experiences

Getting in front of the right people, successfully communicating your vision and getting them to buy into it is the big hurdle. Then, it's a crap shoot as to whether they decide to go for it or not.
—*Student from my UCLA class*

I asked a group of filmmakers, including both my clients and others, to relate their experiences when raising money from equity investors. The participants included Joslyn Barnes, Co-Founder of Louverture Films with Danny Glover; Tony Whalen, Canadian Producer, *All the Wrong Reasons*; Joel Eisenberg and Tim Owens, EMO Films; Patricia Payne, NoHo Films International; April Wade, Woman On Top Productions; and Jay Spain, Producer, *Moving Midway*.

LL: What are the top questions that investors asked?
Joslyn: Who's in the film from a talent standpoint? How are you going to get my money back and when? More recently we've been getting sophisticated questions about soft monies, tax incentives, and various gap and super gap lending frameworks. Investors are quite savvy that their equity participation is a hard thing to find at this time, and therefore equity financing is becoming more expensive.

Tony: The top questions from investors were (1) Who wrote the script?; (2) Who's directing the film?; (3) Are there any cast attached?; (4) Who's producing the film?; (5) Is there any funding already in place?; and (6) What have the writer, director, and producers worked on previously?

Joel and Tim: Our potential investors didn't know what questions to ask. Since they had already worked with Tim in real estate investing, they had a comfort level with him and his advice. As experienced investors, however, they wanted to know all the risks. Joel spoke several times about studio films and independent films. He did general education about film and the entertainment industry being sure they knew all the risks in independent film. He also told them there were several thousand films a year that don't get any distribution, and the worst-case scenario that they might not make any money.

Patricia: Who are the actors? Who is the director? Have your previous projects made money for investors? Give me reasons why I'd want to invest in films. Why do you want to make this film? Who is your audience? Do you have a distributor? They also ask about what type tax write-off or benefits they will get; will there be any income generated from the project and when will it start and how much to expect. Is there information available to substantiate their backgrounds? Is there a prospectus and material supporting this project, and is it currently available? As an investor, do I get the first right of refusal on any subsequent projects? Would there be a role for my daughter/son/wife?

April: These are basic, but they are pretty much the only questions I get asked when looking for money: Who is in it? Who is directing it? Where are you shooting? They don't ask me about myself, and they ask about the movie only generally. I find that with the one that I am currently working on getting funded, they have a lot of specific questions about the mood of the piece, since it is a "non-traditional rock-film" about a very dark topic. Otherwise, "who is the audience," "what are your plans for distribution," etc. has not really been asked of me yet.

Jay: Most of our investors are North Carolinians. Moving Midway had tremendous local appeal to them. They either knew the family or wanted to participate in history, or both. Having said that, the questions we got most were: How much money do you need? How much have you raised so far? Who else has invested? How much did this or that person invest? During the first round of fundraising, we told everyone we had a business plan—with, of course, your credentials, the limited liability company (LLC) paperwork, and who our attorney was. I know a few of them read the paperwork, but I don't think most did. Only a few asked about return on investment. I don't think most cared. One of them told me that he thought it was just the right thing to do. Otherwise, there were a lot of reasons: the Academy Award potential, preserving history, education, and race relations. There were a lot of reasons that were not about making money. I think our biggest investor did it mainly for the arts. During the second round of fund-raising after we asked you to update the plan, more people read it and commented. Most of the questions then were making sure they understood what was there. Between the plan and the LLC and the distribution deals, I feel like I got an Entertainment Law degree. [LL: As happens in many documentaries, events prevented finishing the project in the original timeframe planned; therefore, we updated the financial tables.]

LL: Is there a difference between U.S. and Canadian/European/ Asian investors?
Joslyn: Yes, mainly it is the expectations that are quite different. U.S. investors expect to recoup against all world sales on a pro rata pari passu basis, and expect to be in first position behind only the standard P&A expenditures, sales fees, and taxes. They also expect a premium on their investment upfront and to see their names prominently displayed in the credits. European investors expect to recoup against specific territories and are used to international co-productions with many producing partners. There does not seem to be as much of an emphasis on personal credits, though there are arguably many people interested in being involved with quality, prestige vehicles, red carpet opportunities, and networking with film stars. This last applies to the United States, as well. The other significant difference is the approach to content. European and American investors and filmmakers have cultivated different tastes and audience bases over the decades. Europeans are used to auteur-driven filmmaking as much as they can also appreciate a Hollywood blockbuster. I don't think the reverse can be said of Americans, and American audiences are notoriously allergic to subtitles and dubbing—English-language rules, despite emerging successes in the Spanish-language market, which is finding its clout. As a result, U.S. investors tend to shy away from foreign films. And the American indie market, with its white bourgeois male twenty- to

thirty-something bias, has also shrunk dramatically. On the doc side, you will find engaged U.S. equity investors ready to put up monies for issues they sincerely care about if they feel the films have a chance of being distributed/seen. In Europe, equity investors for docs are extremely rare, as most docs are for broadcast and funded via broadcast networks and the many soft monies available to filmmakers in Europe. U.S. filmmakers do not have access to as much soft money, few foundations support film at a level that really makes a difference, and those that do tend to fund at the seed stage or the outreach stage rather than to fund production itself. This is actually I think a smart approach given the limited funding available and the demonstrable need; but the lack of soft money in general in the United States to support the arts is egregious and frankly outrageous when compared with other industrialized nations.

Tony: I can speak to the difference with Canadian investors. Basically, most Canadian independent films are financed with public funds. In our case, 80 percent of the funding comes from federal and/or provincial government entities. The only money that was raised outside Canada for us came from our U.S. sales agent.

LL: How did you find your investors?

Joslyn: When we launched our company we were quite clear about our intentions, and we have been fortunate to work with producer colleagues and superb filmmakers who have realized those intentions successfully. We have been able to attract investors as a result. We are of course in a privileged position as Mr. Glover is a well-known and well-respected film star, so it has been easier to navigate the usual channels of social networking than would likely have been the case otherwise. The key, however, has been building a brand, and we have done that through clarity of intent, adhering to certain principles, and sheer sweat equity!

Tony: The film has been in development for a few years, and we were able to secure development funding along the way from Telefilm Canada, New Brunswick Film, and Astral's Harold Greenberg Fund. Those three funding sources served as the starting point. From there, we were able to get equity from our home province of New Brunswick. We were also able to include tax credits from the provinces of New Brunswick and Nova Scotia. We went on to secure pre-buys from two broadcasters in Canada (TMN & Movie Central), which were taken to our Canadian distributor for an advance. Our Canadian distributor was affiliated with a U.S.

sales agent, who they came onboard with another advance. All of this funding was included in our application to Telefilm Canada for production funding, and we were successful in receiving that. The final piece of the puzzle to close out our funding was a producer investment. The final investment percentages of our production budget (just over $1 million) were Telefilm Canada Equity, 39 percent; Nova Scotia Tax Credits, 22 percent; Distributor Pacific Northwest Pictures Advance, 9 percent; Province of New Brunswick Equity, 9 percent; Province of New Brunswick Tax Credits, 6 percent; International Sales Agent Myriad Pictures Advance, 5 percent; Government of Canada Tax Credits, 4 percent; Producer Investment, 4 percent; and Astra's Harold Greenberg Fund Investment, 1 percent.

Joel and Tim: We didn't solicit investors at the group. The first person who put money in came up to us after the meeting. That led to another and to another, etc.

Patricia: That's a difficult one for me to be specific. Having been in the industry for many years working in several countries, I have gathered contacts both in and out of the film industry. I never ask a relative or friend to invest in my own projects. It's been doctors, dentists, real estate developers, hoteliers, actors/estate agents, government film agencies, an advertising company, commercial radio, and television stations. I also have approached banks for gap financing. There were professional fundraisers at a brokerage firm (in Australia) where I worked some time ago who raised several million dollars for me from 147 investors. In the latter deal, there were a few substantial investors seeking a tax break and many smaller investors along for the ride and a tax break. However, the tax structure has changed in Australia since this project was funded. They didn't solicit investors at the group.

Jay: Our investors were mostly friends of the Executive Producer, Bernie Reeves, or Godfrey's (Cheshire, the Director), or mine. Many also came in by word of mouth from our investors. Each had to have a net worth of $1 million minimum. We did have some donations also through our fiscal sponsor, the Southern Documentary Fund in Durham.

LL: What suggestions do you want to make to filmmakers in approaching investors?

Joslyn: Do your due diligence. Make sure that your project is sound. Do you have a great script, a feasible production schedule, and an accurate budget? Do you have people with the necessary talent and skills to execute your project at a professional level? Are you sure of your financial model insofar as possible? Have you tested your sales estimates? Have you vetted your investors? Are you 100 percent sure they are for real? Do they have the monies they say they do? What is their reputation? Have they worked in film before or not? What business do they work in? Seek investors with common interests and goals to your own so that expectations at all levels dovetail. Most people in a position to invest monies in films have made those monies because they are quite savvy business-people. In our experience, such investors appreciate down-to-earth, informed presentations where risk is laid out honestly alongside efforts to mitigate that risk. You may need to educate them about the film business and the kind of flexible mindset it requires. Build long-term relationships. Don't focus on short-term quick fixes. If you burn through investors, you are not helping anyone, including yourself. Building long-term relationships implies honesty, respect, transparency, delivery, and accountability.

Tony: My suggestions would be to put together a detailed business plan that includes:

- Backgrounds of the writer, director, and producers (and samples of previous work)
- A list of attached cast with backgrounds
- A director's vision
- A detailed distribution and marketing plan

Joel and Tim: You have to know what you are doing or work with someone who understands and can explain the business and marketing of film. Before we took any money, we had an operating agreement for our LLC and a private placement with subscription docs. We also decided to become investors by leaving our finder's fees for raising the money in the film. [LL: As executive producers, they raised the money for *April Showers*, a film that April Wade produced. It is coincidental, however, that I have answers from all three. Patricia, who has known her for a long time, asked her to participate in this section.]

Patricia: Know your stuff, and be able to present it cogently. Many potential investors invest for a living or a tax break. The filmmaker's responses should be substantial and relevant; your enthusiasm for the project should be coherent. It helps to have name actors, a director with some experience, and personnel— creative and production—on board who have track records. Not only do these people help get the film finished but also they are pitch points up front when raising money. Less detail about the script itself is better, as it often loses something in the telling particularly to nonindustry folk. Just hit the main pitch points and know them backward. If the investors want to know more about the script, they'll ask. Other potential investors may be real estate developers, doctors, dentists, or a neighbor. Many of these folks don't know much about the film or television industry other than viewing the finished product. Be prepared to explain the project and the deal in terms each individual can understand. When dealing with tax incentives, you are dealing with governments and taxpayer funds. Film commissions need to answer to their state or federal government as to why this production and investment is worthwhile for their state or country. All government agencies want to see the merit of investing taxpayer dollars, and they want all the reassurance they can get.

Jay: Three words: DO YOUR HOMEWORK!

COMMUNICATING EFFECTIVELY

> *The biggest problem with communication is the illusion that it has taken place.*
> —*George Bernard Shaw*

No matter how great your film project is, you may be unable to gain your goal—raising the money—unless you can communicate well with others. When you have a meeting, you think that the goal is to get money for your film. It is actually to communicate with the other person. Communication is a two-way street. You need to understand and think about what the other person is saying, in addition to how you are going to explain your project. Go in with a plan, but let the other person go first. You will probably give your short pitch first, but I advise letting the other person be first to speak about a potential deal. There may be a counter proposal you can make, rather than having the meeting end abruptly. Here are a few suggestions to aid your meeting style:

1. Don't interrupt: Let the other person finish what they are saying before you speak. I'll admit that one of my failings with clients is to interrupt due to my "psychic ability" to know what they are going to say next. Even if I am right, the rudeness tends to put people off.

2. Take a breath before speaking: Think about what you have just heard. It lets your investor know that you are taking what she said seriously; or, alternatively, gives you time to form a reply. This comment applies to serious conversation, not if the other person merely says "hello," or asks if you would like coffee or water.

3. Observe nonverbal cues from their mannerisms, tone of voice, gestures, and so on. At the same time, try to be aware of your own. Are you relaxed and smiling? Try nodding once in a while to show you understand what they are saying. Of course, be sure you do understand.

What They Say and What You Hear

A wise old owl sat on an oak, the more he saw the less he spoke. The less he spoke the more he heard. Why aren't we like that wise old bird?
—*Edward H. Richards*

Why am I quoting a nursery rhyme? No matter how old we get, we often seem to forget the art of listening to what other people are saying. Or to be more exact, we think we are listening but don't really hear what the other person is saying. It is the same whether it is an equity investor, the executive at a big production company, or a teacher in the classroom.

What they say: It is an interesting script, but not the kind of project with which I want to be involved.

What you hear: He will give me the money if I rewrite the script and have Jennifer Lawrence, Bradley Cooper, and Johnny Depp in it

(Go on to the next potential investor. Unless he says anything after that sentence, don't spin your wheels.)

What they say: I've got $100,000 for development. Why don't you start pre-production, and we'll negotiate later.

What you hear: It's a done deal.

(It is a done deal when you have a signed agreement, and the cash is in the bank. Do not go forward until then.)

What they say: I've signed the agreement you gave me, and here is a check for $4 million.

(You heard correctly. As soon as that check cashes, happy filming!)

What you hear: It's done deal.

There are many good websites devoted to this subject. I suggest an hour browsing the Internet. In addition, have someone with business experience who can advise you. It is often difficult to be objective and separate reality from fiction.

Common Sense Is More Important Than Rules

The variety of possible conversations is too broad to make a lot of hard-and-fast rules for you to follow. That gets us back to the sticky point that the desire to raise the money for your film may chase all rational thinking out the door. As with the filmmaker's experiences mentioned earlier, I would rather offer observations:

1. If an investor asks a simple question, give a simple answer. For example, if you are asked the total budget number, just say it. You'll have plenty of time to go into other items in your pitch. A client was asked the budget of a film four times. She talked about all the wonderful qualities of the film but didn't answer his question for 30 minutes. He finally ended the meeting.
2. What not to say is almost as important as what to say. Don't be the first to bring up negative news reports. On the other hand, be ready with a response to items that you know have been in the news. If someone has heard that statement and asks you, agree that there is no guarantee that a film will make money. Then go into a short explanation of your financials.
3. Although you are a salesperson in this instance, the motto that "No is only an opportunity" usually doesn't apply in this situation. Sometimes no means no. Thank the person for their time and leave. Later you can assess how the meeting went. You may find better ways to present your material. Then you can choose whether to go back to that person or apply your new knowledge at the next appointment.

Index